GENTLEMAN JAKE

THE SUCCESS AND TRAGEDY OF THE DEADBALL ERA'S GREATEST FIRST BASEMAN

The life story of Jake Daubert, who left the coal mines of Pennsylvania to become a two-time major league batting champion.

HARRY J. DEITZ, JR.

Mechanicsburg, PA USA

Published by Sunbury Press, Inc.
Mechanicsburg, PA USA

www.sunburypress.com

Copyright © 2023 Harry J. Deitz, Jr.
Cover Copyright © 2023 by Sunbury Press, Inc.

Sunbury Press supports copyright. Copyright fuels creativity, encourages diverse voices, promotes free speech, and creates a vibrant culture. Thank you for buying an authorized edition of this book and for complying with copyright laws. Except for the quotation of short passages for the purpose of criticism and review, no part of this publication may be reproduced, scanned, or distributed in any form without permission. You are supporting writers and allowing Sunbury Press to continue to publish books for every reader. For information contact Sunbury Press, Inc., Subsidiary Rights Dept., PO Box 548, Boiling Springs, PA 17007 USA or legal@sunburypress.com.

For information about special discounts for bulk purchases, please contact Sunbury Press Orders Dept. at (855) 338-8359 or orders@sunburypress.com.

To request one of our authors for speaking engagements or book signings, please contact Sunbury Press Publicity Dept. at publicity@sunburypress.com.

FIRST SUNBURY PRESS EDITION: August 2023

Set in Adobe Garamond Pro | Interior design by Crystal Devine | Cover by Lawrence Knorr | Edited by Lawrence Knorr.

Publisher's Cataloging-in-Publication Data
Names: Deitz Jr., Harry J., author.
Title: Gentleman Jake : the success and tragedy of the deadball era's greatest first baseman / Harry J. Deitz, Jr.
Description: First trade paperback edition. | Mechanicsburg, PA : Sunbury Press, 2023.
Summary: Gentleman Jake Daubert escaped the dangerous coal mines of Pennsylvania to become one of the greatest players of baseball's Deadball Era, but his career and life were cut short by an undiagnosed genetic condition. Despite setting a National League record for career sacrifices that still stands and winning an MVP award, two batting titles, two NL championships and the 1919 World Series, he isn't in the Hall of Fame.
Identifiers: ISBN : 979-8-88819-120-0 (paperback) | ISBN : 979-8-88819-121-7 (ePub).
Subjects: BIOGRAPHY & AUTOBIOGRAPHY / Sports | SPORTS & RECREATION / Baseball / History | SPORTS & RECREATION / Baseball / General.

Product of the United States of America
0 1 1 2 3 5 8 13 21 34 55

For the Love of Books!

On the cover: Jake Daubert during the 1913 season when he won the National League batting title and most valuable player award. Restoration & Color by They Played in Color Galleries, www.theyplayedincolor.com

For Andrea, Jason, and Megan

"HE PLAYED THE GAME
UNDER GOD'S RULES –
PLAYED TO WIN ON
THE SQUARE"

— Engraving on the side of Jake Daubert's tombstone

Contents

Foreword	ix
Preface: Another Baseball Champion From Shamokin	xi
Chapter 1: A Future Star Is Born	1
Chapter 2: Digging Out of the Mines and Minors	16
Chapter 3: Rapidly Rising Star	26
Chapter 4: A Champion and a Gentleman	43
Chapter 5: Building a Winner Amid Conflict	73
Chapter 6: Turning the Corner	87
Chapter 7: Raising a Pennant	97
Chapter 8: War, Contract Battle, and Trade	115
Chapter 9: World Series Champion and the Black Sox	136
Chapter 10: Not Ready to Quit	165
Chapter 11: "Not a Staller"	186
Chapter 12: Memories and Memorabilia	209
Chapter 13: In Others' Words	220
Chapter 14: Jake's Own Words	225
Chapter 15: By the Numbers	235
Afterword: No Call From the Hall	244
Endnotes	250
Acknowledgments and credits	261
Bibliography	262
About the Author	263

Foreword

As a sports fan and great-grandson of "Gentleman" Jake Daubert, I was enthralled by Harry Deitz's writing. I have read much about the accomplishments of Jake Daubert from sportswriters and heard about his influence on the baseball community from fans, family, and those who had grown up watching him play and following his career. But what impressed me about this book was Jake's relevance in today's world.

When I think of world-class athletes, I have been inspired by the limited great professional players who competed professionally in their 40s. Players like Jack Nicklaus in golf, Tom Brady in football, Gordie Howe in hockey, Roger Federer in tennis, and Bernard Lagat in running continued to excel in their sport even as they got older. When Jake Daubert died at 40, still playing the game, he was the oldest active professional baseball player to pass away.

In addition to professional longevity, I greatly admire the professional athletes who double as great ambassadors for their sport. Peyton Manning (football), Mia Hamm (soccer), Serena Williams (tennis) and Derek Jeter (baseball) come to mind. To this point, Jake was committed to fighting for players' rights as one of the organizers for the Baseball Players Fraternity, today's MLB Players Association. He took a stand for players' rights when he sued Brooklyn owner Charles Ebbets to honor his full contract after the major league baseball season was cut short due to World War I.

As a man, I was inspired by the reoccurring theme guiding Jake's professional and personal life: doing what was best for his family, fellow players, and fans. Baseball writers bestowed the nickname "Gentleman" on Jake Daubert based on his integrity, work effort, and ability to converse on many levels. In the current climate of over-sharing and braggadocios, I admired this man's trait of quietly overperforming while praising the skill and efforts of his fellow ballplayers.

Mr. Deitz's book offers insight into the biographical history of Gentleman Jake Daubert and his legacy in baseball. The only question I have has to do with induction into the Baseball Hall of Fame: Why is this man not in the Baseball Hall of Fame when the BBWAA Rules for election clearly state that "voting shall be based upon the player's record, playing ability, integrity, sportsmanship, character, and contribution to the teams on which the player played"?

Jack Daubert
Great-grandson of Jake Daubert

Preface

Another Baseball Champion From Shamokin

Cultivate the acquaintance of experienced players and listen to them carefully.
Observe the rules of the game.
Never bait an umpire.
Behave like a gentleman.
Play hard to win and never give up.
Keep regular hours.
Let "booze" strictly alone.
Don't smoke to excess. Better not at all.
Learn the inside of the game.
Practice all you can.

—Jake Daubert's baseball advice[1]

There was no life after baseball for Jacob Ellsworth Daubert. He died on October 9, 1924, 19 days after playing his final major league game. He was 40 years old and left behind a wife, two children, and a major league baseball career worthy of induction into the National Baseball Hall of Fame.

Jake was the greatest first baseman of baseball's Deadball Era during the first two decades of the twentieth century. Like many others from the Anthracite coal fields of Pennsylvania during that time, Jake used baseball as a diversion from long and dangerous days working in the mines. He was among the fortunate men for whom baseball provided a path out of the mines.

It would have been no surprise if Jake's death was related to his work as a coal miner, which he was from 1896 at age 11 until 1906. There were many threats to the lives of the men and boys who traveled deep into the narrow tunnels to collect Anthracite coal and bring it to the surface. If explosions or cave-ins didn't cut short their lives, black-lung disease from inhaling the coal dust likely would. The sad irony was that Jake escaped the dangers of the mines but couldn't overcome an undiagnosed genetic disorder that cut short his life.

I learned about Jake's successful career and tragic death when I was doing research for *Covey: A Stone's Throw from a Coal Mine to the Hall of Fame*, my 2022 book about the life of spitball pitcher Stan Coveleski, who was from my hometown of Shamokin, Pennsylvania. I discovered Jake was one of four other Shamokin natives who played in the major leagues during the early days of baseball.

Stan's brother Harry had an 81-55 record in nine years as a pitcher for the Philadelphia Phillies, Cincinnati Reds, and Detroit Tigers, for whom he was a three-time 20-game winner. He is best remembered as the "Giant Killer." In 1908, he was called up by the Phillies near the end of the season and pitched and won three games in five days against the New York Giants, denying them the National League Pennant.

Two other players from the Deadball Era were born and buried in Shamokin. Harry Budson Weiser played in 41 games as an outfielder for the Phillies in 1915 and 1916. He is fondly remembered for his name, Bud Weiser, not his .162 batting average. George Gilham played in one game in the 1920 and 1921 seasons as a catcher for the St. Louis Cardinals and was hitless in four at-bats.

Although Jake was born in 1884 in Shamokin, he lived most of his life in Llewellyn and Schuylkill Haven in Schuylkill County. For a few months after Coveleski was born in 1889 and before Daubert's family moved to Llewellyn early in 1890, Shamokin unknowingly was the home of two of the greatest players of the Deadball Era.

I was fascinated by the similarities between Jake and Stan beyond their birthplace. Both quit school to work in the mines around the age of 11. Both were pitchers at the start of their professional careers, although Jake became a first baseman because of an arm injury. Both were shy but extremely confident and fiercely competitive on the baseball field. Jake had a .303 career batting average during 15 seasons, won the National League batting title in 1913 and 1914, and was the 1913 winner of the Chalmers Award, an early version of the Most Valuable Player award.

PREFACE

Covey won 215 games and had a 2.89 earned run average during 14 seasons, won three complete games in the 1920 World Series, had five 20-win seasons, and pitched 27 straight scoreless innings in 1923. Each won a World Series and lost another.

Stan spent most of his career with Cleveland. Jake first signed with Cleveland but broke into the majors with Brooklyn. Jake spent his career in the National League and Stan in the American League, so they never faced each other in a major league game.

There was a major difference: Covey remained quiet and withdrawn during much of his life, but Jake became one of the most sought-after players for quotes and commentary about baseball. During my research, I found significantly more written in newspapers and magazines about Jake than I had found about Stan. Some of the most helpful information I found about Jake was in numerous articles written by F.C. Lane over a century ago in Baseball Magazine, which provided insight into his life, personality, and intelligence.

Jake was the team captain and on-field leader during most of his career with Brooklyn and Cincinnati and was one of the most popular players among fans and teammates. That wasn't always the case with team owners, with whom he had numerous disagreements over contracts. He became one of the early leaders for players' rights, eventually leading to the founding of the players union. That may have influenced the lack of support for his enshrinement into the Hall of Fame.

Shoeless Joe Jackson is undisputedly the best player from the Deadball Era who is not in the Hall of Fame. His involvement in the Black Sox scandal in the 1919 World Series resulted in his banishment from baseball. The irony is that Jake Daubert's team won that World Series, which eight Chicago White Sox players conspired to lose in exchange for payments from gamblers. Daubert's Cincinnati Reds team was a talented group in its own right, and Daubert was the star player.

Outside of baseball, he was a successful businessman in Schuylkill Haven and one of the top trap shooters in the state. His community, teammates, fans, and sportswriters respected and admired him. He was known as Gentleman Jake because of the way he dressed, spoke, and acted.

When I started researching Jake's life, I contacted Dr. Ann Yezerski, who did genealogy research and was a valuable help with information about Coveleski's family and early life. She helped to identify and locate some of Jake's descendants, including great-grandson Jack Daubert and his sister, Jill Daubert Malone, who shared some important documents, background, family photos, and memorabilia from Jake's playing days. Ann and I were able to identify the former location of the house where Jake was born in Shamokin and where he lived in Llewellyn and Schuylkill Haven.

We also discovered an unexpected connection to my family, some of whom lived in Llewellyn. The nephew of my paternal great-grandmother married Jake's sister, Anna.

During my research, I visited Jake's grave in the Charles Baber Cemetery in Pottsville, where on the side of his grave marker is engraved: "He played the game under God's rules—played to win on the square." I went to the location of the house where he was born, his childhood community of Llewellyn, and the house where Jake, his wife Gertrude, and children, Louise and George Jacob, lived in Schuylkill Haven, where I met the current residents.

I also learned that there are no markers or monuments for Jake in any of those communities in Schuylkill County, which proudly acknowledges the history of the Pottsville Maroons, who won and then were stripped of the 1925 National Football League championship; Gen. George Joulwan, supreme commander of NATO forces, 1983-1997; Les Brown, the legendary big band leader from Reinerton; and others.

At the Schuylkill County Historical Society, in a beautifully restored building constructed during the Civil War and housed the Centre Street Grammar School in Pottsville, there are few documents or records of Jake Daubert's great accomplishments during the early years of baseball. And in Cooperstown, New York, home of the National Baseball Hall of Fame, there is no plaque signifying Jake's contributions to the great American pastime.

Maybe all of that will change. It should change because from 1910 to 1924, Jake Daubert was the best first baseman in major league baseball and was regarded as one of the best players of his era, which included Ty Cobb, Joe Jackson, Tris Speaker, and Babe Ruth.

PREFACE

Jake Daubert was a fine example who worked hard and escaped from the coal mines to gain national attention and respect.

Jake Daubert showed dedication to clean living, never bragged about his accomplishments, and quietly stood up for what he believed was right.

Jake Daubert should be remembered for all those things and the gentleman he was.

One of the most fitting and succinct tributes to Jake was published in the "Cincinnatus Column" of *The Kentucky Post* on October 9, 1924, the day of his death. It was under the simple heading "Gentleman":

> Jake Daubert, the ballplayer, is dead.
>
> He was a distinguished player in the game, but Cincinnatus prefers to pay tribute to the fine gentleman that he was. Those who knew him well never mentioned him but to speak of his high character, his gentle nature and his lofty standard of sportsmanship.
>
> He played the game that is life faultlessly. He guarded well the base that is character. He batted a high average in the league that is called human relations. The city lifts its hat as he retires from the field.[2]

1

A Future Star Is Born

The small city of Shamokin has two distinguishing landmarks that have long defined it as an iconic community in the Pennsylvania Anthracite Coal Region. One is the remains of the huge culm bank that marks the northern border and is often referred to as the largest man-made mountain in the world. It rose from the discarded dirt washed and screened from the coal removed from the deep mine.

The other is Shamokin Creek, the water of which for decades has been colored rusty-orange from acid mine drainage that carries the pungent odor of sulfur resulting from runoff from the coal mines in the region.

"Acid mine drainage is the result of the exposure of pyrite to oxygen and water," according to the Shamokin Creek Restoration Alliance. "Pyrite is found in association with coal deposits, and when weathered, releases iron and acidity to the waters. Once these waters reach the surface, iron oxidizes and precipitates iron hydroxide (yellow boy) on the stream bottoms, choking out most aquatic life."[1] In recent years, the Alliance has worked to restore the clear waters of the creek that begins its 32-mile path near Mount Carmel, east of Shamokin, and empties into the Susquehanna River south of Sunbury, northwest of Shamokin.

The mountain and the creek remain symbols of Shamokin's coal region heydays more than a half-century ago.

In the early 1800s, farmers discovered a vein of coal in the Shamokin Creek at an area between what would become Spurzheim and Clay streets in Shamokin. Around 1826 John C. Boyd built a quarry there to mine coal and later named the town.² That is significant in the life of Jacob Ellsworth Daubert because the house where he was born on April 17, 1884, was in that same area of the creek where coal was discovered and led to the town's founding.

Shamokin grew largely due to coal mining and was incorporated as a borough in 1864. The population increased from 8,184 in 1880 to 14,403 in 1890 and 18,202 in 1900.³ By the 1920s, Shamokin and the surrounding Coal Township had a population of about 50,000.⁴

There are no remains of the house along the creek where Jake was born and spent the early years of his life, but the location was at what is now Terrace Avenue at Patsy's footbridge, which spans the narrow Shamokin Creek at the end of Clay Street. The row of houses in that area likely were owned by a colliery.

Jake's connection to Shamokin was brief. He was the youngest son born to Jacob Sr. and Sarah (Hoy) Daubert, whose families had lived in Schuylkill County for several generations, including some ancestors who were in America before the Revolutionary War. They married in the mid-1870s and had a combined family of 10 children. Jacob Sr. had two sons with his first wife: William in 1862 and Clifford in 1867. Sarah had two sons with her first husband: (Charles) William in 1869 and Lewis in 1871. Jacob and Sarah had six children together: Irvin in 1877, Anna in 1878, Calvin in 1879, Salome in 1881, Jake in 1884, and Flora in 1889. All of the children except Jake and Flora were born in Schuylkill County.

Census data from 1880 shows Jacob Sr., age 39, working as a coal miner and living in Newtown, five miles west of Llewellyn. Also listed were his wife Sarah (28 and keeping house), his sons William (age 18) and Clifford (14), Sarah's sons William (11) and Lewis (9), and their children Irvin (3), Annie (2), and Calvin (5 months). Jacob's older sons also were listed as coal miners.

The Dauberts moved to Shamokin looking for work in the expanding coal mines between the births of Salome in 1881 and Jake on April 17, 1884. Four months after Jake's birth, his half-brother Clifford, about 17, was killed in an explosion at the Cameron mine.⁵ The family remained in the Shamokin area for six more years. Flora was born about March 12, 1889, but died on July 10, 1890, in Hickory Ridge, also known as Upper

A Future Star Is Born

Sagon, east of Shamokin.[6] That same year, when Jake was six, they moved to Llewellyn in Branch Township, Schuylkill County.[7] Branch Township, a mining and farming community, had a population of 951 in 1890.[8]

The 1900 census lists the household as Jacob Sr., Sarah, Salome, and Jacob Jr. Additional information is unavailable because records of the 1890 census were destroyed in a fire. Jake called Schuylkill County home for the rest of his life.

Jake attended school in Shamokin for about a month before his family moved to Llewellyn, where he continued his schooling for the next six years. At age 11, he began work as a breaker boy at a local colliery, probably the Blackwood Coal Mine near Newtown, several miles west of his home. He continued limited schooling for several years but was destined to follow his father and brothers into the mines.

* * *

Coal mining in the Anthracite region of Pennsylvania expanded rapidly in the 1800s. Thousands of immigrants sailed from Europe to work in the mines in search of a better life. They were joined in the mines by the Dauberts, whose family had settled in the region before the American Revolution, and other families already living in the Anthracite region, which included Sullivan, Lackawanna, Luzerne, Carbon, Schuylkill, Dauphin, Northumberland, and Columbia counties in the northeastern part of Pennsylvania, according to a 1916 report by the Department of the Interior, Bureau of Mines.[9] What they found was a hard and dangerous life.

The wages barely provided enough to support their families, which required most boys to join their fathers in the mines. The 12-hour days of hammering and digging to collect the black rocks deep in the earth hardened their arms and scarred their hands. If their lives weren't cut short by cave-ins or explosions from underground gases, they often suffered from black-lung disease from breathing the coal dirt or from some form of cancer from the tobacco they chewed to battle the dirt in the air.

"During the period 1870 to 1913, inclusive, 17,716 fatalities occurred in and about the anthracite mines, representing a rate of 3.42 per 1,000 men employed. The amount of coal mined per fatality was 124,968 tons, or there were eight fatalities per million tons mined," according to a Department of the Interior, Bureau of Mines report, "Coal-mine fatalities in the United States 1870-1914."[10]

By the late 1800s, workers grew frustrated with the low wages, dangerous conditions, and discrimination against many immigrants. Strikes took place, and violence increased. After mine owners broke the Workingmen's Benevolent Association union's "Long Strike of 1875," the infamous Molly Maguires supposedly emerged in the Anthracite region. According to the Pennsylvania Historical & Museum Commission, the Molly Maguires may have "originated in Ireland in the 1840s as a secret society dedicated to fighting the mounting agricultural oppressions in their country."[11]

Numerous mining officials were murdered, and men believed to be associated with the Molly Maguires were charged. On June 21, 1877, 10 of the 20 accused and sentenced to death were hanged on what was called Black Thursday. By 1903, the Department of Mines was established to monitor safety and record accidents, but mining continued to be dangerous.

* * *

The Dauberts were not spared the pain from the dangers of mining. Two of Jake's brothers died in mining accidents—Clifford in an explosion at the Cameron colliery in 1884, four months after Jake was born,[12] and Calvin in a cave-in at the Blackwood colliery in 1916.[13] At the time, there were few other options for the men in Jake's family. He knew that life awaited him.

"It's in the family," he said years later.[14]

Life for the Daubert family changed after Jake's mother died on March 23, 1897, when Jake was 12. That "completely broke up the family," according to an article by F.C. Lane for *Baseball Magazine* in 1912:[15]

"His older sisters speedily married, and Daubert, as well as his father, went to live with one of the brothers. There was little more schooling for Daubert after his mother's death, though he did obtain three or four months of broken and interrupted learning during the following two years. His 14th year, however, marked the final limit to his school days."

By then, Jake was a coal miner.

A Future Star Is Born

His mother's death had a profound impact on Jake, according to Lane's article. She was a "sympathetic influence" on him. Jake shared with Lane his last memories of his mother carrying him to bed when he had fallen asleep in the sitting room after he came home exhausted from a long day at the breaker.

He began work as a breaker boy, sitting on a platform for 10 to 12 hours daily with dozens of other young boys, sorting and picking rocks from the coal that moved on a conveyor below their feet. But Jake had greater ambitions, even within the limited prospects of mining. After two years as a breaker boy, he joined the men in the mine doing whatever jobs were available, including loading cars, driving mules, and shoring up tunnels with timbers.

At 16, Jake joined the regular miners digging and removing coal deep in the mines. His ambition and resourcefulness in choosing the best available jobs allowed him to double the average miner's $2 per day pay. Jake's limited education didn't hamper his ability to succeed, and the hard work during the next six years strengthened and hardened his body.

Jake's work in the mines laid the groundwork and provided the incentive for the opportunities later when he traded the work digging for black diamonds for one playing on a baseball diamond.

Like many other young men and boys who worked in the mines, one of Jake's few pleasures was playing baseball, mainly on Sundays. He became very good at it, first playing for local amateur teams, including Llewellyn, Shamokin, and Schuylkill Haven, then as a semi-professional player for Pottsville and Lykens. Semi-pro players received some form of payment but did not play baseball full-time.

His first experience as a semi-pro in 1902, however, came with a promise but not a payment.

"It was a small amount they promised me," he recalled years later about the unnamed team. "Perhaps it was a dollar, but the gate was so poor that none of us were paid. That was the first semi-pro game in which I took part. In later contests, however, I drew down small sums that varied from two dollars to five."[16]

Jake, a left-hander who would become one of the top hitters and defensive players during the Deadball Era, began playing baseball as a pitcher because he "always wanted to be where there was the most work."[17]

One of the first newspaper articles about Jake was published in the *Miners Journal* on August 11, 1902:

> The Pottsville team tried a new pitcher on Saturday, and he showed up remarkably well. The new man is Jacob Daubert, of Llewellyn, and previous to Saturday he had been pitching good ball for the minor teams in this vicinity. In the first inning of the game with Shamokin on Saturday the fielding of the Pottsville team was very ragged, and Daubert on account of his newness was a trifle wild. Shamokin put up a good game, however, and were not as easy as expected.
>
> The game was witnessed by an audience of about 600 people and was in all, fairly interesting. Daubert settled down and pitched a good game. In the eighth inning he struck the side out, and made a record of ten strike outs during the whole game. Ten hits were also made off his delivery, but most of them were exceedingly scratchy.

Pottsville won 8-5. Jake gave up ten hits, struck out ten, and walked three in nine innings. He batted ninth, went 0-for-3, was hit by a pitch, and scored a run.[18]

Jake was back on the mound for the Pottsville Buffaloes about ten days later against an excellent Palo Alto team. He struck out the first 12 batters and finished with 23 strikeouts. He allowed only two hits in Pottsville's 9-4 win, although he walked ten and was hurt by his team's five errors.[19]

Twenty years later, in a story published by several mid-western newspapers, Jake talked about another game from 1902. Some of the details appear to be mixed up because of fading memory or poor reporting, including listing the team as Pottstown instead of Pottsville, but it's an interesting story:

> The Shamokin and (Pottsville) Elks got up a game, and there was a great rivalry. I was supposed to pitch . . . and took Tickets Dewald, my catcher, along with me. As I warmed up . . . the

home Elks recognized me and protested on the grounds that I was a pro because of that one game I had pitched for them. "I'll tell you what I'll do." I said. "Let Tickets pitch and I'll catch." They agreed to this. I had caught a little as a kid.

Well, to make a long story short, they had us beaten 12 to 7 at the start of the ninth. Their pitcher was overconfident and a combination of two walks and two hits scored four runs for us. This made it 12 to 11 against us with two out and a man on first.

I came to bat. Our manager told me if I ever did anything to hit that ball. "Do it now if you care for us." he insisted.

I let the first one go by, and the second one was right over. I socked it over the center field fence into the deer yard for a homer. That made it 13 to 12 in our favor, and we held them safe their half of the round.[20]

There were few details of the game in the local newspapers, but *The Philadelphia Inquirer* published a box score on September 14 showing that Jake was the catcher and Dewald the pitcher in a 13-12 Pottsville win.[21]

Jake may have filled in at catcher, third base, and the outfield, but his main position early on was as a pitcher.

"I was a pretty successful pitcher, although I didn't know a whole lot about pitching then," Jake told Ford Sawyer in a 1924 article for *The Boston Globe*. "I used to pitch for Schuylkill on Saturdays and for the Clippers of Pottsville on Sundays. I worked in the mines, and I used to get through work at noon. Then I would hurry home, take a horse and buggy and drive from Llewellyn to Schuylkill or walk three miles to the car line. Then, after the game, I would hop the car and go back home once more.

"I used to get $3.50 for pitching for Schuylkill, but the Clippers paid me $5 a Sunday for twirling. Then Orwigsburg offered me $8 a game if I would pitch for them, but when I told the Schuylkill men of this, they increased my pay to $8. I played three games for Pottsville, in the Pennsylvania State League, in the fall of 1905, and the next year went to Lykens."[22]

Despite Jake's early success in baseball, he expected to remain in Llewellyn, marry and raise a family, and work in the coal mines. On September 5, 1903, Jake married Gertrude Acaley, who also lived in Llewellyn and whose ancestors, like Jake's, had lived in the region before the American Revolution. The couple lived on Willing Street, and their family grew with the birth of Louise Arietta in 1904 and George Jacob in 1905. As much as Jake had hopes of playing professional baseball, his family was his priority, so he continued to work in the mines to pay their bills and played baseball for recreation.

"The fact is I started and slipped back so often that it is hard to tell how," he explained in 1910 after his first season with Brooklyn. "I know that at first, I didn't want to start at all. I loved baseball and played ever since I can remember. I was on the 'first nine' in my hometown when I was 15 years old. But the idea of getting into the big leagues did not come to me for a long time."[23]

The unlikelihood of a successful career in professional baseball hit home for him in 1906 when he was playing for Lykens and injured his pitching arm.

"It is true I am only an accidental first baseman," he said in 1908. "Like many other players who started out in some other position, I have shifted around considerably on the diamond since I broke into professional baseball. When an amateur, I was a pitcher and was considered a fairly good one.

"My breadwinner, however, developed a kink, and as it looked as if it never would get right again, I decided to give up box duty. So I went to third base and played that bag until July 22, 1906."[24]

In addition to the challenge of playing third base as a left-hander, Jake's arm injury was hampering his throws across the diamond to first base, so he considered quitting. The only other option he saw was playing first base.[25]

"Then our first baseman got hurt, and our manager told me to play first until he could get a good man," he said. "I was lucky from the start. Things broke my way, and I must have made good there, for the manager told me to keep on and he would not look for anyone else to play first. Instead, he dug up another third baseman."[26]

A Future Star Is Born

Jake was determined to do well in baseball, just as he did in the coal mines.

"While playing with Lykens, Jake knew that if he were ever to amount to anything worthwhile as a first baseman, he had much to do to improve his play," Ford Sawyer wrote in the August 1, 1924, edition of *The Boston Globe*. "He was weak on 'pick-ups,' and he couldn't run fast enough to rank as a good base-runner. So for hours, he used to throw a ball up against the side of the barn, getting experience in scooping up 'pick-ups' and bounders of all sorts and from all angles. And in the winter months, he donned his spiked shoes and practiced starting and sprinting on an ice-coated road back home until he could get away fast and could run the bases in good time. For an hour and more at a stretch, he went over the strip of road until he was exhausted."[27]

Jake's hard work paid off because he caught the attention of the Kane Mountaineers, a western Pennsylvania team in the Class D Interstate League. When Lykens' season ended on Labor Day, Jake was contacted by Kane to join the team for the rest of its 1906 season. Jake was reluctant to go, feeling responsible for providing for his family. His professional career might not have happened if not for the urging of his wife, Gertrude.

"He didn't want to leave home," Sawyer wrote in 1924. "He was rather bashful and modest as regards his own worth, and he was a little uncertain of his ability to make good. But his wife was confident of his ability, and she wanted him to go. Until 1 o'clock in the morning, she urged and pleaded with him, and, finally, in the morning, he consented to get in touch with the Kane officials.

"The young man sent the club owners a salary demand which he believed they would never accept, a claim for $200 and transportation for the 15 remaining days of the season. But, to his surprise, they accepted the terms and wired him to report immediately."[28]

Jake's professional baseball career had begun. He batted .340 for the brief 1906 season with Kane and was invited back for 1907.

The location of the former house where Jake Daubert was born in 1884, now Terrace Avenue, next to Shamokin Creek. (Photo by Harry J. Deitz Jr)

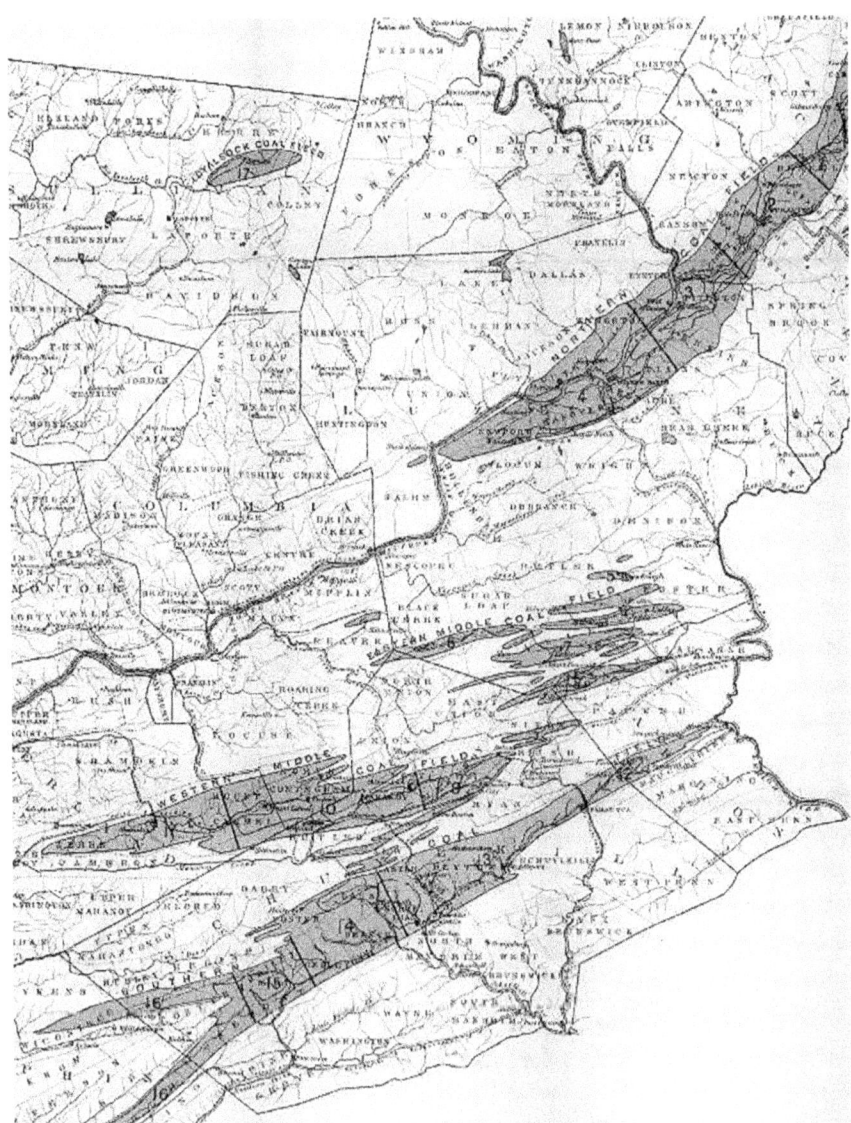

Map of Anthracite Coalfields of Pennsylvania. (Courtesy of Pennsylvania State University Libraries)

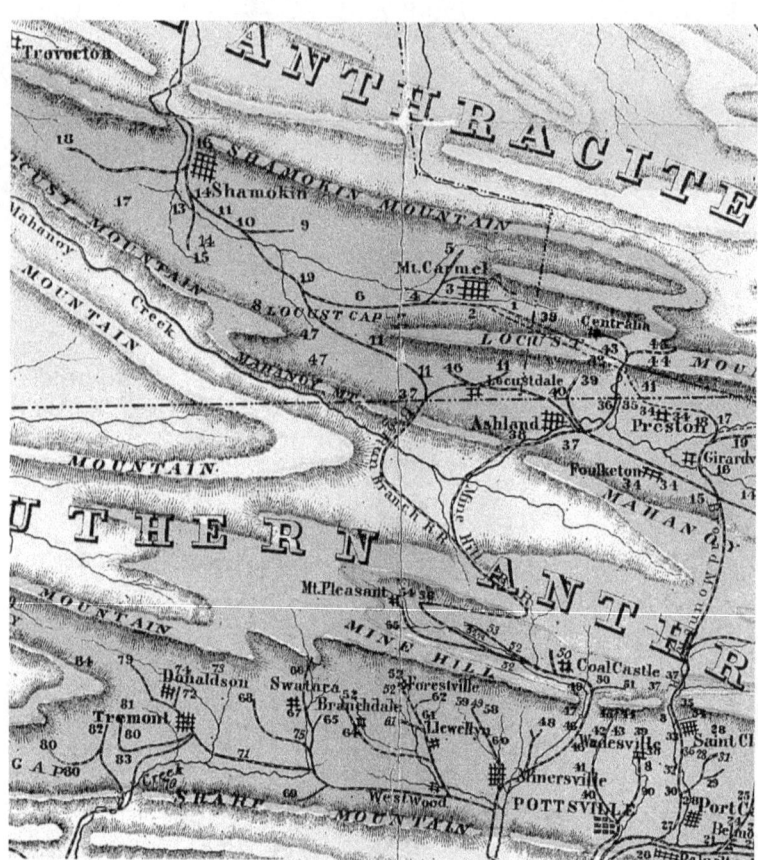

Part of Lower Anthracite Coalfields of Pennsylvania, showing Shamokin and Llewellyn. (Map reproduction courtesy of the Norman B. Leventhal Map & Education Center at the Boston Public Library)

A Future Star Is Born

Breaker boys sorting coal in an Anthracite breaker in 1911. (Photograph by Lewis Hine for the National Child Labor Committee collection. Photo is in the public domain and acquired from the Library of Congress)

Blackwood Breaker near Newtown, west of Llewellyn. (Postcard image from the early 1900s. Photo is in the public domain)

Jake Daubert at 18. (Image from *Baseball Magazine*, February 1914. Photo is in the public domain and from the collection of Cody Swords, Vintage Baseball Memorabilia)

Jacob Daubert Sr. (Image from *Baseball Magazine*, February 1914. Photo is in the public domain and from the collection of Cody Swords, Vintage Baseball Memorabilia)

The 1906 Lykens team in the Williams Valley League. Jake is far right in the front row. (Photo is in the public domain and from the collection of Sally Reiner, Lykens-Wiconisco Historical Society)

The Daubert Brothers around 1902, from left, Irwin, Calvin, and Jake. (Image from *Baseball Magazine*, February 1914. Photo is in the public domain and from the collection of Cody Swords, Vintage Baseball Memorabilia)

2

Digging Out of the Mines and Minors

Jake's arm injury—which ended his days as a pitcher, sent him briefly to third base and finally to first—may have been a hidden blessing.

"I was in the little Williams Valley league down in Southern Pennsylvania and was hitting pretty well, but my arm was bad," he recalled in 1910. "I was a third baseman then and never had played much except as a pitcher and sometimes a catcher or the outfield. I got an offer to go out again when our league went up but wanted to stay at home. I finished up the season there and saw I could hold my own with them, except that my arm was so bad I wanted to quit. I couldn't heave them across from third base, and besides, I didn't know much about playing the game or how to take care of my arm. I went to the manager and told him either I would go home or go to first base. He asked me if I could play first, and I said I thought I could, although I never had tried it, and that a left-handed thrower belonged there rather than at third. He must have liked my nerve, for he gave me a chance, and I made good and hit well."[1]

Jake returned to the coal mine after the 1906 season ended but looked forward to spring and a full season with Kane.

The Kane Mountaineers were formed in 1905 by local business leaders to provide entertainment and prevent ennui, or weariness and boredom, in the isolated mountain region.[2] The team played in the Interstate League in 1906 with northwestern Pennsylvania teams in Erie, Punxsutawney, Bradford, DuBois, Patton, and Oil City, and Olean in southwestern New York.³ Kane is located 90 miles southeast of Erie and on the eastern side of the Allegheny National Forest. It was founded in 1864 by Civil War General Thomas Kane and grew because of the logging of black cherry trees, the supply of natural gas and limestone, and the establishment of the American Plate Glass Company.⁴ Its population peaked at about 7,200 in 1920, twice what it is today.

Jake might have been happy in the area, considering his interest in hunting and shooting, but he focused strictly on making baseball a way to support his family.

The Mountaineers finished 1905 in fifth place with a 40-56 record and improved to 58-58 in 1906. There was reason for hope in the spring of 1907 because of the addition of Jake, pitcher Harry Coveleski, and manager/outfielder Charles Kelchner.

"When Coach Charles Kelchner first laid eyes on Daubert, he stood out like a diamond in a slag heap," Ed Rose wrote in his 2012 article for the Society for American Baseball Research, "Pop Kelchner, Gentleman Jake, The Giant-Killer, and the Kane Mountaineers."⁵

"Pop" Kelchner was a language professor and athletic director at Albright College, located in Myerstown, Pennsylvania, before relocating to Reading after merging with Schuylkill College in 1929.⁶ He was one of the organizers of the Tri-State League and was brought to Kane as the player/manager. His life as a college professor seemed in contrast to baseball then, but he loved the game.

"Professional baseball was far from a gentleman's game, especially as it was played in the low minors," Rose wrote in his SABR article.⁷ "Betting on games was out of control, and fans and players heaped verbal abuse on umpires while heckling relentlessly their foes from other teams. In DuBois, an outfielder with the local Miners club, upset at being called out on strikes, bludgeoned the umpire to death in the batter's box."

Harry Coveleski, like Jake, was born in Shamokin. He was a left-handed pitcher and the older brother of future Hall-of-Famer Stan Coveleski. A year after playing for Kane, he became known as "The Giant Killer" when he was called up by the Philadelphia Phillies in September 2008 and beat the New York Giants three times in five days, denying them the National League Pennant. He bounced around the minor leagues for several years before signing with the Detroit Tigers, where he played from 1914-1918 and was 69-43, including three 20-win seasons. He still holds Detroit's career ERA record at 2.34. In nine years with Philadelphia, Cincinnati, and Detroit, he was 81-55 with a 2.39 ERA and 83 complete games.

All the high expectations for the Kane team were washed away quickly, along with the team itself. Rose quoted from the book "Joe McCarthy: Architect of the Yankee Dynasty" by Alan Levy:

"Day after day, rainouts occurred. One local paper described a steady pattern of 'chilling air and glum skies.' According to the Pittsburgh papers, 'Every team in the Interstate League is losing money, with weather killing off games and attendance. By July 1, Erie was the only club in the circuit not in debt.' Rainouts continued to frustrate the staging of games and promotion efforts."[8]

The Kane team was 17-26 when it folded on July 1. Jake led Kane with a .299 average in 42 games in 1907, Coveleski was 4-7, and Kelchner batted .279. Kelchner returned to teach and coach at Albright until 1919. He became a legendary scout for the St. Louis Cardinals for 40 years. Coveleski finished the summer with an independent team in Wildwood, New Jersey, before catching the attention of Philadelphia.[9]

After the Kane team folded, Jake was sent to the Marion, Ohio, Drummers, who played in the Ohio-Pennsylvania League. Several years later, *The Plain Dealer* of Cleveland recalled Jake's introduction to the Marion team:

> When Daubert joined Marion, he looked like a country boy out for a holiday in town. He wore clothes that had seen better days, a coat that allowed the back of his shirt to show above the trousers when he bent over and looked anything but a minor league player of the first caliber.
>
> Once on the ball field, he appeared transformed into a graceful athlete, fleet of foot and strong of arm. It took the clever left-hander about five minutes to become one of the most popular players that ever wore a local uniform.[10]

The Marion team finished last in the eight-team Class D league with a 48-87 record. Jake had a .283 average in 71 games, but more importantly, his play attracted the attention of Cleveland Indians scout Tom O'Brien, who first noticed him at Kane.

O'Brien had a lengthy conversation with Jake after a game at New Castle, Pennsylvania, on August 6 and wanted him to go to Cleveland, but Jake was under contract with Marion.[11] On August 16, Cleveland reached a deal to acquire Jake in exchange for $1,200 cash and Scotty Ingerton, who had played for Marion in 1906.[12] The money was reported to be the largest ever for a player from the league. Daubert remained with the Drummers until the end of their season because Ingerton was playing for Albany then.

The Marion paper reported: "The local fans will rejoice in the fact that Daubert is to finish the season with the Drummers. It is thought that Daubert will have no trouble in making good with Cleveland. He is a good sticker, fast on the bases, a fine fielder, covers lots of ground and has a good arm and head."[13]

The *Pottsville Republican,* near Jake's home in Llewellyn, reported the signing on August 22 (including misspelling Marion) under the headline "Lajoie Signs Jake Daubert":

> Another Schuylkill County boy has won fame upon the diamond and will play next year with a big league club. The new wonder is Jacob Daubert of Llewellyn, and the eye which singled him out as a coming star was none other than the great Napoleon Lajoie of the Cleveland Americans. The latter club played an exhibition game at Merion, O, last week, and Lajoie noticed the great work of Daubert, who played first for Merion. Immediately after the game, he approached Daubert for terms, and the latter was so pleased to get a chance to play upon a big league team that he told the Naps leader that he would accept any reasonable terms if Larry would secure his release from the manager of the Merion team, George Cartwright.
>
> The manager refused to let him go, so Lajoie was compelled to buy his release, and this could only be done upon the

condition that Jake would finish the season with his team. This was agreed to, and the purchase price was fixed at $3,000, half of which goes to Jake. Daubert is overjoyed at his good luck and will erect a home for his parents at Llewellyn with the money he receives.

Daubert started his base ball career four years ago in Pottsville, riding his bicycle here in order to pitch for scrub teams upon the back lots. Last year he pitched for Schuylkill Haven and started this season with Kane, Pa., which team disbanded several weeks ago. He then went to the Merion, O., team In the Ohio-Penna. League, and now leads that league in fielding. He is also a twirler of great ability, having a good left-hand delivery He has a record of 23 strike-outs at Dolan's Park in 1905 in a game between the Pottsville Buffaloes and Palo Alto, and he also caught an infield fly and assisted in two put-outs at first base.[14]

When the season ended, Jake returned to Llewellyn and worked in the mines until the spring of 1908, when he headed south to Macon, Georgia, with the Cleveland team for spring training. Several years later, he recalled his last days in the mines when, through some carelessness, he was nearly killed. His boss told him if he "didn't stick to baseball and give up mining, he would chase him out of town with a gun."[15]

After only one year in professional baseball, there already were premature comparisons to Hal Chase, the great first baseman for the New York Yankees, especially for his defense.[16] Jake had dreams but knew he needed to improve to reach the next level in baseball.

"I am in good shape now, having been working in the mines until a week ago, when I quit to take up a little road work," he told *The Plain Dealer* of Cleveland in February 1908. "I don't say that I am as good a hitter or fielder as Hal Chase or 'Jiggs' Donohue, but I think I am coming all the time, and perhaps the day will arrive when they will talk about me a little. At least, I hope so. I am willing to learn, and I really think I will be able to hold my end fairly well."[17]

It wasn't Chase of the Yankees or Donohue of the Chicago White Sox who were his competition with Cleveland. George Stovall was the established first baseman for the Indians. Each year he came to spring training and played so hard that he scared off rookies looking to take his job. Stovall admitted later that he saw Daubert as his greatest competition and worked especially hard that spring, making excellent plays and batting around .700 against minor league pitchers. Jake played well but had little chance to replace Stovall, who later said he regretted he had scared Daubert out of the American League.[18]

Stovall played primarily at first base for Cleveland from 1904-1911. He was traded and played for the St. Louis Browns in 1912-13 and signed with the Kansas City Packers in the Federal League for 1914-15. In his 12-year career, he had a .265 batting average but was known more for his defense. He had a .986 lifetime fielding percentage at first base and led American League first basemen in fielding percentage from 1908-1911 and assists from 1909-11.[19] On August 7, 1912, he made seven assists at first base, an American League record that still stands.[20]

Years later, Henry P. Edwards, a sportswriter for *The Plain Dealer*, shared a story about Jake, who, at the beginning of his career, was somewhat intimidated by the veterans on the team and used "mister" when addressing them. He wrote about the reaction of Indians manager Nap Lajoie:

> Jake Daubert found George Stovall and Bill Hinchman also trying for first base. For two days, Jake watched them work out without getting a chance there himself. I asked him why he didn't take some work there.
>
> "Well, Mr. Stovall and Mr. Hinchman are working there all of the time, and when they quit, it's time to go back to the hotel," was his reply.
>
> When Lajoie was informed of Daubert's diffidence, he blurted: "What's that busher want—a perfumed note inviting him to try himself out at first? Tell him to go and tell Stovall and Hinchman to get off first and give him a chance. If he hasn't nerve to do that, I don't want him."[21]

It wouldn't be long before Jake asserted himself on and off the field.

At the end of spring training, Cleveland's owner, Charles Somers, encouraged Jake when he said: "Jake, we have decided to send you over to Nashville for a little more seasoning. You look good to me, but you need more experience. I consider you a dead ringer for Hal Chase, and I believe you will be back to us soon."[22] Jake accepted his assignment to Nashville of the Southern Association, where he worked to improve his skills and gain experience. He batted .262 for the Volunteers, who finished 75-56 and won the championship in the eight-team Class A Southern Association.

Jake was praised that summer by the legendary sportswriter Grantland Rice, who wrote:

> Neck and neck with Bernhard in the popular esteem ranks J. Daubert. The demon first-sacker has handed out some finished articles before, but Hal Chase, at the top of his game, never saw the day when he could have put it on Jake's work of Wednesday. The sidewheeler pulled off plays that looked well nigh as impossible as making money by writing poetry, yanking 'em from midair and out of the soil with equal éclat. Time and again, he figured in the center of a sensation, stretching his system until he looked like a snapshot of the rubber trust in action. Jake certainly had the goods.[23]

Spring training in 1909 was a repeat of the previous year, and Jake was farmed out to Toledo of the Class A American Association. Jake struggled with the Mud Hens after injuring his foot early in the season[24] and batted .186 in 35 games. He was returned to the Indians, and Nap Lajoie gave him to Memphis in the Class A Southern Association. Jake rebounded there, batting a league-leading .315 in 81 games as the star for the disappointing Turtles, who finished 51-88 and in last place in the eight-team league.[25]

"Cleveland got me, and I thought I was started, but somehow they could not see me," he said in the fall of 1910. "I thought I was doing fairly well, but they chased me to Toledo, recalled me, chased me again and finally, I got discouraged and couldn't hit, and everything broke wrong, and I was sent to the Southern League.

"I didn't like the way Cleveland had treated me, and I wanted to show that bunch I could play the game. I worked hard at Memphis and studied the game. I learned a whole lot, and suddenly I settled down and started hitting. After that, I was all right. I began correcting faults and working harder to get along, and pretty soon, Brooklyn grabbed me. That time I was ready and knew I was ready. I had the confidence, and I knew that I could hold my own."[26]

Larry Sutton, a scout for Brooklyn, was watching another player in the Southern Association when he noticed Jake and recommended him to the Superbas. The team selected him in the Rule 5 Draft and signed him on September 1. Jake's days with Cleveland were over, and his major league baseball career was about to begin.

Jake in 1907 when he played for the Marion team. (From the collection of Jill Daubert Malone)

1908 Nashville team. Jake is second from left in the back row. (From the collection of Jack Daubert)

Jake's wife, Gertrude, with their children, Louise and George around 1907. (From the collection of Jill Daubert Malone)

3

Rapidly Rising Star

Jake Daubert made his major league debut in the middle of the Deadball Era, which began around 1900, lasted for 20 years, and was marked by the dominance of pitchers and an emphasis on defense. Many teams played "small ball," putting the ball in play and using speed and aggressive baserunning to score runs. Jake fit that mold perfectly. He was a chop hitter who choked up on the bat, hit line drives, was a good bunter, and used his speed to reach base. And he was an excellent fielder.

Early in the century, a rule change made the first two fouls count as strikes, benefiting pitchers. Previously, batters could foul off pitches until they got one they liked, and only balls that were missed or bunted foul were counted as strikes.

Despite the dead ball, there were many excellent hitters who still are considered among the best in the history of the game, including Ty Cobb, Tris Speaker, Honus Wagner, Nap Lajoie, and Sam Crawford. But the first two decades of the century were dominated by pitchers, especially Walter Johnson, Christy Mathewson, Grover Alexander, Eddie Plank, and Cy Young, all of whom won at least 326 games during their careers.

The period also had a group of pitchers who had excellent careers because of the spitball, which was legal until 1920. Those included Hall-of-Famers Burleigh Grimes, Stan Coveleski, and Red Faber. The spitter—along with other doctored baseballs, such as the emery ball, in which sandpaper was used to scratch the ball; and the black ball, which was marked by licorice or tobacco juice—was another advantage for pitchers because the alterations to the surface of the ball could change the balance and make it break in various directions.

Owners looked to save money, so baseballs were used even after they became darkened, scuffed, and soft. Much of that changed in 1920 after the beaning of Cleveland's Ray Chapman, who was the only player to die due to being hit by a pitch. The Deadball Era also ended because fans—and, as a result, owners—wanted to see more offense. The result was the emergence of power hitters, led by Babe Ruth.

* * *

The Brooklyn baseball team's history began in 1884 when the Brooklyn Atlantics played in the American Association. At various times the team also was called the Grays (the color of their uniforms), Bridegrooms (when six of the players got married in 1888), Grooms, Ward's Wonders (for manager John Montgomery Ward), Foutz's Fillies (for manager Dave Foutz), the Trolley Dodgers (because of the trolley tracks in front of Eastern Park), the Superbas (for a popular Vaudeville act), the Robins (for manager Wilbert Robinson), and The Flock. The team also was informally called Dem Bums, based on a newspaper caricature by *New York World-Telegram* cartoonist Willard Mullins in 1939.[1]

In 1890, the Bridegrooms joined the National League, which was founded in 1876, and won the championship with an 86-43 record in the eight-team league that also included the Chicago Colts, Philadelphia Phillies, Cincinnati Reds, Boston Beaneaters, New York Giants, Cleveland Spiders, and Pittsburgh Alleghenys. The Brooklyn Superbas won the National League title again in 1899 and 1900, then steadily declined during the next few years. They were a struggling team when Jake joined them in 1910. In the previous six seasons, they were 343-569, a .376 winning percentage.[2]

The team originally played at Washington Park I, then Washington Park II and Eastern Park, before moving into Washington Park III in 1898. That field was 335 feet to left field, 500 to center, and 295 to right, and the wooden stadium's capacity was 18,000.[3]

When the Superbas drafted Jake in the fall of 1909, they already had Tim Jordan at first base. Jordan led the major leagues in home runs in 1908 and tied for the lead in 1906 with 12 each season. The situation seemed similar to the previous two years with Cleveland, but Jake had gained experience and confidence during his successful showing with Memphis. Speculation began in early January about Daubert claiming the first-base position over Jordan, along with rumors that Jordan might be traded.

Before Jake ever played a major league game, Charles Somers, president of the Cleveland team, told Charley Ebbets, president of the Brooklyn team, that Daubert has no equal at first base with the possible exception of the Yankees' Hal Chase. "You have a 'jewel' in Daubert if he has improved in his batting," Somers said.[4]

However, Jake was not happy with the initial salary offered by Brooklyn and said he would rather play for Memphis. He returned his contract unsigned. By the middle of February, his differences with the Superbas were resolved for a reported $2,000,[5] and he signed and prepared to head to spring training in Hot Springs, Arkansas.[6]

Jordan arrived at spring training, confident he would keep his job.

"I am in fine shape," Jordan said. "I never felt better in my life. My legs are all right, and even Hal Chase couldn't win my job away from me. You never heard of Chase hitting them over the fence, did you? Well, you know 'Big City' does, don't you? If you don't know, ask some of the residents of the Waldorf flats on First Street. Nobody will get my job; just go put a little bet on that. That's information straight from the feed box."[7]

Several weeks later, the odds of that bet were changing. *The Brooklyn Daily Eagle* reported on March 28:

> Tim Jordan's chances for retaining his job as regular first baseman are going a glimmering. Jake Daubert is so strong with the team that 'Big City' will have to show that his legs are all right before he plays again. Report from Springs has it that Tim's legs are hopeless, but, of course, Bill will have to be shown. In the meantime, Daubert is proving a wonder at first, playing the position on the Tenney-Chase order. He is a left-handed thrower, eats up line drives and hard grounders with lightning speed, and plays all around Big City on inside work, besides hitting about as well. Dahlen has nothing but good words for the new man.[8]

Jake wasn't the only youngster making an impression. Zack Wheat, who had batted .304 in 26 games the previous season, would become the full-time left-fielder.

Brooklyn opened the 1910 season under new manager Bill Dahlen at Philadelphia on April 14. Jake had made the team, but there was no indication who would start at first base. Harry A. Williams later wrote about Jake's first game in the *Los Angeles Times:*

> Finally, the day arrived for Brooklyn to open the season against the Phillies in Philadelphia. Bill Dahlen, the manager, had given no intimation as to who would start the season at first base, and Daubert, along with many others, conceded the place to Jordan.
>
> Daubert worked out with the club during the first half of the preliminary practice and then gave way to Jordan.
>
> Still, there was no word from Dahlen. But when the game started, he ordered Tim to remain on the bench and set Daubert on the first sack.
>
> The shock was considerable to both Jake and Tim. Jordan's confidence, it is said, began to ooze right then, and by that one order, Dahlen practically ended Tim's major league career.[9]

Jake was nervous in his first game and committed an error on his first play. John Titus, the leadoff batter for Philadelphia, hit a sharp grounder to first base. "It was one of the kind that hugs the grass and fairly burns the sod," Williams wrote. "Daubert never did get down on it. It was too swift and shot between his legs." It was not a preview of the level of defense Jake would play for the rest of his career.

Jake batted second and went 0-for-3 in his first game. The next day, he got his first hit, a double that hit the bull sign and earned him a $50 reward. Brooklyn won the opener, 2-0, behind Nap Rucker, who pitched a 2-hitter. But the Superbas lost the next four to the Phillies.[10]

A month later, Jordan was released to Toronto, where he played several years in the minors. Jordan played six games with Washington in 1901 and two with the Yankees in 1903. He had been picked up by Brooklyn in 1906 and became the primary first baseman. He led the league in home runs with 12 in 1906 and 1908. He finished his seven-year career with a .261 batting average and 32 home runs. In the field, he committed 112 errors, had a .980 fielding percentage, and led the league in errors at first base in 1906, 1907, and 1908.[11]

Jake struggled at the plate at the beginning of his career. On May 10, after 21 games, he was batting .194. As the weather warmed up, so did Jake. In the next 22 games, he went 29-for-80, a .362 clip, raising his average to .283. By August, Jake was attracting attention throughout the league. On August 8, *The Brooklyn Citizen* labeled him "Wizard Jake" and reported:

> Some of the fielding plays he has made and is making right along, not even the peerless Hal Chase can eclipse. Not only is Daubert a swell first baseman, but he is a good hitter and clever base-runner as well. One baserunning stunt that he pulled early in the season caused Manager Dahlen to remark that it was as heady a piece of baserunning as he had ever seen. (Al) Burch was taking a long chance on scoring. Daubert, in the meantime, was racing up to second. It was in a game against the Cubs, and (Harry) Steinfeldt, who had got the throw-in from the outfield, could have got Burch easily at the plate. Daubert saw it and calmly turned second and headed direct for Steinfeldt. For just a few seconds, Steinfeld was nonplussed, seeing Daubert racing towards him. Steinfeldt's hesitation was just long enough to give Burch the chance to score. Of course, Steinfeldt got Jake, but the run was home and, but for the great first sacker's quick thinking, Steinfeldt would have easily gotten Burch."[12]

Jake finished the season at .264, second-best on the team behind Wheat's .284. Jake hit 15 doubles, 15 triples, eight home runs, and 31 sacrifices, which was fourth best in the league, in 144 games. He committed 16 errors and had a .989 fielding percentage, second only to the .991 by Ed Konetchy of St. Louis among first basemen in the National League.

"Keep your eye on Jake Daubert," Dahlen said after the season. "He is the best first baseman that has broken into fast company in many years and will be a better fielder than Hal Chase in time. If I had a team made up of Dauberts, Brooklyn would win the pennant in a walk."¹³

The Superbas struggled as a team, finishing in sixth place in the eight-team National League with a 64-90-2 record. The league at the time comprised the Chicago Cubs, New York Giants, Pittsburgh Pirates, Philadelphia Phillies, Cincinnati Reds, Brooklyn Superbas, St. Louis Cardinals, and Boston Doves.

Jake spent the offseason in Schuylkill County, hunting and trapshooting. He didn't forget his hometown friends and held a banquet where he presented them with souvenir baseballs from the 1910 season.¹⁴

1911 SEASON

In just over a year in the majors, Jake had gained the respect of most of the players in the league. Charley "Red" Dooin, a catcher who played most of his 15-year career with the Philadelphia Phillies and became that team's manager in 1910, was among those impressed by the young Daubert.

"Show me something that Daubert cannot do," he said. "He can hit harder than Chase, is just as fast on the bases, and I think he has something on Hal in fielding. That may not go with some people, but I stick by it. He has Chase beaten at his own game—throwing to second or third on a bunt or ground ball to the right side of the diamond. Daubert can hit them as hard as any man in the game and always makes his hits just when they are needed. As for handling thrown balls—well, he seems to get them any place. I have played a bunch of games against Brooklyn since Daubert broke into the league last season, and in all that time, I have seen Daubert miss just one throw that was anyways near him, and he saves that infield a bunch of errors."¹⁵

Jake's nervousness at the start of the previous year was long gone when the 1911 season began. By the middle of May, he was batting .385 and had an 18-game hitting streak. In a 19-game stretch from April 19 to May 13, he batted .444 (32-for-72) with four doubles, three triples, two home runs, and four sacrifice hits.

There were rumors that Charles Ebbets, the Dodgers president, was looking to trade Jake to the New York Giants for three players, including

Fred Merkle, who had earned his unflattering nickname "Bonehead" because of a base-running mistake in September 1908 during a close pennant race that the Giants eventually lost.

"I hear you are going to trade me for Merkle," Daubert said to Ebbets after hearing the rumors in May 1911.

"Nothing doing," Ebbets said. "I wouldn't trade you for Muggsy McGraw himself."

"Well, I just wanted to know," Daubert replied. "You see, my descendants would not be very proud of me if they had to tell folks that their father or grandfather was traded to New York for the man who lost a pennant for Gothan because he didn't touch second."[16]

Ironically, Merkle was traded to the Dodgers in August 1916 and played for them in the World Series, one of five losing World Series he played in during his 16-year career. Jake frequently defended Merkle and believed it was unfair that he was labeled because of one bad play.

Jake played in 149 of Brooklyn's 154 games in 1911. He missed several games in Boston at the end of May because of an illness—variously reported as tonsillitis,[17] a cold,[18] or sickness caused by Boston beans.[19] By July, he had cooled off to .267 but came back to finish the year at .307 and ninth in the most valuable player voting. He finished over .300 for 10 of the next 12 years.

The team, which adopted the Dodgers nickname, had another disappointing season, finishing in seventh place with a 64-86-4 record. They split their first four games and never reached .500 again, ending the year 33 ½ games behind the league-champion New York Giants.

1912 SEASON

Two significant announcements were made in January 1912. Charley Ebbets unveiled plans for a new stadium east of Prospect Park.

The other news was the naming of Jake as captain of the Superbas, replacing John Hummel.[20] It was part of a move by Dahlen to change the attitude of the team. *The Brooklyn Citizen* reported on January 21:

> It wasn't so many years ago when the Superbas were looked upon as a "joy club." Every season attempts were made in the spring

RAPIDLY RISING STAR

to get the team out of the old rut, but the club was shy on good playing material, and each year the Superbas finished always classed a "joy" outfit.

Dahlen, to get rid of that spirit, kept on weeding out the old-timers, replacing them with what "Bad Bill" calls "human crabs." Jake Daubert is a good example of the "crab" ballplayer. Jake doesn't take kindly to watching his team beaten day after day.... He wants to win, and if all hands are not showing the proper spirit, he doesn't hesitate to say it.[21]

The season wasn't any better for the Dodgers, who were 58-95 and again finished in seventh place, 46 games behind the champion Giants. Brooklyn fans began to hope better days were coming because of the play by Jake and Zack Wheat. Jake led the team with a .308 batting average, and Zack was second at .305. Jake finished eighth in the most valuable player voting.

Wheat played 18 years with Brooklyn before his final season in 1927 with the Philadelphia A's. He led the National League in batting in 1918 with a .335 average and had a career average of .317. Like Jake, he was an excellent fielder with a .966 career fielding percentage, mostly in left field, led the league among left-fielders in 1918 (.978) and 1922 (.988), and finished in the top five in left field 14 times. Wheat remains the Dodgers' franchise leader in hits (2,804), doubles (464), triples (171), and total bases (4,003). The Veterans Committee voted him into the Hall of Fame in 1959.[22]

By the summer of 1912, in only his third season, Jake was already considered by many to be the best first baseman in baseball. He raised his batting average to .409 during the first week of the season and remained above .300 for the rest of the year. Twice he had five hits in a game, and five times he had four.

His fielding was at least as good as his hitting. He committed only ten errors during the season and led National League first basemen with a .993 fielding percentage.

Jake missed two games at the end of April after he injured his thumb making a spectacular play at first and injured his hand sliding into second on April 23 in a 7-0 win over Boston Braves.[23] *The Brooklyn Citizen* reported:

> Jake has made some great fielding plays since joining the Superbas, but he made a stop yesterday that eclipsed anything that even he has ever made. It was a terrible drive over the bag, and how Jake ever got to it, not to mention how he ever stopped it with one hand, will always remain a mystery. It was easily the greatest fielding play made at Washington Park in years.[24]

He also missed six games at the end of July because of a sprained ankle.

As captain, Jake filled in as manager while Dahlen was fined $100 and suspended from April 23 to May 4 after he was accused of hitting umpire Cy Rigler on April 20 during a dispute after the umpire ruled a walk-off home run by Art Wilson of the New York Giants. Dahlen believed the ball was foul.

In addition to the ongoing rumors about Jake being traded, there were reports that he would replace Dahlen as player-manager. Those stories were prevalent during July and August when the team went 20-40. Ebbets insisted Dahlen would return as manager next season and, when pressed about the rumors concerning Jake, replied, "That is nobody's business."[25]

Jake denied he was lobbying to replace Dahlen. "This talk about me visiting Ebbets and telling him about the weakness of certain Brooklyn players is not true," he said. "It puts me in a bad light with them."[26]

Jake didn't need to worry about being in a bad light with fans. At the end of the season, he was voted the most popular player on the Brooklyn team in a contest sponsored by the "999" Clothing Store and was presented a loving cup.[27]

The next few months were busy for Jake. After the season, he led many of his teammates as the Daubert Dodgers on a barnstorming tour that included games in Schuylkill County. *The Call* in Schuylkill Haven reported on one of those games played on October 12 and won by Brooklyn, 12-3:

Rapidly Rising Star

The largest crowd of base ball fans and base ball enthusiasts, both chivalry and beau, ever in Schuylkill Haven, or for that matter, ever in this section of the county, was that which gathered on the local base ball park on Saturday afternoon last, to witness one of the biggest base ball attractions ever secured for Schuylkill Haven. The attraction was big enough, Jake Daubert with the Brooklyn Nationals, in fact, most too big for the local team, as the home players appeared to have a bad attack of stage fright and nervousness, with the result that they did not play their usual fast game and the Brooklyn bunch had most too easy a time of it. As the game progressed, it became most too one-sided to be of any real interest or produce the desired base ball thrill or excitement.

No one thought or expected the locals should or would defeat the Brooklyn Nationals, but quite a few fans sure did expect them to put up a better fight than they did. Nevertheless, the stage fright was, to a certain extent, warranted as the Schuylkill Haven men are not used to performing before an audience of eighteen hundred people or against a strong National League team.

Daubert, the Hal Chase of the National League, who hails from Llewellyn and who, prior to his getting into big company, wore a Schuylkill Haven base ball uniform and done it proud, was given an ovation by the crowd when he stepped to the plate in the second inning.

He promptly raised his cap in acknowledgment of the same and also heartily thanked the donor, D. Kaufman, a base ball manager under whom he worked years ago when he was presented with a huge bouquet of roses and carnations.[28]

Jake also became one of the leaders of the newly formed Baseball Fraternity. The union was organized in August and incorporated on September 6 to protect players' rights. According to an article in *The Evening World* of New York on October 21:

> Their main object is to improve the general morale of the players and to protect the men from unjust discipline. They expect it

to do away with the tyranny of fines and suspensions without a hearing. No attempt was made to fix a wage scale, as the "stars" would never have aided in the organization had this been one of its objects.

The article also reported:

> Resolutions were passed requesting the National Commission to give umpires authority to have ejected any spectator who taunts or abuses a player during a game. Such power will prevent such incidents as resulted in Ty Cobb assaulting a spectator and the subsequent strike of the Detroit team because Cobb was suspended.
> The fraternity passed resolutions opposing all forms of contract violations and all kinds of rowdyism on or off the field and against anything else having a tendency to impair a player's ability or injure the sport.[29]

Jake was elected secretary of the group. Former Yankees outfielder Dave Fultz was named president, and Christy Mathewson and Cobb were among the vice presidents.

Daubert attended the annual National League meeting on December 10 but wasn't impressed. "This is the first time I've ever been at one of these meetings, and can't say that I see anything in them," he said. "Outside of looking the boys over, it doesn't interest me in the least to be here. I thought there were high jinks at these gatherings and that I would be entertained, but unless there is something doing up in the meeting rooms, and I can't get in on that, this is about as lively a place to be at as a funeral. I think I'll beat it over to Brooklyn and sell a few hundred cigars and then go back to the missus and tell her all about the fine time I didn't have."[30]

Before the end of the year, Charley Ebbets announced that Dahlen would return as manager for 1913, at least temporarily ending speculation that Jake would replace him.[31] Ebbets also signed Jake to a three-year contract. The terms weren't announced at the time but may have been for $4,500 per year.[32] That investment would begin to pay off in 1913.

Undated photo of Jake and Gertrude. (From the collection of Jill Daubert Malone)

Jake in 1910, his first season with Brooklyn. (Photo is in the public domain and acquired from the Ernie Harwell Collection at the Detroit Public Library)

Bill Dahlen, Jake's first manager in the major leagues. (Photo is in the public domain and acquired from Wikipedia)

American Tobacco Company card from 1911. (Photo is in the public domain)

RAPIDLY RISING STAR

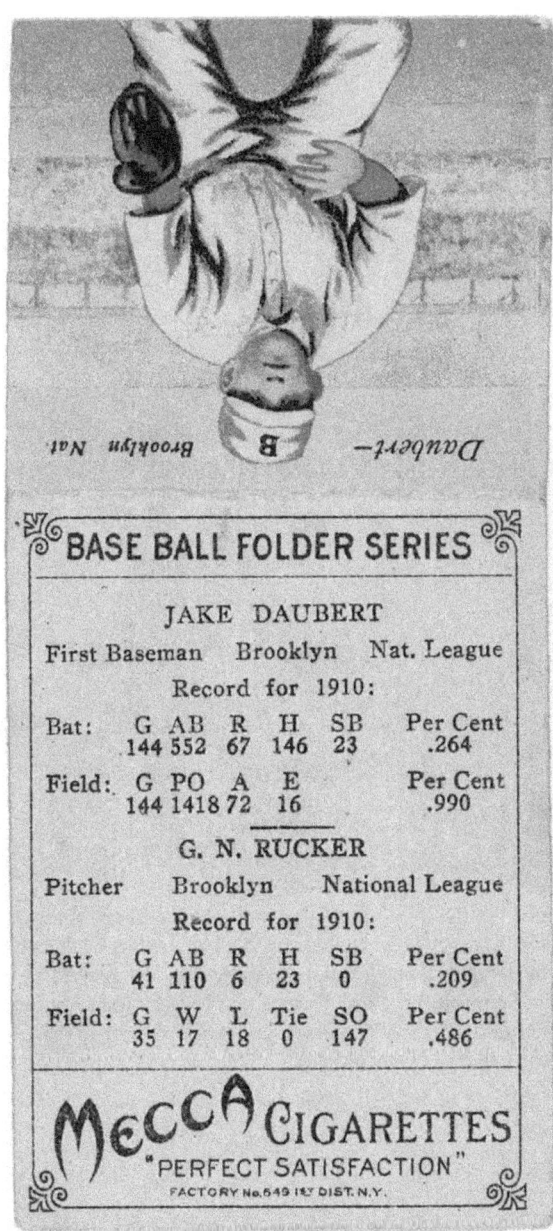

Card issued by Mecca Cigarettes in 1911. (Photo is in the public domain)

Jake, left, with members of the New York Giants on board the Creole of the Southern Pacific line to head for New Orleans by boat on February 22, 1911, before taking a train to Hot Springs, Arkansas, for spring training. Most of the other Brooklyn players traveled directly to Hot Springs by train. From left, Jake, Josh Devore, Larry Doyle, Rube Marquard, Art Devlin, and Fred Merkle. (Photo is in the public domain and acquired through the George Grantham Bain Collection at the Library of Congress)[33]

Jake was voted the Most Popular Player on the Brooklyn team in a contest sponsored by the "999" Clothing Store and was presented a loving cup on October 3, 1912. (Image from *Baseball Magazine*, February 1914. Photo is in the public domain and from the collection of Cody Swords, Vintage Baseball Memorabilia)

Brooklyn Robins in 1912 at Hot Spring, Arkansas, for spring training. Jake is far right in the fourth row. The boy in the front row is believed to be Jake's son, George. (Photo is in the public domain and acquired from the Library of Congress)

Members of the Brooklyn Robins, possibly during spring training in the early 1910s. Jake is standing third from the left. (From the collection of Jack Daubert)

4

A Champion and a Gentleman

Three years after Jake broke into the major leagues by allowing a ground ball to go through his legs, he became one of the game's stars. He was among the leading hitters, fielders, baserunners, and bunters. And if there was any doubt about Jake as the best first baseman in the National League, he erased it in 1913, when he won the league batting title with a .350 average and was named the Chalmers Award winner as the league's most valuable player.

To appreciate Jake's success meant understanding his motivation. He refused to be mediocre and took a no-nonsense approach to baseball. He was determined not to fail, driven mainly by his responsibility to provide for his family. Jake never took his success for granted, and his memories of working in the coal mines remained with him all his life and inspired him to succeed in baseball.

"Look at these hands," he said in 1912. "See those black marks? That's from mining, and even now, when I look at them, I sometimes am afraid for fear that all my success is a dream and that I will wake up in the darkness of the mines again."[1]

With those reminders, Jake worked hard to improve his baseball skills. He played aggressively, evident in his 165 career triples, 29th all-time. He sacrificed and did the little things to help his team win. That was best shown in his 392-lifetime sacrifice bunts that remain a National League record and are second only to Hall-of-Famer Eddie Collins, who had 487 in 25 seasons with the Philadelphia Athletics and Chicago White Sox, ten more years than Jake played. Jake's 237 sacrifices with Brooklyn are still a Dodgers record. He had great bat control and often bunted with two strikes, catching the opposition off-guard.

"In 1914, when I led the league, I bunted a third strike in three straight games," he said. "The first was against the Giants. There was a man on first at the time I bunted the third strike. I advanced the runner to second and beat out the throw to first. The next man up hit safely, scoring the winning run from second base. Next day, with no one on and two strikes on me, I beat out a bunt and finally scored the winning run. That night we went to Boston. Next day Bill James was pitching and had a lot of stuff. I laid down a bunt that was just about right on a third strike, but it rolled foul."[2]

Jake's ability to make contact with the ball and hit it where he intended with two strikes was a skill he developed during his early years in baseball. He averaged fewer than 33 strikeouts per season.

"I'll concede that a bunt on the third strike is a bit risky for some—but I never regard it as a risk with me," Jake said in 1924. "Every ball player tries to be special in at least one thing. My specialty was bunting.

"In all my batting practice in the early years, I strove for one thing beyond all else. And that was to make a ball roll fair when I laid it down for a bunt. Even after I could do it eight out of ten, I kept on practicing it so that, in the end, I had it down as close to perfection as possible.

"Therefore, when I did bunt a ball on the third strike, it wasn't a great risk for me. Practice had made it possible for me to drop that ball into safe territory upon most occasions. Of course, there were times when my bunt on the third strike rolled foul. I was called out, and the customer felt I had made a boob play. But that didn't happen very often.

"A bunt on the third strike is the unexpected play in baseball. And it's those unexpected plays that result in hits or win ball games. I gained a reputation as a third-strike bunter, and sometimes the infields would be playing in for me. When they'd do that, I'd cross them and aim to drop the ball back of the infield.

"Whatever batting success I have had—and the batting championships I won—were due to a variety of things but the most important of all was that I learned how to make a perfect bunt—and then consistently 'crossed' the enemy infields by bunting on the third strike."³

As good as he was as a batter, he was even better as a fielder. He had a .991 lifetime fielding percentage, led National League first basemen in 1912, 1916, and 1922, and was in the top three for 13 years. Jake weighed about 160 and was listed at 5-10 ½ in height, but he was said to have a nine-foot reach when catching balls thrown by other infielders to first base. It was especially true for high throws, which saved a lot of errors.⁴ And that was before the development of the larger first basemen's mitts.

"I think I was naturally a pretty fair fielder, and, of course, in the amateur games we had in the mining country, I was as good a batter as the rest," Jake said in the spring of 1912. "But that wasn't saying very much. It is true when I was a minor leaguer, I seemed to be able to hit, but that doesn't carry a man very far in the majors. And I don't mind saying that any ball player, whoever he is, would rather be able to hit than anything else."⁵

Jake's hands may have been blackened and scarred, but overall he was a ruggedly handsome athlete.

"Daubert is a very pleasant appearing young man, about 5 feet 10¾ inches in height, and weighs ordinarily about 162 pounds," F.C. Lane wrote about Jake in the July 1912 issue of *Baseball Magazine*. "He has pale blue eyes, which are very frank and straightforward looking. His whole appearance gives the impression of many years of hard work. He is, in all ways, a quiet, unassuming and very likable player. He is extremely popular among his teammates and throughout the circuit, particularly in Brooklyn."⁶

He also had become a sharp dresser off the field, no longer looking "like a country boy" and wearing "clothes that had seen better days," as he was described by *The Plain Dealer* of Cleveland when he joined the minor league team of Marion, Ohio, in 1907. When he received the Chalmers touring car for being the MVP during a ceremony before the first game of the World Series between the New York Giants and Philadelphia Athletics at the Polo Grounds on October 7, 1913, he was dressed in a well-tailored suit and tie, long top coat, and bowler hat. His popularity was evident in the ovation he received from players on both teams and the 38,000 fans.[7] He also was at the series to provide a daily player's perspective for fans in the pages of the *New York Tribune*.

His classy demeanor, intelligent insight, and clean living earned him the enviable nickname "Gentleman Jake." He was a role model for youngsters and an example for anyone struggling to overcome difficult or unfortunate circumstances.

"Jake Daubert, the star first baseman of the Brooklyn National Club, is a player with whom the public should become better acquainted," F.C. Lane wrote about him in the July 1912 issue of *Baseball Magazine*. "His career is a story of hardship and struggle, in which he rose from the lowest rounds of the industrial ladder in a Pennsylvania coal mine to one of the most prominent positions in the world of sport. His record should serve as a model and inspiration for the thousands of would-be big leaguers scattered throughout this country who feel discouraged through lack of opportunity. There are no obstacles, so Daubert's life has showed, which may not be overcome by anyone who has native ability and is conscientious and persevering."[8]

His approach to baseball—and life—was serious, and fans loved him for his intensity on the baseball field. But there was a warm side of him that not everyone got to know. His friends in Schuylkill County knew it because he spent the offseason there. So did his teammates and sportswriters, who often asked him to share the fine points of playing first base, preview and analyze World Series games, and explain the art of hitting.

"One of the first impressions is that life has been rather a serious matter with him," Harry Williams wrote about Jake in 1915. "He stands out as a man who has taken some hard knocks. There is something there that makes you think he may have taken on the responsibilities of a man while still a boy. Possibly it is the imprint left by the early underground days in the mines. There is just a trace, a mere shadow of the expression that you see in the faces of laboring men who are very tired—and possibly a bit discouraged—which years of success and prosperity have not entirely erased.

"This, however, is misleading, for Jake has a very sunny disposition, and in conversation, he becomes radiant."[9]

Jake also was fiercely loyal to those close to him, and he never shirked the responsibility he felt for them, which was why he played the game so hard.

"His leading ambition is to make enough of a success in life so that his son will not have to work in the mines as he had to do," Lane wrote. "Daubert's aged father is no longer dependent on the precarious work of the underground, for when Jake received his contract from Brooklyn he decided once, and for all that, his father should not work anymore in the coal shafts. For fifty-seven years, his father had been a miner, passing through all the grades from breaker boy up, and he had seen most of his early companions blown to pieces in gas explosions or buried under caving roofs. He himself, when still in his prime, had been terribly injured in an explosion, so that his spine was wrenched apart and he was unable to work for fully three years; but now he is permitted to share in his son's success and enjoy a little of that leisure which had been denied him all his life."[10]

Lane asked Jake in 1912 about his plans after his playing days were over.

"I have no plans," he said; "I do not know that I am fitted for anything. I only know two things, mining and baseball, and I hope I shall be able to save enough money while I am an active player to provide for my family. So long as they are taken care of, I am not worrying about myself."[11]

Again, Jake undersold himself. He became a very successful businessman in the Schuylkill Haven area. He owned a coal washery, movie theater, ice company, and billiard parlor. A store in Brooklyn named a cigar for him, he was featured in advertisements for sporting goods (D&M Sporting Goods, The "Lucky Dog" Kind) and a bat by Louisville Slugger (Jake Daubert pattern), and he endorsed a shotgun made by Remington UMC, a "Radiolite" watch by Ingersoll Waterbury, and a Cole 8 motor car.

There were reports that Jake made as much in his businesses as he did playing baseball and that halfway through his career, he didn't need to play the game to support his family. But baseball was what Jake enjoyed most and where he gained his greatest reputation.

And yet Jake's success didn't lead him to believe he was better than he was, even though he was better than he believed. Even after batting .307 in his second season in 1911, he didn't see himself as a .300 hitter.

"Three hundred and seven was my last season's batting average, but I am not a three hundred hitter," he said. "I would like to think I am, but I have no reason to. Last year I admit I reached that mark, but everything broke just right for me. To tell the truth, I was very lucky, for I know that my average batting gait is nowhere near three hundred. I think I am about a .250 hitter. I cannot claim to be any more, but of course, I shall always do my best."[12]

His obvious modesty prevented him from speaking candidly about his greatness as a hitter, but he did share his theory of the reasons for his success, which included batting over .300 for 10 of his 15 years in the majors.

"I used to dream about hitting .300 in the majors, but I never expected to get there," he said. "I believe three things accounted for my success last year: First, luck; second, the knowledge experience had given me; third, simply trying to do my best at all times."[13]

Jake studied the game and knew a lot about hitting. Although he refused to brag about his accomplishments, he often was anxious to talk about his philosophy of hitting. Because he was so intelligent and well-spoken, people listened.

"The secret of .300 hitting is in the eye," he told Lane in 1914. "All batters know this, and it is rather hard to explain why one man can hit twice as well as another who seems to be just as capable in every way. When I say that a player has a good batting eye, I don't mean that he has better eyesight than some other player. True, the keener his eyesight, the better, but that in itself isn't enough. The eye, the brain and the muscles must all work together in the same fraction of a second, or the eye alone is useless. For instance, your eyesight is probably as good as mine. It may be better, for all I know. If I should take you to the Brooklyn ballfield and we should both take turns with the bat against some good pitcher, you would probably miss altogether what I would consider a very easy strike. And that wouldn't be any fault of your eyesight, but the fact that your arms and hands would not swing the bat quite quickly enough, that is, they would not work with your eye. You might know everything that was necessary to know about meeting that ball with the bat just as well as I would, but the chances are the wrists and shoulders wouldn't be exactly geared to your eye. In other words, you wouldn't have what I call a good batting eye. I admit I would be taking you at a disadvantage in such a test, but if you should ask me to read a column in the newspaper, I might know the meaning of every word in that column as well as you, but you would probably be able to read that column at least twice as fast as I could. There your eye would be much quicker and better than mine."[14]

When Jake wasn't playing baseball or running one of his businesses, he hunted and was one of the top trap shooters in Pennsylvania. He compared the eye-hand coordination of shooting live birds to hitting a baseball.

"Shooting birds on the wing is a good illustration of what I mean," he said. "The amateur can point a shotgun at a quail as accurately as the crack marksman. His eyesight may be just as good, but his finger on the trigger doesn't work when he tells it to. It may be only a hundredth part of a second behind. That is perhaps enough. He pulls the trigger and misses the shot. The crack marksman has absolute mastery over his muscles. His finger on the trigger and his eye work together, and he doesn't miss." [15]

For someone with limited education, because he quit school at age 12 to work in the mines, Jake was a deep thinker who had a profound way of sharing his knowledge. Much of what Jake knew and shared was captured by F.C. Lane, the prolific writer and editor for *Baseball Magazine* from 1912-1937.[16] Lane interviewed Jake numerous times and wrote extensive feature articles about him, exquisitely capturing Jake's personality and understanding of baseball. He included Jake's expanded explanations of hard work, experience and confidence, and luck, which Jake credited for his success.

Jake spoke to Lane about the importance of hard work:

> I think a man must have some natural ability as a batter to start with, but the rest depends upon the use he makes of it.[17]
>
> When I worked in the mines, they used to have to pound the jumper. That is, one man would hold a heavy iron peg and the

rest would swing on it with sledge hammers. If you tried it, you probably couldn't hit it at all, and yet those men who are used to such work can keep pounding away with their full strength and never miss, though they hardly have their mind on the work at all. It is just practice, like everything else, and there is no doubt that practice has made a better hitter of me than I was before.[18]

Jake spoke about the importance of experience:

> None of us are any more than human. No batter is so great at the start that he can't improve with experience. That is my belief, at least, but I will speak for myself at any rate and say that, in my own case, I would put confidence first.
>
> When I joined the Brooklyn team, the pitchers looked about ten feet high, and, as for me, I felt about so big (placing his hand about a foot above the floor). That was my first trouble, lack of confidence.
>
> Confidence is the foundation of all batting. I have gained confidence now, or I would never have been able to keep above the .200 mark. By confidence, I do not mean that every time I step to the plate, I expect to hit safe. I do expect to make a try for it and generally do at least hit the ball. I know now that all pitchers, even the greatest, are only human beings like myself, that they are not half as much to be dreaded as I thought they were once, and that there is nothing supernatural about their skill.
>
> I remember very well the first time I ever faced Christy Mathewson in the box. He looked to me as big as a house. You see, I was over-awed by my opinion of his ability more than by the man himself. That is not saying that Mathewson is not a wonderful pitcher, because he is, but I was guilty of the same error which makes nine-tenths of the young batters so much clay in a master-pitcher's hands. They exaggerate the pitcher's ability and underestimate their own. The cure for this is confidence.[19]

And Jake spoke about luck:

A Champion and a Gentleman

I cannot claim that I have really earned my success. I am not trying to say, of course, that success is anything unusual, but to me, it seems great compared with what I hoped to do when I was a coal miner. It is so much better than anything I supposed possible for me that I cannot believe it is merely the result of my own efforts. True, I have worked hard at all times and have always played my best. But I consider myself a very lucky man.

Luck is a big item in baseball. I will not say it is the most important thing in the game because I do not believe it is, but I know that it is a great deal more important than many people suppose, and I think it has done better with me than I deserve.

The infield hit helped me as much as any one thing to win the batting championship. The infield hit is mostly luck. People may tell you differently, but they don't know what they are talking about. Does anybody suppose that when I, or any other batter, drive a slow roller to shortstop and manage to beat the throw to first that that is what we are trying to do? Anybody with any intelligence knows this is not so. I will not speak for other players, but I will speak for myself. When I swing at a pitched ball and connect with a hit of this kind, it means only one thing. It means I have absolutely failed to do what I was trying to do. What I actually had in mind was to drive the ball through the infield. No batter in his senses, unless he was trying to bunt, would have anything else in mind. I swung at the ball, and instead of doing what I had in mind without first hitting it hard, I almost missed it. As soon as I swung, I knew that I had missed it, but the only thing for me to do was to drop the bat on the instant and run as fast as I could to first base. This is the only thing any batter can do in such a case. All the time I am covering that long 30-yard distance between home plate and first, you can picture me blaming myself for making such a bad swipe at that ball, and all the time, I well know that, outside of my own speed, the only thing that can mend matters now is the slowness with which that ball travels to short or wherever it is hit, and the difficulty the receiver may have in getting hold of it in time to catch me at first. Now, if I go to first on a play of that kind, the official scorer will call it a hit. It is a hit, but it was caused by no ability on my part. Remember that I had failed to do what I intended. As far as my ability went, I had no license to reach first base at all, but luck stepped very kindly on the diamond and took things out of my hands, so to speak, and changed a very bad play on my part into a hit. If that isn't luck, what is it? Of course, people will say that a man's speed must be allowed for in a case like this. I have already admitted that speed was a valuable thing for any batter to have. It is true that a fast man can beat out an infield hit that a slow man would fail on, and you can call that special talent if you want to. But I claim that a fast man, no matter how great his speed, has no more license to make errors like this than a slow man. It takes more than speed to beat out infield hits. They are failures on the batter's part, pure and simple, and I, for one, am willing to admit that when I make one of these so-called hits, I have been helped one step up the batting ladder by pure luck.

I remember once, when I was at the plate, the pitcher sent in a vicious drive which looked to me as though it would hit me in the face. I stepped back to dodge it and involuntarily raised the bat to protect my face. I had not the slightest idea of even trying to touch the ball, but it struck the upraised bat exactly square and bounded into the outfield so hard that I was able to get to second base before the fielder could catch it. That was a two-base hit in the records, but how much of the credit of that hit belonged to me, and how much to luck? When I say that I have been lucky this year, I mean, for one thing, that I beat out more infield hits than I ever did in a single season.

Luck doesn't always favor the batter, of course. Sometimes she works directly against him. Take another case. Suppose I am at the plate, and the ball comes in. I judge it exactly right. This time I swing my shoulders to the one-hundredth part of a second, meet the ball with the bat fair and square and drive it straight with my full strength. Here, I have actually done what I set out to do. I have actually done all that any batter could do; all that lies within the possibilities of human skill. But what happens? The ball travels straight into some infielder's hands or curves into the far outfield near enough to one of the outfielders so that he can catch it. The result? I get no credit in the batting records for doing all that a human being could do. That is, meeting the ball square and driving it hard. So you see, luck doesn't always favor the batter. But what I mean to say when I claim that I have been lucky in making some evidently real hits is merely this: I made more than my fair share of these lucky raps and believe I was no more unlucky in hitting balls to the fielders' hands than the average batter, so I am willing to admit that luck ought to get some of the credit for whatever might seem above the ordinary in my batting record for 1913."[20]

Many baseball experts believe players make some of their own luck through the way they play. Jake may have been a perfect example. He was a contact hitter rather than a slugger and struck out only 489 times in 8,749 career plate appearances, an average of 5.6 percent.

Even with a body hardened from working in the mines, he did not consider himself exceptionally strong or heavy enough to be a power hitter. Instead, he choked up on his 34.5-inch-long, 32-ounce Ash bat, concentrated on making contact, and relied on speed and getting a fast start out of the batter's box, which showed in his career home runs—30 of his 56 were inside-the-parkers.[21]

"Look at the manner in which Jake Daubert faces the pitcher," Lane wrote. "The Brooklyn Captain is too light and too slender to be a slugger of the Crawford or even of the Joe Jackson type. Wiry and strong he is, but he lacks the weight. Jake, therefore, for a variety of reasons, is not a natural slugger, and we are not surprised to see that he grips the bat well up, almost choking up on the stick. Jake holds it with a resolute, firm grasp at a low Speaker angle, watchful, crafty, eager to hit and, once met, off like the wind for first base. Like Cobb, Jake bats with his feet and utilizes to the most his great speed. He beats out an incredible number of bunts and infield hits, but he is not commonly a long-range hitter and is noted far more for his singles than his home runs. Jake's bat is sadly battered and well-reinforced with tape, and Jake is gripping the handle with all the strength of his wiry wrists. Once a two-fifty hitter, Jake has made himself one of the league's great batters by conscientious effort and utilizing to the full, all the gifts which he possesses."[22]

Jake also studied the game and developed a philosophy that led to his success, which he shared with Lane:

> They will tell you that every batter has his weakness. The pitchers are supposed to study this weakness and pitch accordingly. Now I am not denying that every batter would like to have the ball cross the plate at some particular elevation a little better than any other, but at the same time, I think every good batter should be able to hit a fair strike that crosses the plate, inside or outside, or at any elevation, with about equal ease. I don't think a man can call himself a star batter unless he can do this. I am not placing myself in that list, but at the same time, I do not think it makes much difference to me where the ball crosses the plate, so long as it crosses it.
>
> I have just said that it does not make much difference to me where the ball crosses the plate, but it does make a good deal of difference how it crosses the plate. That is, it makes a good deal of difference to me whether the ball is a fast, straight one, a sharp curve, or a spitball. Here, I think every batter has his preference and his weakness. I have always been able to hit speed better than anything else, and I suppose I might be ranked as a speed hitter. I think I can hit a curve about as well, except one with a sharp break just before the plate, which is a bad ball for any batter to hit. The spitball, when it breaks right, has always been hard for me to hit, and most batters have the same opinion. The slow ball is bad solely because one is not looking for it. Even Mathewson's fade-away would not bother the batter so much, in my opinion, if he knew it was coming, and that leads a good many people to what I think is another error.
>
> They tell you that there is always a war of wits going on between the batter and the pitcher. The pitcher is always trying

to outguess the batter while the batter is trying to do as much with the pitcher. They will tell you to study the pitcher's style of delivery, which is all right and good sound advice. They will also tell you that the batter at the plate is always trying to guess what kind of a ball the pitcher is going to give him next, whether it will be a ball or a strike, fast or slow, and so on. I know that a good many batters, perhaps the great majority, try to outguess the pitcher. It may be useful to them, but it was never of much good in my own case. Perhaps they can read the pitcher's mind and foresee what kind of a ball he is going to pitch next, but I have no such second-sight power myself. I know I never try to outguess the pitcher save as a kind of by-play once in a while, just as you might predict it would be a fair day tomorrow. If I had depended on my ability to foresee what the pitcher had in mind, I would have been lucky to bat upon the .200 mark. I am not laying this down as a rule for anyone else to follow. There may be batters who help their averages by ability at this kind of guesswork. I have no such ability myself and will not claim to have it. I am merely giving my own experience, understand. I may be wrong. My system may seem too simple. It is simple. When I am at the plate, instead of trying to figure out what the pitcher has in mind, I am keeping myself alert and ready to take a swipe at any kind of a ball that comes along. All the energy that I might put into this mind-reading stunt seems better placed to me when it is in my wrists or shoulders, where I can get at it handy whenever I want to use it quick. You see, I have the notion, when I am at the plate, that the main thing for me to do is not to hypnotize the pitcher, but to hit the ball. But I admit I may be all wrong.

Once in a while, somebody who ought to know better makes a few remarks about place-hitting. It seems, according to these people, that there are batters who can not only hit the ball but make it go about where they want it. There may be such players. I have never met them. I know I have no such ability.

Once or twice in a whole season, a batter may meet a ball that is just to his liking and drive it through the particular gap in the infield he aims for. That is place-hitting, and I won't say it does not exist. But it is the rarest thing in the world. The most any batter can ever expect to do, as a general thing, is to drive the ball, at will, either to right or left field. That is not place-hitting in any sense of the word, but it is as near as any batter can come to directing the course of the ball after he has swung on it with the bat.

I believe a great many fans give the batter a number of special talents which he would be the last one to claim for himself, and while there is a good deal of truth in all of them, I have never paid much attention to them myself, and do not believe they have helped me any in whatever batting success I may have gained.[23]

* * *

Jake's philosophy and approach to baseball worked for him, especially in 1913, when he had his best season. He batted a career-high .350, had an on-base percentage of .405 and an OPS (on-base plus slugging) of .829. He was second in the league in hits with 178. His .991 fielding percentage matched his career number. Jake was above .300 all but four days during the season, the lowest at .289 in mid-May, and never dropped below .344 after July 1.

He won the National League most valuable player award with 50 votes. Philadelphia's Gavvy Cravath, who was second with 40 votes, led the league in home runs (19), runs batted in (128), and hits (179) and was second in batting at .341.

The Chalmers Award was established in 1910 by Hugh Chalmers, the president of Chalmers Motor Car Company, to recognize the player with the highest batting average. The prize was a Chalmers Model 30 luxury car. After a controversial race in which Detroit's Ty Cobb edged Cleveland's Nap Lajoie for the award, the Chalmers Award was changed to recognize a player in each league who "should prove himself as the most important and useful player to his club and to the league at large in point of deportment and value of services rendered" and voted by baseball writers. Because of an economic recession, the award ended after the 1914 season but was the forerunner for the MVP awards presented by the leagues beginning in 1922.[24] Jake's biggest challenge after receiving the Chalmers car was learning to drive.

Baseball Magazine also selected Jake as the all-star first baseman, an honor he earned eight times (1911 and 1913-1919).[25] In its all-star team story in 1913, the magazine also supported the Chalmers award Jake received:

> If ever a gift was deserved, it was this—endowed to an unusual degree with all the talents that make a first baseman a star, fast, a brilliant and spectacular fielder, a heady baserunner, an aggressive player who is in the game every moment, a strong, earnest, popular leader on the field, a conscientious workman in every particular, one of the finest fellows in the world personally, and, in addition, a slugger who virtually led his league in batting.
> These are qualifications enough to assure anyone instant recognition on the crack team of the year.[26]

As well as Jake played, his Brooklyn team, which sometimes reverted to the Superbas nickname, remained mediocre. It appeared Jake would play his career without a championship.

The Superbas opened the 1913 season on April 9 at their new Ebbets Field, 55 Sullivan Place, where they lost to the Philadelphia Phillies, 1-0. That was not the first game played at the stadium. On April 5, before 25,000 fans, Brooklyn beat the cross-town rival New York Yankees in an exhibition game, 3-2, on a walk-off hit by Red Smith that drove in Zack Wheat, who had reached second on a bunt and throwing error and moved to third on a sacrifice by Jake. Brooklyn scored its first two runs on home runs by Casey Stengel, the future Yankees manager, who hit an inside-the-parker, and Jake, whose drive to center field was the first ball hit out of the park.[27]

The original dimensions of the steel and concrete stadium were 419 feet to left, 450 to center, and 301 to right. The stadium cost $750,000 and listed a capacity of 23,000. The stadium featured a double-deck covered grandstand, an exterior of brick arches, and an 80-foot rotunda made of Italian marble at the entrance.[28] The first game was moved up one day so the league season would start in the new stadium. Originally the teams were to open on April 10 in Philadelphia, and the first game at Ebbets Field had been scheduled for April 17. Before the game, players from both teams marched to the center field flag pole, where the American flag was raised as Shannon's Twenty-third Regiment Band played the Star Spangled Banner.[29] Fans presented a gold bat and two large horseshoes of flowers to Jake as the team captain. Attendance was about 10,000, less than expected because of the cold weather.[30]

The Superbas lost their first four games at the new stadium, including the first three by 1-0 to Philadelphia. Jake scored the first run for Brooklyn in the new stadium, but it wasn't until the fourth home game, a 2-1 loss to the Phillies.

As the weather warmed up, the team became comfortable in its new home, going 14-4 at the start of a long home stand in late April and May, and shared first place on May 19, percentage points behind Philadelphia. But the Superbas faded and were out of contention after an 8-20 July. They finished in sixth place with a 65-84-3 record, 34 ½ games behind the New York Giants, who won the National League championship and lost in the World Series for the third straight year.

Jake again gained some experience running the team when he filled in for Manager Bill Dahlen several times during the season, including in August when Dahlen was ejected by umpire Bill Klem and then suspended for three days for delaying the game after Klem ejected third-baseman Red Smith.

Jake also had a run-in with Klem on May 21 when he argued over a called third strike, resulting in Jake's first ejection, a three-day suspension, and a rain of boos upon Klem from the fans.

Although Jake didn't get to play in the World Series, he did attend the games and provided commentary in the *New-York Tribune*. The newspaper reported:

> In this way, the fans and other readers will get the opinion of a man who knows what it is to be on the field of play, the obstacles and difficulties to be overcome, and all the intricacies of latter-day inside baseball.

A Champion and a Gentleman

No player, perhaps, is better qualified to watch the games and pass judgment. He ranks among the greatest first basemen in the history of the sport and, as a field leader, has few equals. When it comes to baseball, his keen brain seems to work automatically, while his quick perception and sound judgment, to say nothing of his consistent hitting, has counted largely for the Brooklyn nine this season.

Jake Daubert is popular, not only with the fans of Brooklyn but with lovers of baseball in this city, as much for his forceful if usually quiet demeanor on the field as for his remarkable skill in fielding his position and slamming out the ball when at the bat. He is the type of ball player that commands admiration, and for that reason, his opinions are bound to be respected.[31]

Jake provided interesting commentary, even though he picked the National League's New York Giants to win the series. The Philadelphia Athletics won in five games. The experience gave Jake a new perspective.

As he headed out of Newspaper Alley after Game Two at Philadelphia's Shibe Park, where the Giants got their only win of the series, 3-0, behind Christy Mathewson, Jake said: "I want to get rid of this headache. I think, for the first time in my life, I realize what it means to be a 'fan.' I never had a headache from playing the game, but I've got one now from watching one. There are tense situations on the field, but the tension is greater up here. Believe me; it's better for the nerves to be in the thick of the fight than looking on."[32]

Jake missed the final game of the World Series on October 11 because of a previous commitment for his barnstorming team to play a Lykens team near his home in Llewellyn. The game had been scheduled for the previous day, but when Jake was unable to attend because he was at the World Series, the Lykens team refused to play. Jake headed to Lykens Saturday so his Brooklyn teammates would not lose their share of the gate money.[33] Jake had five hits, and his team won, 9-4, before 2,000 fans.[34] He shared his thoughts about the end of the series by telephone.

Already rumors were swirling that Dahlen would not return to manage the Superbas, and again Jake's name surfaced as a likely replacement.

But two days after Charles Ebbets fired Dahlen on November 17, he announced Wilbert Robinson as the new manager. That surprised Brooklyn fans, many of whom wanted to see Jake as the player-manager. Robinson had spent the previous four years on the coaching staff of the New York Giants and had a history of developing young pitchers. Ebbets wanted a non-playing manager rather than placing that additional responsibility on Jake.

Brooklyn was 251-355-9 in Dahlen's four years as manager, finishing sixth and seventh twice. Dahlen's aggressive managing style and rowdy behavior, including being ejected 65 times by umpires, earned him the nickname "Bad Bill."[35]

Dahlen, however, laid the groundwork for the improvement that was to come for Brooklyn. He weeded out players that had caused the Superbas to be labeled a "joy club." He also set Jake on a path to stardom, establishing him as the starting first baseman in his rookie season and naming him the captain the next year.

Robinson acknowledged Dahlen's good work when he was hired: "Bill Dahlen left the foundation of a mighty strong team, and I hope to complete the task so ably started."[36]

While all that was happening, Jake was in Cuba, where he had taken some of his Brooklyn teammates as part of his annual month-long barnstorming tour that earned each player $600. He was joined on the trip by his wife and son.

Shortly before the end of the trip, the players presented Jake with a pin with 16 diamonds but not before playing a joke on him. The story was reported in the *New-York Tribune* from a clipping Jake shared from the *Havana Post*:

> Mr. Daubert was sitting in his room yesterday morning at the Plaza with his young hopeful and heir on his knee, teaching him his lessons so that he would not be behind in classes when the team returned to Brooklyn when someone knocked. He called, "Come in," and in stalked the entire body of Brooklyn players as solemn as if they were pallbearers at a funeral.
>
> "What's the idea?" Daubert inquired.

"It is like this," explained one of them. "We are on strike. We came down here on a contract to play twelve games, and as we have played that number, we are all agreed that we want to go home."

"Well, I am sorry to hear that," Daubert replied. "I think you recall we contracted to stay here thirty days, didn't we? And we haven't done that. Besides, Manager Jimenez has been real decent with us, and he is a good fellow, and I don't like to see him put in bad."

"We know," replied the spokesman, "but we just feel like we want to go home. It's getting cold up there, and we want to feel some cold weather, so we thought we would let you know about it."

"Well, if that is the way you feel about it," replied Daubert, "why, you can go, for I can't keep you, but I am going to stay here and see Jimenez through if I have to stay by myself and get together another team."

"Now, we will tell you what we are here for," said the spokesman to Daubert. "It is for the purpose of presenting you with this diamond pin as a little token of how much we think of you."[37]

They arrived home on December 5, and three days later, Brooklyn fans honored Jake and welcomed Robinson at a banquet at the Waldorf-Astoria, where Jake was presented a $1,000 gift. The most encouraging part of the evening was the positive interaction between the team's manager and captain.

"I won't be foolish enough to promise a pennant winner," Robinson said, "but am confident that with the help of Daubert, whom I consider the best first base man in baseball, and working in harmony with President Ebbets, I am sure we will have a winner and finish higher next year than Brooklyn did in 1913."

Jake said: "I will go a little stronger and say that with the working together of the players we now have, and Manager Robinson and the club, we will not only enter the first division next year but will make a fight for honors away up in that division.

"Someone has spoken of my career as from a breaker-boy in the mines to champion batter. As a breaker-boy a few years ago, I little thought that I would have been one of the guests of honor at such a gathering of representative citizens as that are here tonight. It seems like a dream to me. I can hardly realize where I am, and when I wake up, sometimes I have to think for a minute before I understand that I am still in Brooklyn."[38]

Two weeks later, Jake and his family made a 12-hour drive in their Chalmers car from their home at 721 Coney Island Avenue in Brooklyn[39] to Llewellyn for Christmas.[40] It was an amazing year for Jake, but there were even better things ahead for the former breaker boy.

"My wife was talking over our circumstances the other evening," Jake said a couple of months later, "and she said to me, 'Jake, perhaps the number 13 is unlucky for some people, but it hasn't been for us. This is the first year, Jake, that we have been able to take things easy. Do you know, I am sorry to see the old year slipping away, for I am afraid we may never see another year that will be quite so good to us as this has been,' and she was right. Everything seems to have come our way this year. Our Cuban trip was very pleasant and a success. We won most of our games, made some money, and the boys were satisfied. I had a good year in baseball, no doubt much better than I deserved, but I am afraid it will not last. It seems like a dream to me. It was only yesterday that I thought I would always be a coal miner. I never expected to be anything else, and even now, I don't feel any too sure of things. It doesn't seem right that I should be so fortunate. I never expected to be so fortunate, never supposed it was possible, and I am afraid it can't last. I can't help feeling it will all slip away from me some day and that I shall finish my life where I started, in the coal mines."[41]

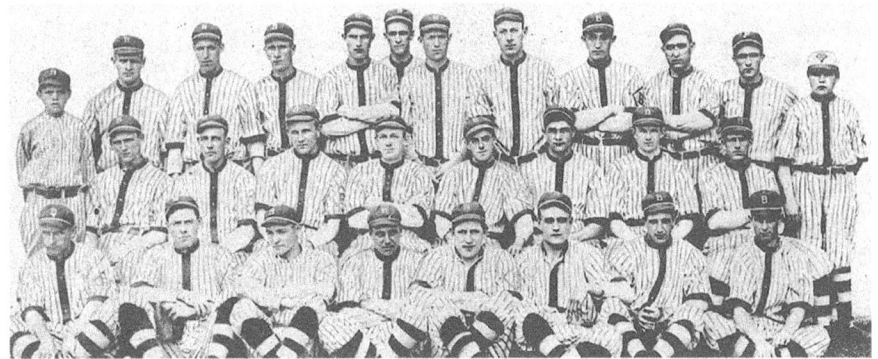

1913 Brooklyn Robins. Jake is far right in the second row. His son, George, is far right in the third row. (Photo is in the public domain and acquired from the Ernie Harwell Collection at the Detroit Public Library)

Ebbets Field on opening day, April 9, 1913. (Photo is in the public domain and acquired from the Brooklyn Public Library)

When Ebbets Field opened on April 9, 1913, Brooklyn fans presented a gold bat to Jake in appreciation for his play. (Image from *Baseball Magazine*, February 1914. Photo is in the public domain and from the collection of Cody Swords, Vintage Baseball Memorabilia)

Jake early in his career with the Brooklyn Robins. (Photo is in the public domain and acquired from the collection at the National Baseball Hall of Fame)

GENTLEMAN JAKE

Jake on the cover of a supplement to The Sporting News, October 23, 1913. (Photo is in the public domain and acquired from the Ernie Harwell Collection at the Detroit Public Library)

Jake in top coat and bowler hat prior to the first game of the World Series at the Polo Grounds on October 7, 1913, when he was presented a Chalmers touring car for being named the National League most valuable player. (From the collection of Jack Daubert)

Jake, Gertrude, and son George during their 1913 trip to Cuba. (Image from *Baseball Magazine*, February 1914. Photo is in the public domain and from the collection of Cody Swords, Vintage Baseball Memorabilia)

Jake was featured in numerous newspaper sketches, including this one published in the *Buffalo Evening News*, July 29, 1912.

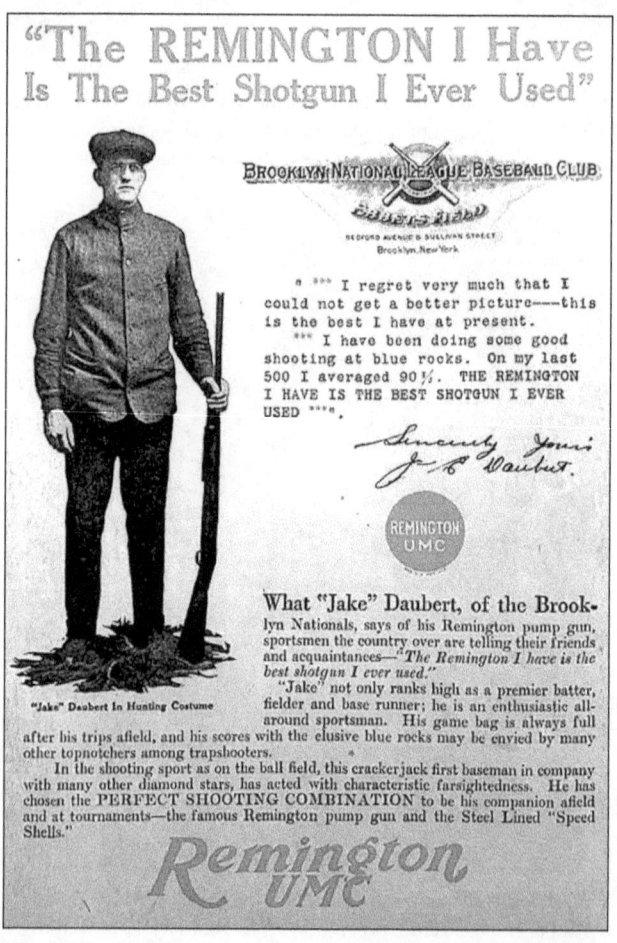

Jake was featured in many newspaper advertisements for endorsing products.

What Jake Daubert Thinks

Robins' Star First-Sacker Says the New "Radiolite" Looks Like a Winner—It's a Glow Dial Watch That Tells Time at Night, and a Hum-Dinger for Looks and Service

By THE MAN BEHIND THE COUNTER

ROBT. H. INGERSOLL & BRO.,
315 Fourth Avenue, New York City.

Gentlemen:
The Ingersoll Waterbury "Radiolite" Watch, one of which I am wearing, is just about the prettiest watch you have ever made. It is a nice size and that glow dial stunt is a real practical help. I notice that wherever you find a baseball crowd you find them wearing Ingersoll watches and for good reasons. This is a fine watch for a huntsman.

Jake E Daubert

Copyright, International Film Service, Inc.
Jake Daubert

WHEN the game is called on account of darkness, it doesn't bother Jake Daubert any. He can still tell when it's supper time by his Ingersoll Waterbury "Radiolite" watch. You've heard of Waterbury watches? Well, the Ingersoll Waterbury "Radiolite" is a new model under that good old name—a handsome, thin, four-jewel, four-dollar watch—a trifle smaller than the ordinary size, and its hands and figures are coated with a substance that shines brightly in the dark. The light-giving power of this substance is radium in minute proportions.

I figure that Ingersoll "Radiolite" watches ought to be just about fifty per cent more useful to a fellow than ordinary daylight watches. They're handy motoring, camping, in the dark movie theatre, under the pillow at night—everywhere in the dark. There are other Ingersoll "Radiolites" beside the Waterbury: the regular "Radiolite," $2.00; the Radiolite" Two-in-One, for pocket or to stand on bureau, $2.25; and the "Radiolite" Strap Watch, for wrist, especially fine for motorists and athletes. I'll invite you to a treat—come in and let me show you the "Radiolites"—they're beauties, every one.

Please mention Baseball Magazine when writing to Advertisers.

The Attraction of Achievement

KINDRED likes and dislikes separate one group of men from another.

That is why it is customary to judge men by the company they keep.

Is it not conceivable, then, that the potential qualities that make for human success are strongly attracted by equivalent qualities in the makeup and performance of a motor car?

Is it not possible to judge motor cars by the men who own them?

Consider the range of achievement represented by this brief selected list of recent Cole buyers in Brooklyn.

J. E. BAILEY, Naval Constructor In Charge of the Construction of the Battleship Arizona.	Lieut.-Commander SWEET, Steel Expert In Charge of the Wireless Station of the U. S. Navy.
BIRD S. COLER, Banker Ex-Controller of the City of N. Y.	WILLIAM E. KELLY, Postmaster City of Brooklyn.
BERT ALLEN, Champion Bowler and Golfer.	JAKE DAUBERT, Ball Player Champion Batter of the National League.
EDGAR N. FINN, Lawyer Assistant Corporation Counsel, City of New York.	Dr. A. L. TALLMADGE, Physician Health Dept., City of New York.
WILLIAM P. THOMPSON, President Thompson Drug Company.	H. C. BOHACK, President H. C. Bohack Co.

Cole 8 cyl., $1,785 f. o. b. Detroit
Cole 4 cyl., $1,485 f. o. b. Detroit

BISHOP, McCORMICK & BISHOP, Inc.

Distributors of Cole and Dodge Brothers Cars.
18-20 HALSEY STREET, BROOKLYN, N. Y.

Bayshore Motor Sales Co.,   Elbert Tappan,
Bayshore, L. I.   Oyster Bay, L. I.

JAKE DAUBERT, Cincinnati First Baseman
First played professional baseball with Kane, Pa.

Dry Slitz STOGIES

JAKE DAUBERT

Now 3 for 10c
ON SALE IN THE BEST STORES

The Perfecto Cigar Co.
"DISTRIBUTORS"
Main 6006   39 E. Chestnut St.   Citizens 7365

—PLAY BALL—

You will find in our Sporting Goods Department the most complete stock of Baseball Goods in the city. We are agents for the famous D. & M. Baseball Goods that are used by many of the Big Leagues in preference to any other make.

Louisville Slugger Bats

No. 40 JD—Jake Daubert pattern	$2.00
No. 40 TC—Ty Cobb pattern	$2.00
No. 40 BR—Babe Ruth pattern	$2.00
No. 20—Bing-Go, golden finish, highly polished	$1.50
No. 11B—Semi-Pro, brown stained hickory	$1.00
No. 4—Jr. League, made of hardwood	50c

D. & M. BASEBALLS

No. 150 D. & M. Official League Ball. This is without question, the best baseball that was ever guaranteed to go through eighteen innings without a rip. The cover is genuine horsehide, sewed with heavy, fine cord, Sea Island cotton. Put up in individual boxes and sealed. Regular $2.00 ball, priced at $1.75

No. 100 D. & M. College League. Official for any game, price $1.50

Other well made balls ranging in price from .... 20c to $1.00

D. & M. BATTER'S MITTS

No. 70½—A large size molded mitt, made of soft brown Wapiti elk. Light in weight and easily broken in. The ends of the fingers and thumb are reinforced with strap leather. Regular price $14.00, our price $12.00

No. 72½—Made of tan colored cowhide on a large molded pattern, price $8.50

No. 732—A molded mitt with light tan cowhide palm and fingers and strong leather back. Priced at $6.75

No. 706—A medium sized youth's mitt made with leather palm and fingers $1.00

D. & M. BASEMEN'S MITTS

No. 647—Light tan horsehide, lightly padded in palm, well padded around thumb and heel. Regular price $9.00, our price $8.00

No. 695—Large size baseman's mitt with black horsehide palm and leather back. Sole leather protection over end of fingers. Either right or left hand glove $5.00

D. & M. FIELDERS' GLOVES

No. G40—Made of tan colored full grained horsehide. Full leather lined and laced $5.50

No. G79—Long fingered black horse hide glove, leather laced, well padded and leather lined. Either right or left hand, price $4.00

No. G35—Well padded, genuine horsehide gloves, leather laced and leather lined $2.75

D. & M. CATCHER'S MASKS

No. M10—Open vision, spitter model with double wire frame. Double leather forehead and chin strap and has extension neck protection. Regular price $8.00, our price $6.00

No. M4—A boys' mask with continuous, hair stuffed pad. Priced at $2.25

D. & M. PROTECTORS

No. 75—Made of heavy brown waterproof khaki, fitted with elastic harness $5.60

We also carry Aluminum Pitchers Toe Plates, Umpire Indicators, Score Books, etc.

S. S. BRYAN— Sportsman's Headquarters

GENTLEMAN JAKE

JAKE DAUBERT AND HIS COLE EIGHT

Jake Daubert, captain and first baseman of the champion Superbas, has long been the owner of a Cole Eight. He uses it daily when at home, in going about his business, driving to the ball park, etc. During the World's Series games Jake's big car was very much in evidence. In the picture shown above are seen Daubert and a party of his associates on the Brooklyn team, who have just returned from a ride. They are, from left to right, Nap Rucker, Casey Stengel, Duster Mails, Jack Coombs, Jeff Pfeffer and Daubert himself.

5

Building a Winner Amid Conflict

Brooklyn began 1914 with hopes of breaking a string of 10 straight losing seasons. That didn't happen, but there were positive signs for the Superbas/Dodgers, who were now called the Robins in honor of their new manager. Although the Robins finished in fifth place, their 75-79 record was an encouraging improvement over the previous ten years when they averaged 59-92, including 104 losses in 1905 and 101 in 1908, and never finished higher than fifth.

The "joy club" had disappeared, and Jake's determination, intensity, and leadership played a big part. Jake didn't match his previous season but won his second straight batting title with a .329 average.

Hiring Wilbert Robinson as manager in November was the start of a busy offseason for Brooklyn and Jake. On December 12, 1913, Brooklyn president Charles Ebbets acquired shortstop Joe Tinker from the Cincinnati Reds.[1] Tinker had played for the Chicago Cubs along with second-baseman Johnny Evers and first-baseman Frank Chance in the famous Tinkers-to-Evers-to-Chance double-play combination from 1902-1912. The Old-Timers Committee inducted the trio into the National Baseball Hall of Fame in 1946.

The Cubs had traded Tinker to Cincinnati after the 1912 season, and he became the player-manager. His brief managing career was disappointing, as the Reds finished 1913 in seventh place with a 64-89 record, and Tinker was sold to Brooklyn for $15,000. Ebbets offered Tinker a $10,000 contract, but the shortstop never played for the Robins. He jumped to the new Federal League to manage and play for the Chicago team.[2]

The Federal League was organized in 1913 as a six-team minor league. The next year it proclaimed itself a major league of eight teams owned by wealthy businessmen and began offering contracts to established major league stars in a plan to compete against the National and American leagues.[3]

At the same time, the Players Fraternity had gained some traction in dealing with owners of the National and American leagues. A forerunner to the eventual Major League Baseball Players Association, the Players Fraternity had been formed in 1912 and by 1913 had about 700 members. That number and the threat of the Federal League no doubt led owners to be receptive to players' concerns when a six-man committee, including Jake, presented a list of 17 requests and demands during a January 6 meeting with the National Baseball Commission. The owners agreed to 11 of the petitions, including that a player who has served ten years will receive his unconditional release if no major league team desires his services—baseball's reserve clause. Previously players were bound to a team for life unless traded or released by that team. Six requests were held for further consideration.[4] Despite the progress, owners still held a lot of control over players.

On January 9, Jake told *The Brooklyn Daily Eagle* that when he was in Cincinnati for the meeting with the Baseball Commission, he had been offered a $30,000, three-year contract by the Pittsburgh club of the Federal League. Daubert was still under contract with Brooklyn but did not immediately reject the Federal League offer.

"I do not think I can be expected to turn down a small fortune for three years' work, when I am now drawing ordinary pay for the same work," Jake was quoted in *The Eagle*. "Any man, for instance, drawing a weekly salary, who was offered a fortune in hand, with yearly pay greater than he was getting, would look after his own best interests and accept. That is my position and I feel that I have a right to help myself.

"I know the Federals have been quoted as saying that they would not go after players under contract and would sign only those who were under reserve, but I have never been told that they were making that their definite policy. They approached me in Cincinnati, and I naturally listened to what they had to say. Several of their clubs were after me, but the talk was rather general until I received the letter from Mr. Barbour, whom I will meet in Brooklyn next Sunday or Monday to discuss details."[5]

That same day James Gilmore, president of the Federal League, declared that Pittsburgh could not sign Jake because he was under contract with Brooklyn. "Make it as strong as you like," Gilmore said, "but this goes, and my managers must understand that what I say goes in his regard, that no player under contract will be signed by any Federal League club, and furthermore, as soon as any manager learns that the player is under contract he must stop all negotiations with him.

"I have no objection to my managers going after players who are merely held by the reserve clause, but as to signing a contract player, that is a different matter."[6]

Jake obviously was concerned when he read the story that he might break his contract and the negative impact on Organized Baseball. The day after *The Eagle* story, *The Brooklyn Citizen* reported: "Jake Daubert Says Story He Will Jump Is Fine Little Fake" and the "'Small Fortune' Offer Was Never Made."[7]

Jake sent a letter to Ed McKeever, vice president of the Brooklyn team, that he would honor his contract:

Brooklyn, January 10, 1914

Edward J. McKeever, Esq., Vice President
Brooklyn Ball Club, Brooklyn, N.Y.
Dear Sir: I deem it my duty to notify you that I have received a telegram from John B. Barbour, president of the Pittsburg Federal League team, asking me to wire my best terms to play and manage the Pittsburg Federal League team, and that I have sent him this answer:

> John B. Barbour, President
> Federal League, Pittsburg, Pa.:
> Your telegram received asking for best terms to manage Pittsburg Federal League team.
> Replying, would say that I will not play outside of organized baseball.
>
> J. Daubert

Wishing you all success for the coming season, I am, respectfully yours,

Jake E. Daubert[8]

"I will not desert organized baseball," Jake told *The Brooklyn Daily Times*. "I am pleased with Brooklyn and its treatment of me, and I am not thinking of leaving."

But in an article in the same edition, headlined "Daubert's Wife Wants Him to Join Federals," Gertrude Daubert said: "My husband would like to remain in Brooklyn. We have our own house here and like our surroundings, but if Mr. Daubert is so valuable to the Pittsburgh Club, he is just as valuable to Brooklyn. He has a letter in his pocket accepting the Federal League club offer, which he will forward unless the Brooklyn Club meets his offer at a conference this afternoon with the McKeever brothers."[9]

Ed McKeever defended the salaries paid to his players: "Daubert is under contract, which has two more seasons to run, and the terms are satisfactory to him. Knockers have been constantly handing out a lot of fake yarns about the poor pay the Dodgers receive, but none of those scandal-mongers has ever asked the players whether they were pleased or displeased. The club pays a man according to his value, and no club in either league pays better salaries than Brooklyn. As our standing in the league improves the salary of the players will advance also. Any player the club keeps gets a good salary. The club is willing to go the limit to get good players and will pay them accordingly."

Jake pointed to his three-year contract as his reason for not leaving Brooklyn.

"My contract with the Brooklyn team has still two years to run," Jake said. "I have always received considerate treatment from the club, and I feel that I owe it to my own honor and conscience to finish out my time.

"I am opposed to contract jumping. It comes to no good, and is fair neither to the man himself nor to the club employing him. I do not refer to the reserve clause in the contracts. That is merely a more or less necessary evil of organized baseball, which operates as much as a check on the magnates as on the players, and which I do not consider binding.

"If I were bound to the Brooklyn team only by the reserve clause I might have jumped at the offer of the Pittsburgh team of the Federal League. It was certainly most tempting."[10]

When asked about Gertrude's comments about a letter he had written to Pittsburgh, Jake said his wife didn't realize what she was saying, and he never wrote a letter.[11]

Charles Ebbets had been on vacation in Puerto Rico during the controversy, and when he returned, he praised Jake for his loyalty to the team: "It was a manly act of Captain Daubert's to turn aside the offer of the Pittsburgh club of the Federal League. I do not recall a player who ever was placed in a similar position who acted so promptly and to the point. It was a big thing for organized baseball to have Daubert exercise such quick and excellent judgment, and the Brooklyn club not only appreciates what he did but will not forget Daubert."[12]

That loyalty was rewarded in May when Brooklyn signed Jake to a new five-year contract[13] at $9,000 per season. It did not include the 10-day release clause. That five-year contract would be at the center of an even more intense conflict for Jake four years later.

Jake wasn't the only star player targeted by the Federals. In addition to Tinker, Hal Chase and Mordecai "Three Finger" Brown were among the initial 59 major league players who joined the new league,[14] which also made unsuccessful efforts to sign Ty Cobb, Walter Johnson, Honus Wagner, Christy Mathewson, and Casey Stengel. The result was a baseball war that included a black list of players who joined the Federals.

The Federal League began play in 1914 with eight teams in Brooklyn, Pittsburgh, Baltimore, Buffalo, Indianapolis, Chicago, St. Louis, and Kansas City. The Indianapolis Hoosiers won the championship that year. After the season, Eddie Plank and Chief Bender, star pitchers for the American League champion Philadelphia Athletics jumped to the Federal League.

The new league filed an anti-trust suit against the National and American leagues in federal court. Judge Kennesaw Landis, who later became commissioner of baseball, presided over the case and urged the leagues to come to a peaceful settlement. With the oncoming World War and declining attendance, they reached an agreement, including that Federal League owners in Chicago and St. Louis would be permitted to buy the Cubs and Browns in those cities. Some Federal League players were sold to the highest bidders, but others, including Joe Tinker and Three Finger Brown, were not allowed to return.[15]

When the 1916 season began, the Federal League was done.

Just when it appeared things had calmed down, there was a new controversy for Jake. Brooklyn opened the 1914 season on Tuesday, April 14. That morning Jake was summoned to court for violating New York state's Blue Laws, which prohibited playing professional baseball on Sundays. The Oakland Baseball Club, a semipro team for which Jake was part owner and operator, had played against the Brooklyn National Yanigans, which included Jake, on Sunday, April 12. Teams often skirted the Blue Laws by accepting donations instead of charging admission. In this case, a magazine called *The Oakland*, which contained Jake's life story, was sold for admission. After some confusion and a hurried drive, Jake arrived late at the magistrate's office. He pleaded not guilty and was paroled in time to play in the season opener.[16]

Jake had a triple, single, and sacrifice in the opener, which the Robins won, 8-2, over the Boston Braves.

About a week later, Jake dropped his connection to the Oakland team, believing his involvement prevented the team from playing Sunday games.[17] On May 6 in the Court of Special Sessions, Jake was found guilty of playing baseball on Sunday. His sentence was suspended.[18] The New York state law banning Sunday baseball remained in effect until April 19, 1919.[19]

Following the offseason drama, the 1914 season was a mixture of success and suffering for Jake. He played very well on the field, batting .329 and winning his second consecutive batting title.

"It isn't hard so hard to get to the head of procession as it is to keep there," said "Shoeless" Joe Jackson, whose .356 career batting average included .408 in 1911, when he finished second in the American League to Ty Cobb's career-high .419, and whose career average is the third-best in major league history behind Cobb (.366) and Rogers Hornsby (.358).[20]

Jake suffered from a combination of injuries and suspensions, causing him to miss 28 of the Robins' 154 games. He was out of the lineup for six games at the beginning of June because of tonsilitis, and he missed six games in July with a sprained left ankle, which he hurt sliding into home with the winning run in the second game against Boston on Saturday, July 4.[21]

His most serious injury occurred on August 14 against Philadelphia, when he hurt his leg beating out a bunt in the third inning. He stole second and then reached third but was limping badly and left the game. In the same game, Robins rookie Ollie O'Mara, who took over at shortstop after Tinker signed with the Federal League, broke his leg and was lost for the season.[22]

In a doubleheader sweep over Philadelphia the next day, Jake was hobbling but had six sacrifices, including four in the second game, a major league record that still stands. Jake played the next three games and went 5-for-12, but when the team headed from Chicago to St. Louis on August 20, Robinson sent Jake back to Brooklyn to rest his injured leg. In Chicago, he consulted three specialists who diagnosed a pulled tendon and said he needed rest to avoid permanent injury.[23] Jake missed the next six games.

He still limped a week later when he joined the team in Pittsburgh, but he went 9-for-24 as the Robins won five of the next six games. The injury remained a problem for the rest of the season and caused him to miss eight of the last 12 games, although there were accusations later that Jake may have sat out those games to protect his league-leading batting average.[24]

Jake also missed a couple of games for non-injury reasons. His "gentleman" moniker didn't mean he wouldn't protest or stand up for things he believed were wrong. In addition to confronting owners as one of the leaders of the Players Fraternity, he had numerous run-ins with umpires. During his 15-year career, he was ejected eight times, including three in 1914.

On June 16, Red Smith complained that umpire Ernie Quigley was positioned between second and third, distracting his view of the pitcher. When Quigley refused to move, Smith argued with umpire-in-chief Mal Eason. Jake and Manager Wilbert Robinson got involved, and Jake was ejected, then suspended for two games and fined $25.[25]

On September 4, Quigley again ejected Jake after he aggressively protested a call at first base. Shortstop Dick Egan and Robinson also were ejected in separate incidents during the game.[26]

Umpire Bill Klem sent Jake to the bench on September 14 for protesting a called third strike.

Brooklyn was a season-worst 15 games under .500 on September 17 before an 11-game winning streak. The Robins went 19-13 in September, but it wasn't enough to overcome their 9-15 record in May. Their 75-79 record and fifth-place finish was an improvement over the 65-84 and sixth place in 1913, as Robinson had hoped, but it did not put them in the top half of the league as Jake had expected.

There were encouraging signs. Brooklyn had four of the top five batters in the National League. Jake won the batting title by .004 over Philadelphia's Beals Becker (.325), followed by Robins outfielders Jack Dalton (.319), Zack Wheat (.319), and Casey Stengel (.316). In his first full season, Jeff Pfeffer led the pitching staff with a 23-12 record and a 1.97 earned run average.

Wheat batted .317 during a 19-year career, mostly with Brooklyn, and was elected to the Hall of Fame in 1959. Stengel batted .284 during 14 years with five teams but made his mark as a manager for 25 years, including 12 with the New York Yankees, who won seven World Series championships and 10 American League titles. He was voted into the Hall of Fame as a manager in 1966. Dalton joined the Federal League in 1915 and was out of baseball by 1916. Pfeffer was 158-112 with a 2.77 earned run average during 13 seasons.

The high expectations for the team at the start of the year created another issue: The rumors about Jake becoming the team manager continued throughout the season. In mid-June, with the team below .500 and dropping in the standings, rumors surfaced that Robinson had been asked to resign and would be replaced by Jake.[27]

On June 19, Charles Ebbets dispelled the rumors: "Robinson is going to continue as manager of the Brooklyn team, and Daubert is not going to take his place. There is absolutely nothing to the rumor. Robinson's work suits me, and it suits everyone else connected with the Brooklyn Baseball Club, and I think that ought to be enough."[28]

Ebbets was angry about the ongoing rumors and issued a vote of confidence for Robinson. "Our team has had a lot of hard luck, and it has also thrown away games which should have been won, but that is part of baseball," Ebbets said. "Robinson is not to blame, and I know it. It would be absurd for me to change managers in the middle of the season because the team has struck one of those streaks that come to all baseball outfits at one time or another. No man can prove his merits as a manager in less than a year or two years, and to discredit Robinson because this team has not set the league on fire in his first three months would be bad presidenting on my part. The Superbas have the natural ability, as Robinson has pointed out, and a change for the better is bound to come. If it does not, the fault will not be that Robinson does not know baseball or that the men are not trying their best to win for him. For that reason, I would keep him if we did not win another game all season."[29]

Jake denied his interest in Robinson's job and endorsed his manager: "President Ebbets will bear me out when I say I never had managerial designs. It will be time enough for me to think of trying my had at that game when I have come to the end of my rope as a player. I am under contract to Brooklyn for five more years. By that time I will know a whole lot more about baseball than I do now.

"Every player on the Brooklyn Club is with Robinson heart and soul. He is a fine fellow and thoroughly competent to get the very best results out of the material on hand. Brooklyn is not going to finish in the ruck for him, take it from me. We are going to do our level best for Robby."[30]

Despite the statements by Ebbets and Jake, the rumors persisted into August. Jake was tired of the stories that were written, including reports of dissension on the team, which he denied. Jake addressed the reports along with Ebbets and Robinson on August 11.

"I think those stories are pretty shabby treatment to hand to me when I have been working my head off to help the team win. While the stories are so ridiculous that I should not waste my time denying them, it has reached a stage now that if I did not enter a denial, the fans might begin to believe there was really some truth in the stories.

"Manager Robinson and myself are the best of friends, which makes the yarns all the more annoying. I never was a double-cross in my life, and I don't intend to start now. The thing that has worried me the most is the fear that someday I might play a poor game and instantly there would be cries that after all there was some truth in the stories that Daubert was not giving the Brooklyn club his best services because he was piqued over not getting the management of the team. I want to say right here and now that I have never looked for the job, and what is more I wouldn't take it if it were offered to me.

"I don't know what I have ever done to warrant such treatment. I have given the best that was in me and if that is not good enough then I don't know what to do. But irrespective of all these wild yarns, Jake Daubert will be out there every day doing the best he knows how, and as for the job of manager of the Brooklyn team I want to repeat, I wouldn't take it if it was offered to me on a silver platter."[31]

The stories didn't end after the season, and there were reports that Jake wanted to be the manager and that players had signed a petition to have Robinson removed or they would jump to the Federal League.[32] Robinson remained in charge, and most players remained with the team.

After the season, Jake went on his annual barnstorming tour with Brooklyn teammates, did a lot of trapshooting, and took a several-weeks family vacation to Great Cacapon, West Virginia, with teammate Ed Reulbach and his family.[33] Reulbach, a pitcher who had starred for eight-plus seasons with the Chicago Cubs before being traded to the Superbas in 1913, was released by Brooklyn in February 1915 and then signed with Newark of the Federal League. Along with Jake, he was a leader in the Players Fraternity. Reulbach was 18-24 with a 2.46 earned run average in a little more than a year with Brooklyn, but there was speculation that his union activity affected his release.

Jake on the cover of *Baseball Magazine*, February 1914. (From the collection of Cody Swords, Vintage Baseball Memorabilia)

Wilbert Robinson was hired as Brooklyn manager for the 1914 season. (Photo is in the public domain and acquired from Wikipedia)

Manager Wilbert Robinson, second from left, with Charles Ebbets, Steve McKeever, and Ed McKeever, owners of the Brooklyn team. (Photo is in the public domain and acquired from the George Grantham Bain Collection at the Library of Congress)

Jake is tagged out at home plate by the New York Giants' Chief Meyers in 1914. (Photo is in the public domain and was by the American Press Association)[34]

Jake at first base for the Brooklyn Robins in 1914. (Photo is in the public domain and acquired from the George Grantham Bain Collection at the Library of Congress)

6

Turning the Corner

The Dauberts spent some time during the winters in Llewellyn, but most of the year, they lived at 721 Coney Island Avenue in Brooklyn, where Jake rode the trolley about two miles to Ebbets Field. Their home was located over a funeral home.[1]

"Brooklyn was like a big country town," George Daubert, Jake's son, told Richard Goldstein, a former sports editor for *The New York Times,* for his 1991 book *Superstars and Screwballs.* "There were a lot of beer gardens on the corners with German brass bands playing and free lunch and nickel beers."

"When you went to New York, you went to 'the city.' Brooklyn wasn't considered a city in that sense. On rare occasions, dad would pack my sister, mother and I into the car and drive to New York City, an exhilarating and spine-tingling experience. It seemed that every street crossing was a challenge between car and trolley. The conductor rang his bell, dad honked his horn, but neither slowed, creating an unbearable period of bated breath, followed by a long sigh of relief from the passengers accompanied by a few shouted insults by the drivers of both vehicles directed at each other."

George recalled how fans would approach players on the streets to talk about baseball.

"My dad commuted to the ballpark by trolley," George told Goldstein, "and for the longest time he would complain about some baseball nut who always waited for him when he got off the trolley after the game, usually tired and hungry. It was impossible to evade this portly, stuttering, nail-chewing baseball nut without being rude, so dad would listen."

Jake and Harry Blair, who owned the funeral home below the Daubert home, became close friends and partners in a real estate deal. George called Blair "Uncle Harry."

"Uncle Harry would take me with him to ballgames, where he chain-smoked Between the Acts cigars, chewed his fingernails, and fidgeted in his seat if Brooklyn was losing," George said.[2]

On April 1, 1915, *The Brooklyn Daily Eagle* reported that Jake had offered his house on Coney Island Avenue in Brooklyn for sale and that he and his brother-in-law bought 40 acres in Mercedes County, California, where they planned to raise hogs. The newspaper wrote that Jake was building a house there.[3] But there was no indication Jake ever lived in California.

In spring 1916, Jake confirmed his family would make their permanent home near Pottsville.

"I hate to take the step as I have many friends in Brooklyn," he said, "but I must. I figure that all going well; I have seven years of baseball left in me. If I am to remain in the game that long, I must spend my winters in a less rigorous climate."[4]

On June 23, the *Pottsville Daily Republican* reported that Jake solicited bids to build a $12,000, three-story brick house, with stone trimming and a large plot of ground, in the western part of Pottsville.[5] But in the spring of 1917, the Dauberts purchased the Reed homestead in Schuylkill Haven[6] and were living at 217 East Liberty Street in Schuylkill Haven, according to Jake's World War I draft card, and they remained there for the rest of Jake's life.

George had other fond memories of his time in Brooklyn and his dad's years with the Robins.

"In 1911, at the age of six, my dad parked me on a wooden bench in front of the Brooklyn clubhouse in the old Washington Park," George told Goldstein. "The clubhouse attendant was enlisted as a babysitter for the duration of the game. He explained to me that Pittsburgh was the visiting team and, as the players emerged from their clubhouse, he pointed out a player and told me his name was Honus Wagner. That bit of information meant nothing to me until a few years later, but I was intrigued by Wagner's bow legs and long arms.

"I was fascinated by a large Bull Durham sign near the clubhouse in left-center field. A batter who hit the sign received a prize of fifty dollars. My dad's first base hit in the major leagues struck the Bull Durham sign for two bases."

When Robinson became the manager in 1914, he named George, then nine, the team's batboy.

There were some bad moments, he told Goldstein, especially regarding players' superstitions. "A player would grab me and give me a barber's rub, rubbing my head hard with the knuckles," George said.

At one point during a losing streak, one of the pitchers said they should remove the batboy to change their luck.

"The team lost eight or nine games in a row, and I was chased off the bench by Jeff Pfeffer, a burly pitcher," George recalled. "I spent the day in the runway playing back there by myself. My dad didn't interfere. He didn't say, 'Let him sit here.' He said, 'Go on back there,' so that's where I went. But they lost anyway, so I reclaimed my spot on the bench the next day."

* * *

The 1915 season began with more optimism, and Robinson predicted a finish in the first division.

"Jake Daubert has been a big help, too," Robinson said. "It makes me hot to hear or read those stories about Jake being sore that he has not got my job. Why we are the best of friends and are working hand in glove."[7]

The year was a turning point for the Robins. They were in contention during most of the season and finished in third place with an 80-72-2 record, ending a string of 11-straight losing seasons.

The season had a rough start. In spring training, Jake sprained his right ankle sliding into third base on March 29 in Daytona and was out for about two weeks. The Robins lost the opener to the New York Giants, 16-3, with Jeff Pfeffer giving up seven runs in just two innings. They lost six of their first seven games, continued to struggle for the first three months, and were in last place on June 29 with a 26-34 record.

Jake missed the first three games of the season because of his sprained ankle but didn't miss another game. He had a 15-game hitting streak beginning on May 15, during which he went 22-for-54, a .407 average. The team went 10-5 during that stretch. By June 10, he was batting .380 and leading the league. He cooled off but never dropped below .300. Jake finished the year at .301, fifth best in the league, and set career highs in walks (57) and sacrifices (39). He led the league until early August, but any chance he had of winning a third-straight batting title ended when he batted .231 in the final 17 games. He would have won the batting title with ten more hits during the season.

After a doubleheader sweep over Philadelphia on June 2, the Robins were 20-18 and in second place, 2 ½ games back of Chicago. An eight-game losing streak dropped them to 24-32 and last place on June 24. The Robins' turnaround began on June 30, when Pfeffer pitched a two-hitter and beat the Giants 7-0.

On July 19, they were 43-37 and tied for second place with Chicago, one game behind Philadelphia. They went 22-9 in July and remained in second place through the rest of July and most of August and September. For two days in mid-August, they were tied for first place, .002 behind Philadelphia. On September 7, they were one game back, but that was the closest they came because of a 13-13 September that dropped them to third place.

Brooklyn was 47-39 on July 24, when Jake shared a theory that if the team won 44 of the remaining 66 games, it would win the pennant.[8] That would have been true, but the Robins went 33-33 in those final games. They finished the season 10 games behind the Phillies, who won the National League title by seven games over Boston.

Jake was the only player on the team to hit over .300, but there were encouraging signs from the pitching staff, led by Jeff Pfeffer (19-14, 2.10 ERA), Jack Coombs (15-10, 2.58), Sherry Smith (14-8, 2.59), and Dell Wheezer (11-10, 2.34).

Now in his sixth season, Jake not only was a star and the team leader, but he also was learning the intricacies of dealing with umpires.

On April 26, umpire Lord Byron ejected Jake when he argued the Giants had brought in a dead ball in the eighth inning. Robinson joined the argument and also was kicked out. Byron again ejected Jake on September 4 for arguing a called third strike. Jake claimed Boston catcher Bert Whaling tipped his bat as he was about to swing.

"That's the old alibi," Byron said. "That's what you guys always say."

"Where are your eyes that you didn't see him tip my bat?" Jake asked.

"You're out of the game," Byron replied.

Jake continued to protest, resulting in a $50 fine but no suspension.[9]

He learned that it was wiser to limit his protests and remain in the game where he could help his team. On May 13, 1916, against the Chicago Cubs, he began arguing a close call at first base before quickly calming down and avoided being ejected. Brooklyn won the game, 3-2.[10]

Jake would be ejected from only two other games in his career. One was the following July 19, 1916, by Mal Eason after a called third strike. The final one was on September 21, 1922, by Barry McCormick after a call at second base.

Jake's limited education didn't mean he wasn't a quick learner. That also was evident in his successful businesses, and he gained the respect of players, fans, and other citizens in his community.

Several Brooklyn newspapers reported on September 2, 1915, that the Flatbush Democratic Club had chosen Jake to run for Alderman in the Eighteenth Assembly District, and he wired his acceptance.[11] But *The Daily Standard Union* of Brooklyn reported that Jake had wired he "will not accept Alderman at present" and he was too busy with baseball to get involved in politics. Jake showed no interest in the campaign and lost by 1,500 votes to A.L. Squires in the heavily Republican district.[12]

The Players Fraternity and the Federal League continued to make news in 1915, and Jake addressed the connection between them:

"Reulbach is the only member of the fraternity in good standing in the Federal League," he said. "Ed was released outright by Brooklyn, and there was no objection to him signing wherever he could get the most money. He is still secretary of the fraternity.

"Chief Albert Bender, formerly with the Athletics, whose flop to the Feds was a sensation and whose failure and release have been the talk of baseball, was not a member of the fraternity. He and the other players of the Philadelphia American League team allowed their memberships to lapse, saying they did not need the fraternity to protect them. Hence the fraternity has no interest in Bender's case. It is only fair that his status should be made clear.

"Men who jump binding contracts and join the Feds are automatically expelled by the fraternity, and that also should be made clear. As regards those who jumped the reserve clause, their membership is suspended until they return to the ranks of organized baseball. The courts have held that the reserve clause is not equitable or binding, and the magnates have acted in accordance with that ruling; hence the fraternity has done the same.[13]

The Players Fraternity also pushed to speed up the games' pace, which Jake supported.

"It is a crime against their intelligence and their incomes for ball players to waste as much time as they do now in the course of nine innings," Jake said. "Baseball differs from football, lacrosse, hockey and such sports in that all the participants are not engaged all the time. For that reason it is easy for a ball game to become dreary and draggy, unless all are on their toes and creating the impression that something is going to happen every minute.

"In a close contest, where the pitching is good on both sides and runs are few, the fans may see comparatively little action. The last game at Ebbets Field, in which Brooklyn made one hit off George Tyler, and Boston made two off Jeff Pfeffer, was a case in point. It was a perfect exhibition, yet there were few occasions for thrilling stunts.

"Fans go to a baseball park not only to see the competition, but to enjoy the open air and to have their minds diverted. In other words, baseball is an amusement, with local patriotism as an added zest. That's what spectators pay for, and it is up to the men making a living out of the sports to keep those ticket-buyers interested all the time. When they do not, they are not delivering the goods to the purchasers, who are the fans. I want to see the players go at their work with vim and snap. They should hustle to their positions and from their positions, as if there were going to be big doings right away. No batter should wait to be called by the umpire. When at the plate this useless stepping out of the box and killing time should be forbidden. Also, the pitchers should not be allowed to loaf.

"I have been in some games this season that were a disgrace, and I knew it. I have thought the matter over and am heartily in favor of any scheme which will give someone in authority on the field the power to compel the players to keep the game going under a full head of steam from the first inning to the last."[14]

Daubert seemed to be way ahead of his time, and his assessment of the state of the game displayed his deep thinking and the intelligence he brought to baseball as a game and a business.

"Another angle to the dilatory tactics is that they affect the performers more than you would suppose," he said. "For instance, George Cutshaw and I do not have far to go from the bench, and neither of us is prone to loaf. Not infrequently, we have reached our positions and couldn't see an outfielder, but not often. I have seen it occur much more often on other teams.

"Now, suppose Cutshaw and I are ready, but the outfielders are dawdling to their positions. We naturally begin to talk. He will say, for instance, 'Did you take your family down to that shore dinner at Skeezick's last Sunday?' I might answer, 'No. I found a place that beats Skeezick's a mile. They have a great bathing beach, and they cook fish just the way I want them,' and so on.

"In other words, the delay in starting the inning has taken the minds of the early birds off baseball, and whenever a man on the field begins to think of something besides his signals, the peculiarities of his pitchers, the hitting tendencies of the man at the bat, the sun, the wind, the number out, the number on bases, the count on the batter, the weaknesses and the strong point of the men next to him, and the hundred and one other things a big leaguer or small leaguer, either, for that matter, has to keep at his fingers' ends, then that man's usefulness is distinctly impaired. He may not pull an obvious bone stunt, but he may lose a chance to pull a smart stunt of decisive importance.

"Baseball needs every ounce of ginger that can be injected into it in these hard times, and it will not be the fault of the fraternity if we do not have a marked improvement next year."[15]

Jake at first base for the Brooklyn Robins. (Photo is in the public domain and acquired from the collection of Steve Steinberg)

Jake's World War I draft registration card.

Present-day photo of Jake's house on Liberty Street, Schuylkill Haven.. (Photo by Harry J. Deitz Jr)

7

Raising a Pennant

The 1916 season was a great success for Jake and the Robins, but there was a lot of suffering along the way.

The team won its first National League championship with a 94-60-2 record, and Jake finished with a .316 batting average, which was second best in the league to Cincinnati's Hal Chase at .339, by far a career-best for the .291 lifetime hitter who had just returned after two seasons in the Federal League.

Jake was scheduled to leave on March 2 for spring training in Daytona, but on that day his brother Calvin was killed at the Blackwood colliery near Llewellyn when a large piece of coal fell off a pillar and crushed him.[1] He was the second of Jake's brothers to die in the coal mines. Calvin left a widow and five children for whom Jake was appointed guardian.[2]

On March 14, Jake headed south and was in good shape when he arrived in Daytona. When asked how much he needed to take off to get in condition, he replied, "My winter underwear."[3] He stepped into the lineup and went 4 for 4 the first day.

The Robins started the regular season slowly, losing three of their first four games, but they won 10 of their next 11. They moved into first place on May 1 and stayed there all but three days for the rest of the season.

Jake also was off to a fast start. He was at a season-high .432 at the start of May and .345 on July 1. On April 26 at Philadelphia, Jake recorded the 1,000th hit of his career. It was an infield single in the sixth inning against future Hall of Famer Pete Alexander. Jake went 3-for-4 in the Robins' 6-3 win.

He had a 12-game hitting streak in May and a 17-game hitting streak from June 5-26, when he batted .397 and raised his season average to .355. Jake was having one of his finest seasons and did not miss a game through the beginning of August as Brooklyn opened a five-game lead during a season-high eight-game winning streak.

Everything changed on August 5 in the first game of a doubleheader against Pittsburgh, when Jake pulled a tendon in the second inning and left the game. The injury did not appear to be serious at the time.[4] He originally injured his leg—reported as a charley horse—on August 2 against the Reds when he beat out a bunt. The Robins won that game, 5-4, in 13 innings on a one-out, walk-off double by Jake.

Jake returned to lineup August 12 after missing four games. He went 1-for-3 with a sacrifice in the first game of a doubleheader but went 0-for-2 in the second game, grounding out twice to shortstop, and was replaced by Lew McCarty at first in the top of the fourth inning. The Robins lost both games by 5-4. Jake missed the next eight games.

While he was out, Jake saw a Brooklyn specialist, who determined the problem was in his back, which was putting pressure on his sciatic nerve, and prescribed treatment and rest.[5] He rejoined the team and pinch-hit on August 22 but grounded into a force-out and was lifted for a pinch-runner. He missed the next 11 games, and in late August, Robinson said Jake might miss the rest of the season. With his uncertain status, Brooklyn acquired Fred Merkle from the Giants for catcher Lew McCarty, who had been filling in for Jake at first base.[6]

Jake went home to Schuylkill County after Brooklyn's game at Philadelphia on September 2. The *Pottsville Republican* reported the injury was to his spine:

> When greeted by friends and congratulated for the stand his club is making, Jake just hung his head and declared he was broken hearted. It has been the one ambition of Daubert to win a pennant and now when they were going at a fast clip, a thing like this forced him out of the game. Daubert fears that he will never be able to play ball again and at least will be out for the remainder of the season . . . Jake says he would give his entire year's salary just now to be in the game.

> The injury to Daubert's spine is a repetition of practically the same sort of an injury earlier in the season. A portion of a bone is affecting the spine and there is a grave doubt if Jake will ever be able to don the uniform. There is talk in Brooklyn now of making Daubert manager of the club, and in that event Jack Coombs, to whom belongs the credit of the pitchers good work, will be made captain.[7]

Jake returned to the lineup for the next game on Monday in Philadelphia. He went 0-for-4 in the first game of a doubleheader on September 4 and sat out the second game.

Despite the injury that threatened to end his season, Jake gradually was working his way back. His doctor advised more rest, but Jake refused. "Our club simply must win," Jake said, "and I'm going to work until I fall down."[8] He went 2-for-5 on September 5, 1-for-3 in the second game of a doubleheader on September 6, 0-for-3 on September 7, and 1-for-2 with a triple and sacrifice in the second game of a doubleheader on September 8. He missed only two more games the rest of September.

On September 19, Brooklyn was 83-55 and led Philadelphia by two games and Boston by 2 ½. Jake was back and feeling confident about his team's chances.

"I am sure that we can win the pennant this year with anything like an even break in the luck of the game," Jake said. "We have the power, and now it would seem that it is being properly applied. One might ask the cause of my confidence after the team slumped so on the Western trip. Paradoxical as it may seem, that slump rather tended to increase my confidence in the Brooklyn team.

"You see, all through that trip, we played .500 percent baseball, yet we managed to come back to Ebbets Field in first place. Of course, we owe a debt to the Giants for licking the Phillies, but then, it must be remembered that we helped ourselves by beating Boston.

"If the players would stop and think just what to do in the event of certain situations arising, many misplays would never be made. To be sure, one may think a situation all out, but the way in which a ball is hit will make one change plans entirely.

"Just as an example, consider runners on first and second and a ball hit between the box and first base. If the ball is hard hit, there is a fine chance to get the runner at third, but if it be tapped slowly, often there is time only to get the man at first. You have to think all those things out for yourself. It is a good thing to hold little conferences when the game is tight, and one play may decide it.

"But our chances to win this pennant are bright. Our pitchers are going nicely again, and pitching is a great asset. Larry Cheney is back in his best form, and Pfeffer has returned after a bit of a slump during the Western trip. The work of Marquard has been first-class, and Jack Coombs has pitched some wonderful baseball. Jack has been unfortunate in the matter of winning, but to appreciate his work full, check up the number of earned runs made off him and then see how many runs were made behind him.

"Any outfield with a Buck Wheat in it is strong. I hold Zack to be the best hitter in the league. All his safe drives are real drives. He beats out mighty few weak taps. Moreover, I think he is one of the best fielders in baseball, and his base running is improving all the time. Stengel and Jimmy Johnston rank right up there, and the three present a formidable front, indeed.

"There are hitting strength and defensive skill as well, and that is all one can ask for any combination. Our infield has been playing steady ball and good ball, too. Merkle has given us strength, for Fred cannot only play first base like a real champion, but he is an outfielder of ability and a dangerous hitter. The other men are up on their toes, fighting for every break, every man with the other, and all working with one idea. That is: 'Win that pennant!'"[9]

At end of September, Philadelphia won two of three over Brooklyn to pull within a half-game. Brooklyn then won three of four from New York in October, while Philadelphia lost four of six to Boston. In the final 15 games of the season, Jake batted .400 with nine sacrifices. Beginning September 19, he had a 10-game hitting streak. Despite his injury, Jake played in 127 of 156 games (two games originally ended in ties) for Brooklyn.

The Robins clinched the National League pennant on October 3 when they beat the New York Giants, 9-6, while the Phillies lost a doubleheader to the Boston Braves, 6-3 and 6-1.

There was controversy after the Robins clinched because Giants manager John McGraw didn't believe his team played as hard as he expected. There were suspicions that the Giants favored the Robins to win the pennant because Robinson, Brooklyn's manager, previously was a coach under McGraw.

"I am not accusing anyone of anything wrong, but I will not stand for that sort of ball playing," said McGraw, who was annoyed and left the field in the fifth inning. "I do not believe that any of my players deliberately favored Brooklyn, but they did not obey my orders. When Perritt took a windup with a man on first, permitting the runner to steal second, I lost my patience and quit the bench. I'm through with baseball for the year. I have worked too hard this summer to tolerate that stuff."

Robinson disputed McGraw's take on the game. "Does anybody think we would have spotted them three runs in the first inning if there was anything wrong?" he asked.[10]

Jake also believed New York was playing to win because of a financial incentive for finishing in third place. The Giants finished in fourth place behind Boston.

"The Brooklyn players believe that the Giants did all they could to win," Jake said. "New York players told me last night that they were going to try to win in every way they know to beat us. They said President Hempstead had promised them $250 each if they finished in third place. To beat out the Braves, they had to win from us. I think they tried, but we got the breaks and outplayed them."[11]

Jake at .316 and Zack Wheat at .312 led the team in batting, but a big reason for the Robins' success was the pitching staff, led by Jeff Pfeffer, who went 25-11 with a 1.92 earned run average. Larry Cheney was 18-12 and 1.92, Sherry Smith 14-10 and 2.34, Rube Marquard 13-6 and 1.58, and Jack Coombs 13-8 and 2.66. Jake also led all first basemen in the league with a .993 fielding percentage.

The Robins were the underdogs in the World Series against the defending World Series champion Boston Red Sox. Boston was 91-63 and finished two games ahead of the Chicago White Sox in the American League. From August 9 on, the Red Sox were in first place all but two days. They clinched the pennant on October 1 when the White Sox lost to the Cleveland Indians, 2-0, in the first game of a doubleheader.

The Red Sox were led offensively by third-baseman Larry Gardner, who batted .308. They had a loaded pitching staff of Babe Ruth, who was 23-12 with a 1.75 earned run average and 23 complete games in this third season; Dutch Leonard, 18-12, 2.36; Carl Mays, 18-13, 2.39; Ernie Shore, 16-10, 2.63; and Rube Foster, 14-7, 3.06. Manager Bill Carrigan was in his fourth season.

Jake believed the Robins matched up well against the Red Sox, despite predictions and odds to the contrary.

"We have the advantage inasmuch as we have everything to gain and nothing to lose," Jake said. "You will see the Superbas out there on the field as cool and collected as if just an ordinary game were to be played. On the other hand, I expect to find the world's champions nervous and fretful. They have everything to lose. Don't mind the fact that the Brooklyn boys do not cut up and explode with enthusiasm; they save all this to put into play. They are game beyond all question of doubt. They have demonstrated it time and again all through the season just closed. We are a better hitting team than the Red Sox and have just as good, if not a better twirling staff. Take Marquard in the form he showed against Philadelphia and New York, and there is not a team in the world that has a look-in with him. If Rube is right and Manager Robinson works him tomorrow, it looks like a cinch for Brooklyn to win the first game."[12]

Jake's outlook for the first game and the Series proved to be wishful thinking. Boston won the best-of-seven series in five games to claim its third of four titles in a seven-year span beginning in 1912.

William Phelon, who analyzed the Series in the December 1916 edition of *Baseball Magazine*, wrote that the outcome wasn't in doubt before it began:

> The Red Sox worked like a smooth, well-oiled machine, and the Robins, in a vague, disjointed manner. Carrigan's men seemed sure of their ground at all times; Robbie's men seemed worried, easily rattled, and too much inclined to parlor baseball. Politeness and silence may meet the requirements of the ultra-fastidious,

but they don't win world's series. Go get 'em, as the Braves got the Athletics two years back. That's the way to play the big annual games, and Brooklyn, distinctly, didn't play that sort of ball.[13]

Game One
Boston 6, Brooklyn 5
October 7, at Braves Field, Boston
Time: 2:16, attendance: 36,117

The Robins left for Boston on October 6, and many of the players' wives and fans joined them on the train. Gertrude had planned to accompany Jake, but she hurt her arm and had to remain at home.[14]

In the opener, Brooklyn outhit Boston, 10-8, but was hurt by four errors, including two by shortstop Ivy Olson. Jake's bat was mostly silent.

Boston threatened in the first inning when Tillie Walker tripled to left-center with two outs, but Rube Marquard got Dick Hoblitzell on a grounder to second to end the inning. The Red Sox had the bases loaded with one out in the second, but Ernie Shore was called out on strikes, and Harry Hooper flied out to deep left-center. They finally broke through with a run in the third when Hoblitzell hit a two-out triple and scored on a double by Duffy Lewis, who then was picked off second.

Brooklyn tied it in the fourth when Casey Stengel led off with a first-pitch single and scored on a triple by Zack Wheat on the next pitch. But Boston regained the lead in the fifth on an RBI single by Walker, then added three more in the seventh on one hit with the help of errors by Olson at shortstop and George Cutshaw at second on ground balls. They scored again in the eighth against reliever Jeff Pfeffer on a throwing error by Stengel in right field.

The Robins trailed, 6-1, in the top of the ninth but didn't quit. Jake, who had struck out on three pitches in the first and again in the third and had grounded out in the sixth, led off the ninth with a walk on four pitches from Shore. He moved to second on a single by Stengel, then was forced at third on a grounder by Wheat. After Cutshaw was hit by a pitch to load the bases, Mike Mowrey was safe on an error by second-baseman

Hal Janvrin, allowing Stengel and Wheat to score. Olson singled to third, reloading the bases. After a popup for the second out, pinch-hitter Fred Merkle walked to force in another run. Carl Mays came on in relief of Shore and gave up a single to Hi Myers, pulling the Robins within one with the bases still loaded.

That brought up Jake for the second time in the inning with a chance to be the hero.

The Sun of New York sportswriter "Daniel" described the scene in prose reminiscent of the famous poem "Casey at the Bat" by Ernest Thayer under the pen name Phin in 1888:

> Not a sound could be heard in that huge amphitheatre as, with two men retired and the bases full, Jake Daubert strode to the plate in the ninth inning. Four runs had already been registered, and now came one of the strong batsmen in the National League. The situation presented a world of possibilities, most of them contrary to Boston welfare.
>
> But as is often the case when the big call comes, the weak become strong and the mighty lowly. Daubert stood by while Carl Mays, who a few moments before had relieved Shore, spun a strike across the plate. Still, there was yet hope for Brooklyn. Its famous field leader had not obtained a hit in four previous attempts, and in the vernacular of the diamond, he was "due."
>
> Idly Daubert stood by while Mays sent a ball over and then another that was too wide of the rubber. The fourth pitch was met, but not squarely. Daubert topped the ball in a vicious swing, and the horsehide sped on to Everett Scott at shortstop. The blow carried speed and sting, but Scott made a fine stop and whipped the ball to Dick Hoblitzell. Hoblitzell had to stretch for the throw, but he got it before Daubert reached the bag. For Brooklyn, the day was lost.[15]

Jake hit the ball to the third base side of Scott. It went past Gardner, but Scott dug it out and made a perfect throw to first to get Jake, who dove head-first for the bag.[16]

"If my legs had been made of rubber, we'd have brought home that old ball game," Jake said. "Couldn't stretch another inch, and Scott's throw just beat me by inches."[17]

Despite the result, Jake continued to voice confidence in his team.

"Do you think that failure to quite come through in the ninth worried us or broke our hearts?" he asked. "If you do, you are a mistaken young man, for that gave us the idea that this Red Sox team isn't made up of unbeatable men. It was just what we needed, I guess, for we feel a whole lot more confident than we did when we started the game."[18]

A ticket scandal surfaced after the game. Boston had announced that all 42,000 seats were sold, but it was just over 36,000 when official attendance was announced. That would mean less money paid to the players. In addition, Brooklyn players were upset that friends and family members had trouble getting tickets.

"I'd like to know just what will be done with regard to those tickets which were sold but for which no accounting has been given," Jake said. "It is true that the Jewish holy day kept the attendance down to some extent, but even if the people did not attend the game, the tickets were purchased. The players are supposed to receive 60 percent of the gross receipts of the first four days, regardless of the attendance, and they want their full share.

"There is another point that I would like to have cleared up, and that is the matter of tickets sold at the box office. I had some friends who came up here, and shortly before noon, they went to the grounds in an endeavor to purchase seats. They were informed that every ticket had been sold. Yet after noon, just before the game started, I learned that seats were to be had."[19]

Game Two
Boston 2, Brooklyn 1, 14 innings
October 9, at Braves Field, Boston
Time: 2:32, attendance: 41,373

Following an off day on Sunday, Brooklyn looked to bounce back and go home after a split in Boston. The Robins took a 1-0 lead in the top of the first. After Jimmy Johnston flied out to deep center and Jake fouled out to third, Hi Myers drove the ball deep to right-center and circled the bases for an inside-the-park home run. Boston tied the score in the third when Everett Scott led off with a triple and scored on Babe Ruth's grounder to second.

After that, Brooklyn's Sherry Smith and Ruth locked up in a scoreless duel for ten innings. The Red Sox threatened in the fifth when Pinch Thomas tripled with two outs, but Smith struck out Ruth to end the inning. The Robins had a chance to take the lead in the eighth when they had runners at second and third with one out, but Mike Mowrey was thrown out at home on a grounder to Scott at shortstop, and Johnston grounded to the pitcher to end the inning. Boston attempted to end it in the bottom of the ninth, but Myers caught Dick Hoblitzell's line drive to center, then threw home to get Hal Janvrin.

With darkness threatening to stop the game, Boston won it in the 14th when pinch-runner Mike McNally scored on a one-out single to left field by pinch-hitter Del Gainer.

Smith threw 142 pitches, gave up seven hits and six walks, and struck out two in 13 1/3 innings. Ruth threw 144 pitches, allowed six hits and three walks, and struck out four in 14 innings.[20]

Jake had another disappointing game, going 0-for-5 with a walk and a strikeout.

The bright spot for him came in the 11th when he made an over-the-shoulder catch of a foul popup.

The Robins were in a 2-0 hole after the pair of one-run losses but were happy to be heading home for the next two games.

"Yes, we'll do a lot better," Jake said. "For one thing, I'm going to start in and hit. I don't like going through two games like this without making a single hit. It doesn't make me feel good."[21]

Game Three
Brooklyn 4, Boston 3
October 10, at Ebbets Field, Brooklyn
Time: 2:01, attendance: 21,087

In the first two games, Jake was 0-for-9 with three strikeouts. He stranded four runners, including two in scoring position. When the Robins returned home, Jake started hitting. He went 3-for-4 with a triple in Game Three, which the Robins won, 4-3.

Jake had a bunt single to the pitcher in the first inning but was stranded at third when Mike Mowrey was called out on strikes with the bases loaded. He singled to right field in the third, moved to second on a groundout, and scored Brooklyn's first run on a single by George Cutshaw. Jake grounded to shortstop to end the fourth inning after Jack Coombs' RBI single gave the Robins a 2-0 lead.

In the sixth, Jake tripled to left field against reliever Rube Foster and was thrown out at home on the play. According to the report in *The Brooklyn Daily Eagle* the next day:

> Daubert slid into the plate in a slow and extremely awkward manner. He did not go in briskly, feet first, in the usual manner, but lit on his side and rolled. Umpire O'Day call him safe, but Dick Hoblitzell and other Red Sox let out a yell. They pointed to Thomas' foot and asserted that it was a physical impossibility for Daubert to have been safe, as the said foot of Thomas completely blocked the pan. O'Day was convinced and reversed himself, calling the runner out. The Superbas, naturally, made a violent but withal gentlemanly kick. It did them no good, but the decision did them no harm.[22]

Brooklyn took a 4-0 lead in the fifth inning on a two-run triple to left field by Ivy Olson. Boston scored two in the sixth inning on a walk to Olaf Henriksen, a triple by Harry Hooper, and a single by Chick Shorten. The Red Sox added a home run to right field by Larry Gardner in the seventh.

Jack Coombs started for Brooklyn and allowed all the Boston runs before tiring after Gardner's homer. Jeff Pfeffer retired the last eight Red Sox batters. Submarine pitcher Carl Mays, who got Jake to ground out to end Game One, took the loss, allowing seven of the Robins' 10 hits and all four earned runs.

Jake may have found a good omen before the game, according to *The Brooklyn Daily Eagle:*

Fanatics at Ebbets Field yesterday were surprised to see Jake Daubert, prior to game time, rush over to a field box and make, as though to strike a bald-headed man right on the bald spot. The man with the high forehead made no resistance, and the watching fans then saw that Jake was lovingly rubbing his bat o'er that bald spot.

No explanation of his extraordinary action was asked or given until the game was over, and Daubert had made three hits in four times at bat. Then it was discovered the bald head came from Minersville, Pa. (near Jake's home town), in company with a large delegation of Daubert's friends from the same place.

His name is John Geier, and despite his bald bean, he is a young man, and an enthusiastic rooter for Jake Daubert. Following the game, Daubert requested Geier to stay over until today's game, so he could rub the bat over that bald cranium again. Geier was non-commital.[23]

There was another report that before the game, Jake had received a package from Pottsville that included good-luck charms—a four-leaf clover, metal horseshoe, rabbit's foot, and silver baseball and bat.[24]

"I'm not trying to brag, but I think we've started," Jake said after the game. "I'm going to hit now. You wait and see. About the game, there's only one thing to say. The team found itself and played a great game. We got a few breaks, for which much thanks. Ivan Olson certainly was there with the stick, and that sort of thing helps a lot."[25]

Game Four
Boston 6, Brooklyn 2
October 11, at Ebbets Field, Brooklyn
Time: 2:30, attendance: 21,662

With a few breaks, Brooklyn could have been looking at clinching the World Series in Game Four after the three one-run games. Instead, the Robins were all-but finished when the game ended.

Jake didn't need Geier's bald head or other lucky charms for Game Four because he didn't play. Despite Jake's strong showing in Game Three and the fact that Jake would finish his career with a higher batting average against left-handers (.305 vs. .298),[26] Robinson sat Jake in favor of righty Fred Merkle against left-handed pitcher Dutch Leonard.

Robinson's move appeared to work when the Robins took a 2-0 lead in the bottom of the first. Jimmy Johnston, who started in place of lefthanded-hitting Casey Stengel, opened the inning with a triple to center and scored on a single by Hi Myers, who later scored on a ground-ball error by second-baseman Hal Janvrin. But Leonard blanked Brooklyn the rest of the way.

The Red Sox took the lead in the top of the second against Rube Marquard when Dick Hoblitzell walked, Duffy Lewis doubled, and Larry Gardner drove them home on an inside-the-park home run to left-center. Marquard gave up an RBI single to Bill Carrigan in the fourth, then was lifted for a pinch-hitter in the bottom of the inning. The Red Sox added two runs against reliever Larry Cheney. Marquard, Cheney, and Nap Rucker combined for 11 strikeouts, a World Series Record.[27]

Game Five
Boston 4, Brooklyn 1
October 12, at Braves Field, Boston
Time: 1:43, attendance: 42,620

A Red Sox championship seemed inevitable when the series shifted back to Boston for Game Five. *Baseball Magazine's* Phelon described the scene:

> When the gong rang for the fifth tussle, at Boston on Wednesday, October 12, the wisdom of Garry Herrmann was again apparent. This was Columbus Day, and Garry had asserted that there would be a huge attendance at the obsequies. So there was—the biggest crowd ever officially counted at a ball game—42,620 paid admissions! They came as in duty bound to attend the funeral, for a funeral none doubted it would be. The practice before the game seemed strangely prophetic, and was enough to put the final damper on any National League partisan amid the mighty crowd. Over on the sunny side of the field, with the bright rays glowing

fair upon them, practiced the Boston crowd. Many of them were arrayed in flaming red jackets, and the white and scarlet figures, dancing in the sun, were the embodiment of happiness and self-esteem. Over on the dark side of the park, the Brooklyns, clad in sombre gray, worked slowly and despondently— a troop of gloomy forms, without life, vigor, or vitality. The contrast between the gray-clad men over in the silent shadows, and the white and scarlet forms that leaped and tumbled in the golden sunshine, was the strongest and most striking that I ever saw in my long years of world's series games—it told the final issue more forcefully than trumpets could have brayed it from the stands.

Brooklyn again took an early lead—and again lost it. The Robins scored a run in the second without a hit against starter Ernie Shore when George Cutshaw walked, was sacrificed to second, moved to third on a groundout, and scored on a passed ball by Forrest Cady.

Boston tied it in the bottom of the inning when Duffy Lewis tripled on a ball misjudged by Zack Wheat in left and scored on Larry Gardner's sacrifice fly. It was all-but over in the third when the Sox scored two runs with the help of two errors by Ivy Olson on one play. After Cady singled and Harry Hooper walked, Olson booted a grounder on a sure double-play ball by Hal Janvrin. Then, with the runners safe, Olson threw the ball past second, allowing Cady to score. Chick Shorten's single scored Hooper. It would have been worse if Brooklyn catcher Jack Myers hadn't thrown out two runners attempting to steal second in the inning. The Red Sox added a run in the fifth on an RBI double by Janvrin.

Boston pitcher Ernie Shore didn't need much help. He limited the Robins to three hits on 80 pitches.[28] Brooklyn's first five batters went 1-for-19, including Jake, who was 0-for-4 on four groundouts.

Jake went 3-for-17 in four games with a triple, two walks, and three strikeouts. He batted .176. Wheat also struggled, batting .211 (4-for-19) in five games. Stengel led the Robins with a .364 (4-for-11) average in four games, and Jimmy Johnston was .300 (3-for-10) in three games. The Robins batted .200 as a team and scored 13 runs in the five games. They committed 13 errors, including four by Olson. Jake had a 1.000 fielding percentage.

The Brooklyn pitchers had a combined 2.85 earned run average. Pfeffer was a respectable 1.69, but Marquard was 5.73 and Coombs 4.26.

Boston had a .238 team batting average, led by left-fielder Lewis at .353 and right-fielder Hooper at .333. Gardner batted .176 but had two home runs. Shore, who won two of the games, had a 1.53 ERA. Ruth was 0.64 in winning the 14-inning second game, and Dutch Leonard was 1-0 with a 1.00 ERA. Mays took the only loss and had a 6.75 ERA in two games. Their combined ERA was 1.65.

"You can say this for me, that Ernest Shore has the best break on his fast ball I ever saw," Jake said. "It puzzled me in the first game. You will remember that I struck out the first two times up. I remember it anyway. I saw that ball fall away off the plate, but do you think I could keep away from it? I was hypnotized. I swung in spite of myself and then I looked foolish, I guess. At any rate I felt so."[29]

Wheat, along with Jake, was considered a disappointment in the series.

"They will say the Brooklyn team isn't game, I suppose," he said. "It is easy to say those things. Personally I am much disappointed in the result, but I will say we played our best under the circumstances. We had a hard fight for the pennant, and when we won, I believe all the boys relaxed a little, unconsciously. I know I am not given to worry, but for ten days before we won that pennant, I couldn't sleep nights. I know some of the other boys were the same way. Having won the pennant, we went to pieces and never found ourselves again. The Red Sox didn't have so close a finish, were more used to winning than we, and were not under the same strain. They were more fit, but I do not want to detract at all from their showing. They are a great team with a lot of reserve strength that looks deceiving on paper. And Shore has the best fast ball I ever saw. If we faced him regularly, I believe we could fathom it, but in a short series, he had us guessing."[30]

Attendance for the five games was 162,859, and receipts were $385,590.50. The players' share, based on the first four games, was $162,927.45. Brooklyn players each took home $2,715.41, and Boston players $3,332.94.[31]

Brooklyn would not win a World Series until 1955.

GENTLEMAN JAKE

Jake on the cover of *Sporting Life* magazine, January 1, 1916. (From the collection of Cody Swords, Vintage Baseball Memorabilia)

1916 Brooklyn infielders: Jake Daubert, first base: George Cutshaw, second base; Ivy Olson, shortstop; and Mike Mowery, third base. (Photo is in the public domain and acquired from the George Grantham Bain Collection at the Library of Congress)

1916 Brooklyn Robins. Jake is fourth from the right in the front row. (Photo is in the public domain and acquired from the Ernie Harwell Collection at the Detroit Public Library)

Jake is tagged out at home by Boston catcher Pinch Thomas in the sixth inning of the third game of the 1916 World Series when Jake tried to score after hitting a triple. (Photo is in the public domain and acquired from the Ernie Harwell Collection at the Detroit Public Library)

8

War, Contract Battle, and Trade

After the World Series, Jake headed home to Schuylkill County, where he hunted birds and rabbits during a busy offseason. He invested some of his World Series earnings in local real estate, including half-interest in the Baker ice plant in Schuylkill Haven.[1] The plant was located on East Liberty Street, near the house where the Dauberts moved several months later. He and Baker also owned a company that reclaimed culm, the byproduct of coal that was extracted from the mines.

On January 15, 1917, the Dauberts avoided a potentially serious accident. Jake, Gertrude, and the children were riding in their car near Llewellyn when it skidded and plunged down an embankment. Jake kept the car from rolling, then drove the car back up the bank. No one was injured.[2] It was typical of how Jake handled challenges in his life and on the baseball field.

There was concern throughout the nation at the start of 1917 over the possibility of the United States entering World War I. That happened on April 6 when the U.S. declared war against Germany. During spring training, players supported the war effort by practicing military drilling. By the end of the season, most minor leagues shut down, and some major leaguers received their draft notices and headed overseas to join the fighting.

With the uncertainty of how the war would impact baseball, especially regarding attendance and the availability of star players, owners began reducing players' salaries. Even though the American Federation of

Labor rejected a charter request from the Players Fraternity, the organization continued to focus on players' rights and was threatening a strike if owners continued to reduce salaries.³ But Jake was not in attendance when members of the Fraternity met on January 25, a sign that the Players Fraternity was weakening.

Owners publicly announced the salaries of their star players, believing that many of them were overpaid because of efforts to keep them from signing with the Federal League. They said the total paid to players in 1916 was $1.5 million, led by Ty Cobb's $20,000. The owners were seeking the support of the public.⁴

"The players were overpaid; there is no doubt about that," Brooklyn vice president Ed McKeever said. "The public knows it, but no better than we do. The salaries paid last year were mostly high because of the efforts of the Dodgers, along with other arms of organized baseball, to hold regular in their berths during the war. We intend paying but one war time price. That is the salary of Jake Daubert.

"In 1914, when the Feds first started their alluring offers, we gave Daubert a five-year contract at $9,000 a year. His contract has two years to run yet. The other men receiving an abnormal return for their services all had contracts which expired last season."⁵

The Players Fraternity essentially disbanded a few months later, which Jake confirmed when he said members were not asked to pay their dues for the year.⁶

Jake was healthy when he arrived for training in Hot Springs, Arkansas, on March 14, but the team was without Zack Wheat, Casey Stengel, and Jeff Pfeffer, who were unhappy with their contract offers. Pfeffer signed the next day, Wheat signed about a week later, and Stengel a week after that. Shortstop Ivy Olson was looking for his release so he could manage the Vernon, California, team in the Pacific Coast League, but he resigned with the Robins.

Owners of the Chicago Cubs offered Brooklyn $25,000 for Jake, but Ebbets refused, saying Brooklyn fans would not support losing Jake. The Cubs then acquired Merkel on April 21 for less than $6,000. That meant Jake would have to face more left-handed pitchers, and the Robins were counting on him to stay healthy. That didn't happen, and Robinson undoubtedly regretted not having Merkel as a backup.

In the first game of a doubleheader on June 25, Jake pulled a tendon trying to beat out a bunt in the third inning.[7] He missed 23 games. After missing ten games, he was tired of sitting on the bench. He played one inning on July 4, following extended rain that softened the field, reinjured his leg, and was out for the next 13 games. Jake came back on July 18 and, one day later, started a 12-game hitting streak, during which he batted .367 and raised his season average from .259 to .282.

Jake's best day was July 26, when he went 5-for-8 in a doubleheader at Pittsburgh. There were some other highlights. On August 3, he went 3-for-4, including a bunt that went past the shortstop and eluded the outfielders as Jake raced to third for a triple in a 3-2 win at St. Louis. And on August 14, he hit a two-run homer in the sixth inning to beat the New York Giants in the second game of a doubleheader.

He missed only one more game for the rest of the year. Overall, it was a disappointing season for Jake, who never reached .300 after April 23. He had another good year in the field, finishing with a .991 fielding percentage, second in the league among first basemen behind Boston's Ed Konetchy at .994

It also was a disappointing season for the Robins, who finished in seventh place with a 70-81-5 record, 26 ½ games behind the National League champion New York Giants. Brooklyn lost its first four games and was 3-7 at the end of April. The Robins briefly were a game above .500 in early August, but by then, they were 15 games behind.

Injuries played a part in the Robins' collapse. In addition to Jake, outfielder Hi Myers was hurt in May and missed two months. Outfielders Wheat and Jimmy Johnston, pitchers Sherry Smith and Pfeffer, and third-baseman Mike Mowrey also missed significant time. Wheat led the offense with a .312 batting average in 109 games. Rube Marquard, at 19-12, was the only pitcher with a winning record.

Jake knew his baseball career wouldn't last forever, so he continued developing businesses around Schuylkill Haven.

In September, Jake sold his half interest in the ice plant in Schuylkill Haven to his partner, E.H. Baker, for $17,500.[8] A month later, he joined Jacob Rettinger in leasing the Euclid Theatre in Schuylkill Haven. After some renovations, the theater opened on October 19 showing the silent film *The Marriage Bond* starring Nat Goodwin, followed by *Neptune's Daughter* starring Annette Kellerman the next night.[9]

After the season, there were reports that Jake's baseball career was over, even though he had one more year on his contract. Baseball writers pointed to the recent injuries that caused him to miss significant playing time and his drop in production. His .261 average was 55 points lower than in 1916, ending a streak of six .300-plus seasons.

"It was a big slump," Jake said. "The papers figured I was nearly through. What was the real trouble? I had a lot of money invested in things that weren't turning out especially well, and I was worried. I had sickness in my family, and that bothered me. I couldn't get these things out of my mind and got run down and off my feed generally. I was lucky to hit .261."[10]

Many athletes refuse to accept when the time comes that their skills have slipped and they should retire. Although others may see it, those star players find it hard to admit their career is near an end. That was not Jake, however, as he would prove during the next few years. He was confident that he would return to the form that made him one of the most feared hitters in the National League. Jake addressed his situation late in the season in an article for *Baseball Magazine* that showed his determination as well as his ability to evaluate himself and intelligently express it:

> When They Say "You're Slipping"
> How It Seems to Hear the Crowd Yell "One Out"
> By Jake Daubert
> When Mark Twain took his first trip abroad some enterprising newspaper man circulated the report that the famous humorist had fallen a victim to a sudden illness. Notices of his own funeral were very interesting reading to Mark. He went through them with his usual thoroughness and then issued his famous comment, "Reports of my death greatly exaggerated."
>
> When a ball player who was once good enough, or lucky enough to hit .350 falls below the .300 mark for some reason that isn't entirely clear to the public, he can be sure that enterprising

scribes will play up that fact for all it is worth. He will be reminded of how "good he used to be." Broad hints that he is going to be traded or sent to the minors will receive free calculation. By and by someone will say openly that he is "slipping" and once he has had that word applied to him it is but a step before someone else says that he is "through."

I can thoroughly appreciate what Mark Twain must have thought when he read about his own funeral. For I am one of the ball players who are supposed to be "slipping." This season so far I have not been able to hit for .300. True I hope to reach that mark before October and am quite sure I will if I can get my eye glued to that old pellet. But the fact remains that, so far, I am on the wrong side of the dividing line, on the side where the great mass of players vegetate and are never heard of.

Now of course I well realize that the time will come when I will be through. Every ball player knows that and also pushes the fatal date as far off as possible. But I am equally certain that the time is not yet. I can say with Mark Twain that the reports of "my big league death are greatly exaggerated."

My principal troubles this season have centered around my leg. I developed a "Charlie hoss" in that leg rather early in the season. They wanted me to get back into the game as soon as possible, however, and I went into the lineup on the Fourth of July.

I hated to do it because the ground was wet and very heavy. But any way I went. The first time I hit the ball and tried to beat out the hit to first, I got into trouble. I struck that soggy, wet, heavy soil and my leg seemed to crumple under me. It made the strain much worse. All in all I was out of the lineup for three weeks. But that wasn't the worst of it. When I did get back, I wasn't myself. My leg was bad, and neither Ty Cobb nor anyone else can beat out bunts and grounders with a bad leg. I will guarantee I have worried and fretted more about my condition than anyone else. But I am at a loss to see why that condition or lack of condition has caused quite the line of comment I have heard recently. I am not the only player who has had trouble with his legs. Few players but have been out of the game from injuries, even in their prime, I well remember a season when Ty Cobb, himself, was laid up through spraining his thumb in a fight with a butcher. Lajoie was out of it for part of a most important season by getting blood poison in his leg from wearing colored Bocks. Frank Baker last year ran into a gate and hurt his ribs but nobody said he was through. Now a "charlie hoss" is about the commonest injury a player can get. I will guarantee that few players have lived through their big league careers without becoming very well acquainted with a "charlie hoss." I am getting my share just now and I hope it will last me for keeps. It's tough to be bothered in this way, I admit, but it isn't anything unusual.

Now it is true that I am getting a good salary with the Brooklyn Club, a bigger salary than I ever expected to get. It is also true that I made that contract with the expectation of delivering my best work. And I have. No one can truthfully say that I have not at all times done my best work ever since I first wore a Brooklyn uniform.

This season, true enough, things have not been very satisfactory. There is a great deal of difference between a pennant winning club and a team which flounders around in the second division. Some of that difference is, no doubt, due to the fact that I am hitting .275 instead of .325. Some is due to Zach Wheat's injury, some is due to other causes. But so far as I have affected the result I can say that I take no responsibility on my own shoulders. I have done my best and if I have been prevented from doing as well as I expected it has been due to injuries over which I have no control, injuries gained on the field in trying to fulfil the terms of my contract.

My bad leg, in itself, is enough to account for most of my batting slump. I used to be very successful in beating out bunts and infield hits. Naturally in doing this you have to use a good degree of speed. If your speed is cut down, even a little, you will get thrown out at first on a close play. I realize all this and know that my bad leg has cut my batting average at least 25 or 30 points.

The other day I went to bat four times and wasn't able to do anything with the opposing pitcher. The fifth time I was the first man up for our side. Some fellows in the stands started to yell "one out." It got my goat. This is my eighth season with the Brooklyn Club. Most of that time I have been captain of the team. An old veteran like myself expects most of his knocks from the crowd when he is on the road. Then he doesn't mind it. But when he is on his home grounds he has learned to depend on the encouragement of his home folks. Well this time I made a hit and when I was safe on first I made a megaphone of my hands and called out to that bunch in the stands, "You can yell yourselves hoarse, but I will be right here next year."

That's my attitude in a nut shell. I have struck a streak of hard luck this season nothing more. I am as good a ball player as I ever was. I can hit the ball as hard and true as I ever could. My leg is rounding into shape and will soon be as sound as it ever was. I am thirty-two years of age, an age when a player ought to be in his prime, I have always lived a careful life, I never take on weight in the winter, which has to be sweated off and weakens a man in the process. I am always in condition, always barring accidents, in a position to play my best ball.

Also, I have had the advantage, though it didn't seem so at the time, of undergoing a very severe and thorough hardening process in my younger days. Anyone who has worked in the coal mines, as I have done, isn't going to be alarmed at the hazards of playing baseball. And whatever you can say against it, breaking rock and shoveling coal in the dark certainly does harden a fellow's muscles as all the gymnasiums in the world couldn't do. My father was not a big man physically, but he worked as a miner for fifty-seven years. That's a pretty long stretch of time when you come to think of it. I am not a large man myself and not very heavy. But my muscles have been hardened and toughened by real work, of the heaviest kind. Does anybody suppose you are going to kill a coal miner by eight years work in the major leagues playing baseball? Does anybody suppose I am through at an age when a man ought to be doing his best?

Well, if they do feel that way about it, I can tell them they are wrong. I was never better in my life, barring this bum leg. And pretty soon, I will be in a position to shake the kinks out of that leg and go after them as I used to do. Then I hope there will be a general let up of that cat call from the bleachers of "one out" when I go to bat.[11]

1918 SEASON

The 1918 season began with numerous question marks beyond Jake's rebound and the Robins' chances of returning to their championship form of 1916. The big unknown for baseball was the impact of World War I.

Many players received draft notices, and others enlisted. Public sentiment was that baseball should be shut down during the war, but owners and some fans argued that baseball raised public morale. Others claimed the owners didn't want to lose their revenue.

"Amid rising cries to halt play, owners made a concession for the 1918 season by reducing the schedule from 154 games to 140," Matt Kelly wrote for the National Baseball Hall of Fame. "It was not enough, however, at least in the eyes of the military. On July 1, 1918, Secretary of War Newton D. Baker issued a 'work or fight' order, stating that all draft-eligible men who worked in 'non-essential' vocations must sign up for war-related work or risk being drafted for battle.

"The game was given a temporary pass, as government officials declined to recognize it as one of the 'non-essential' activities. But Newton's favor turned by the end of July when he publicly recognized that the unusually athletic men on the diamond should be using their talents to help their country on the battlefield. There was no getting around it: Baseball players would have to serve too."[12]

The government and team owners finally agreed that the season would end on Labor Day and the World Series would start on September 4.

There had been a report that Brooklyn president Charles Ebbets had agreed to pay half of the salaries of his players who enlisted or were drafted, but he denied he had made that promise and said the club could not afford that. Jake, Jack Coombs, and George Cutshaw had established a fund to help the families of players who were drafted. It was supported by $500 from the club and about $500 from fans.[13]

Jake registered for the draft, but at age 34 and with two children, he was unlikely to be called to serve. His draft card, signed on September 12, 1918, listed his address as 217 E. Liberty, Schuylkill Haven, his occupation as "operating coal washery," and his employer as "River Coal Co." of "Schuyl. Haven."

Although Jake didn't join the military, he did other things to support the war effort. He led a movement among players to provide an ambulance and driver for service in France, and he was among the players in a friendly competition to sell Liberty Bonds.

"It sort of gets one's goat to hear that professional golf players, billiard players, tennis players, and others who make a living out of athletics are receiving credit for giving ambulances, while the professional ball players are giving nothing," Jake said. "The ball players are not remiss because they are cheap, but they overlooked the responsibilities because they did not know what to do. They will give up money as readily as the next patriot and many a poor fellow will be carried back to the hospitals and repair shops in our ambulance.

"The men who are playing the game in the big leagues are not slackers, but men who have been exempted because they have families. Those subject to Class 1A are going every day or are beating the Government to it by enlisting in the Army or Navy or the tank or aerial service, and no complaint can be made about our being hardy, husky fellows who are not doing their share.

"We are furnishing as much public amusement and diversion as the actors and actresses, and when we give the public something to talk about apart from the war, we have helped the cause. For instance, the scorers gave me an error on a ball that passes through me on Sunday when Mack Wheat (Zack's brother) attempted to complete a double play at first after catching a fly. The scoring of that error, with which I did not agree at all, has caused an immense amount of talk among the fans here in St. Louis. Some of them claim that I was robbed by scorers who were asleep at the switch, while others claim that it was my error. Can you suggest any vaudeville or comic opera act that will stir up the animals that way and create discussion long after the incident has passed?"[14]

Another challenge was the Spanish flu, which surfaced early in the year. It resulted in a restriction of public gatherings and caused in an estimated 675,000 deaths in the United States during the next two years.[15]

After the disappointing 1917 season, the Robins knew they needed to make changes to their roster. With the nation fully involved in the war, baseball owners again reduced players' salaries to offset the decline in attendance. Jake was in the last season of his five-year contract, but the salaries of all the other members of the team reportedly were reduced, some by more than $500. Manager Wilbert Robinson even agreed to a cut.[16]

Jake still believed he had several more good years as a baseball player, but he continued to plan for his family's future. Early in 1918, the ever-enterprising Jake started a company to dredge the Schuylkill River south of Pottsville for coal that had washed out of the mines or fell from barges.[17]

During the offseason, Jake decided to take dancing lessons as a way to test his leg.

"You see, I got a notion in my head that dancing would indicate to me whether my legs would be affected on the diamond," he said. "I had never tripped the light fantastic in my life, but out home in Schuylkill Haven, which, if you don't know, is in the State of Pennsylvania, during the long winter, I decided to give it a trial. So I took one lesson and, progressing favorably, took another. There was not the slightest pain in either leg, for which I was thankful. I think my legs are as sound as a dollar, as they say of thoroughbred horses. But, let me whisper, do you know I became a regular fiend at the dance game. You couldn't keep me off the floor any night we had a spiel. I went in it for exercise and, as I have said to learn about my limbs and came out of it a regular lefthander of a dancer."

He hoped it would help him return to his pre-1917 form.

"The Charlie horse in my left leg last year was the first ailment of the kind I have ever experienced," he said. "The trouble I had in 1916 was with the straight muscle in my right hip. Both have been eliminated for good, I hope. Before leaving home, I was seized with a desire to play a little fungo, the weather being fine. In the three days I was out, my limbs didn't bother me. In the practice here so far, the only effect has been soreness, which all ball players know after they go out for their first work of the spring. I am not going to force my training but shall content myself with getting in condition generally.

"I always wanted to give the public the best I was capable of. The fans expect me to be at my best on the opening day, and that's my object in training by easy stages. When the time comes that I am no longer capable of giving the club and the public a high-class exhibition, I make my exit.

"But gosh, do you know before I retire, I should like to have a .400 year? Impossible, you say? Well, I know in our league that's some notch, and I guess I will be as satisfied with .300. I ought to hit that, too. Last season I was in tough luck. Don't you believe I wasn't. Why, some fielder always got in the way of a ball I hit. As for bunting, do you know Robby was continually warning to be careful because of my legs? It's hard to get away from an old habit or practice, and this year I suppose I will be at it again, trying to beat out taps before the plate."[18]

The Robins' rebuild began January 9, when they traded Casey Stengel and George Cutshaw to the Pittsburgh Pirates for young spitball pitcher Burleigh Grimes, pitcher Al Mamaux, and infielder Chuck Ward. Grimes would go on to a 19-year Hall of Fame career, including nine with Brooklyn, where he was 158-121. In late March, Ward, who was expected to start at third base, was drafted into the Army, although he did play two games for the Robins during a military ceremony in June,[19] and by late April, Mamaux left the team for a job in a shipyard.[20]

Many others with the Robins joined the service. Second-baseman Lew Malone, shortstop John Kelleher, catcher Ernie Krueger, outfielders Jim Hickman and Tom Fitzsimmons, and pitchers Jeff Pfeffer, Sherry Smith, and Rich Durning enlisted. Infielder Ray Schmandt, pinch-hitter Clarence Mitchell, and pitchers Leon Cadore and Johnny Miljus were drafted. Pitchers Dan Griner, Norman Plitt, and John Russell left for shipbuilding yards or ammunition works. Only Jake, shortstop Ivy Olson, second-baseman Mickey Doolin, and pitcher Jack Coombs were above the draft age.[21]

Schmandt was a young player expected to challenge Jake and fill in if Jake missed time because of injury. Jake was helping to coach him and praised the youngster. Schmandt, who also played second base, never turned out to be the replacement for Jake. He lasted five seasons with Brooklyn and batted .270.

In late March, there were new reports that the Cubs were looking to acquire Jake.

"I certainly would not care to leave Brooklyn," Jake said after he was told of the story. "I have played my best baseball in a Brooklyn uniform, and it is my ambition to play such a game in 1918 for Manager Robinson as I did when I was batting .300.

"Physically, I am in the best of shape. My legs have not given me the least bit of bother. The rest of the boys have the best of feeling for Manager Robinson, and I think that this spirit will enable us to rise considerably above the position to which we dropped last season."[22]

As bad as the 1917 season began, 1918 was worse for the Robins, who lost their first nine games and never recovered. They finished the year at 57-69 and in fifth place, 25 ½ games behind the league-champion Chicago Cubs.

Jake batted .308 in 108 games and led the league with 15 triples. He didn't drop below .300 after April. On June 17, he went 4-for-5, raising his average to a season-high .361, and the Robins beat the first-place Cubs, 4-3, on Jake's bases-loaded, walk-off single to center field. He had a 12-game hitting streak from June 20 to July 3, and by the end of June, Jake was batting .356 and leading the league.

Despite his preparation, injuries again affected Jake's season. He missed 18 of 126 games. Jake was hit in the back by a pitched ball on May 8 in Boston and missed the next five games.[23] He returned on May 17 and went 7-for-13 in the next three games with a triple and two sacrifices.

By the end of the month, Jake had raised his batting average to .353, but on May 26 in St. Louis, Jake again hurt his leg. He missed nine games and pinch-hit in three others from May 27 to June 12. The Robins were in last place during most of that time.

In reporting the injury, sportswriter "Rice" of *The Brooklyn Daily Eagle*, wrote about Jake's approach when he was hitting well:

War, Contract Battle, and Trade

> It is easy to tell whether Daubert is in his stride. When such is the case, he consistently hits to left, his best stunt being line singles over the shortstop's head. Occasionally he may pull around over second, or a swing later than usual may crack the ball past the third baseman, but the regular place for his hits is somewhere through or over shortstop. All batters have a tendency to place a great majority of their hits in a particular section of the field. Daubert, being a left-handed batter, and sending so many snappy, clean singles in one direction, advertises that he has his eye on the ball, has confidence, and is hitting naturally. When he is in a slump or is worried, he has an inevitable tendency to lose his natural abandon at the plate and to try to do something extraordinary. That special effort—which is likely to be all to the bad in any batter—brings the bat around harder and faster than is his wont, and the ball has a tendency to go somewhere to the right of second base.[24]

Jake's reliance on his speed helped to make him a success, but it also was part of his downfall because of the injuries he suffered from stress to his legs and ankles.

Zack Wheat won the league batting title with a .335 average in 105 games, and Jake's .308 was fifth. At 19-9, Grimes was the only Robins starter with a winning record.

Many of the New York newspapers reported in late July that Jake left the team briefly to return home because of the death of his father. The reports were inaccurate because his father lived until 1928. It was his father-in-law, Henry Acaley, who died in 1918.

Two months after the 1918 season, the good news of a ceasefire was announced on November 11, signaling the end of the war. That meant baseball would return in 1919, although with a shortened season of 140 games. The Spanish flu would pose a serious threat for another year.

Jake played his final games for Brooklyn in a doubleheader at Philadelphia on September 2. He went 1-for-3 in the first game, which the Robins lost, 4-2, and 3-for-4 with a double and triple in the second game, which they won, 5-3. After the season, Jake returned to Schuylkill Haven to work at his coal business.

When club owners cut short the season, they also stopped the players' salaries for September. Jake believed he should be paid for the entire season based on his contract, which called for him to be paid $9,000 for each season from 1914 to 1918. He was paid $202 on September 2, bringing his total for the 1918 season to $6,850. Jake filed a claim with the National Commission to be paid the remaining $2,150 he was owed. According to the contract:

> The club agrees to pay the player for the seasons of 1914, 1915, 1916, 1917 and 1918, beginning on or about the fourteenth day of April in each of said year, and ending on or about the fourteenth day of October, in each of said years, a salary at the rate of $9,000 per season.
>
> It is further understood and agreed that the services of the part of the second part shall not be released, assigned, traded or transferred without the consent of the party of the second part.[25]

The National Commission, a three-person committee comprising a chairperson and the presidents of the American and National leagues that oversaw baseball before the establishment of a Baseball Commissioner in 1920,[26] ruled against Jake's claim, citing the circumstances related to the war:

> In view of the orders of the United States Government with reference to the playing of baseball, it became necessary to suspend operations of the game on and after September 2 last. The player's service for which he was engaged could not therefore be utilized by the Brooklyn Club after that time. This condition is one that could not have been in contemplation of the parties at the time the contract was entered into on May 15, 1914. Under the circumstances, the player would not have been liable to the club for breach of contract in not continuing to play, nor, on the other side, can the club be held liable to pay him the money agreed upon when his performance under his contract has practically been rendered illegal and impossible.

While it is true that the Brooklyn Club agreed to pay the player his specified salary for the playing season for each of the years in which he was under contract with that club and that the contract recited that the playing season would begin on or about the 14th day of April in each of said years, and end on or about the 14th day of October, there was nothing to prevent the league of which the Brooklyn club was a member, by appropriate action, cutting the season short. This was made necessary by the work-or-fight ruling of the Government herein referred to. The Brooklyn club was unable finish the season because of the impossibility of retaining the service of its players in view of the Government order, and for that reason, that club was within its rights in giving notice of the termination of all of its contracts with its players if it desired to do so.

The claim of the player is therefore dismissed.[27]

Jake contended that the Secretary of War did not order the suspension of baseball after September 2 and that when many of the players left for the service, teams could have continued to play with men under or over the draft age. Following the National Commission's ruling, Jake filed a civil suit in the Supreme Court of New York County.

Other players—including Roger Peckinpaugh, whose claim for $238.98 against the Yankees was dismissed by the National Commission[28]—were watching Jake's case against the Brooklyn team because it could affect their own contracts, but many people expected the matter to be settled out of court.

"I've had hundreds of letters from other ball players begging me to fight the case to the limit and offering to back me financially in the legal battle," Jake said. "Legally, I don't think the club has a leg to stand on. However, if it is going to do the game any good to settle the matter out of court, I am not averse to doing so."[29]

Jake's baseball days seemed to be over. Even though his contract had expired, Brooklyn held the rights to Jake under baseball's reserve clause. That meant if Jake wanted to play, he would have to do it for what Ebbets offered him unless the Robins released or traded him. Speculation was that Jake would be offered $1,200 to $1,500 for 1919.[30]

Despite the stories that Jake and Wilbert Robinson didn't get along, they went on a 10-day hunting trip with pitcher Jack Coombs to Georgia in December.[31]

Jake wanted to continue playing, and he still wanted to play for Brooklyn. "Of all the cities I have played in during my career on the diamond, Brooklyn has suited me best by far," he said. "I have been royally treated by the fans, and you can bet I appreciate it. I should like very much to continue to play under Robby."[32]

On December 12, numerous newspapers reported that the Giants acquired Jake for first baseman Walter Holke and pitcher George Smith.[33] But Ebbets denied Jake had been traded. "Daubert still has a suit against the Brooklyn Club, and I don't believe any club would care to take him until that is settled," he said. "He is still the property of the Brooklyn Club."[34] The next day Ebbets said that trade still was possible.[35]

A few days later, there were reports that Jake would be traded to the Phillies and play for former teammate Coombs, who had been hired to manage Philadelphia.[36] The Boston Braves and Cincinnati Reds also were interested in acquiring Jake. Ebbets said Jake would not be traded until he withdrew his suit against Brooklyn.

Finally, on February 1, Jake was traded to Cincinnati for shortstop Larry Kopf and outfielder Tommy Griffith. But there were problems with the deal. Jake refused to sign with the Reds or drop his suit against the Robins, and Kopf refused to report to Brooklyn and said he would retire.[37]

On the morning of March 3, as Jake's court case against the Brooklyn team was to begin, he reached an agreement on the money he believed he was owed, clearing the way for him to head to Cincinnati.[38] Kopf also wound up with the Reds about a month later when Cincinnati manager Pat Moran got him back from Brooklyn for second-baseman Lee Magee.

Terms of the settlement were not initially released, and Ebbets denied he had settled the claim by Jake. According to later reports, Jake was to receive $1,500—$500 from the Reds and $1,000 from the National League—in addition to a $5,000 salary from Cincinnati.[39]

Brooklyn returned to the World Series in 1920, where the Robins lost to the Cleveland Indians, led by Jake's fellow Shamokin native Stan Coveleski, who won three games in the Series.

Before that, Jake had his own taste of a World Series championship.

The Daubert and Baker coal and ice plant on East Liberty Street in Schuylkill Haven. (Photo obtained by Ann Yezerski)

Jake's coal dredge on the Schuylkill River in 1917. (Image is from a collection donated by Jake's son, George, to the National Baseball Hall of Fame)

Jake, right, with Brooklyn manager Wilbert Robinson in 1917. (Photo is in the public domain and acquired from the George Grantham Bain Collection at the Library of Congress)

Jake on a chilly day while playing for Brooklyn. (From the collection of Jack Daubert)

Jake was a chop hitter who choked up on the bat. (Photo is in the public domain and from the collection of Cody Swords, Vintage Baseball Memorabilia)

Jake during batting practice in 1918. (Photo is in the public domain and acquired from the George Grantham Bain Collection at the Library of Congress)

9

World Series Champion and the Black Sox

Cincinnati joined the National League in 1890 and finished most seasons in the second division. Its best showings before 1919 were four third-place finishes, including 1918, when they were 68-60. The Reds finished fourth in 1917 with a 78-76 record under manager Christy Mathewson. It was their first winning record since 1909.

Mathewson, one of baseball's all-time great pitchers, had a brief managing career. In parts of three seasons, the Reds were 164-176 under Mathewson, a coal region native like Jake, who was born in Factoryville, near Scranton. With ten games remaining in the 1918 season, Mathewson was commissioned a captain in the Army's Chemical Warfare Division and sent to France. There he suffered from influenza and was exposed to mustard gas during a training exercise for which he was hospitalized. Mathewson returned to the United States in the spring of 1919, but the letters regarding his status as manager that he and Reds owner Garry Herrmann had sent to each other were not received. Herrmann needed a manager and hired Pat Moran. When Mathewson returned, he joined the Giants as an assistant manager.[1]

In 17 years as a pitcher, mostly with the New York Giants, Mathewson had a 373-188 record and 2.13 earned run average and struck out 2,507 in 4,788 2/3 innings. He won at least 30 games four times, including 37 in 1908. Mathewson was elected to the first Hall of Fame class in 1936. In 1921 he was diagnosed with tuberculosis. He died in 1925.

WORLD SERIES CHAMPION AND THE BLACK SOX

When Mathewson left for the service in 1918, he was replaced as manager by third-baseman Heinie Groh with ten games remaining in the season. The Reds finished with six straight wins to move from fourth place to third.

Before Moran was hired to manage the Reds, he led the Philadelphia Phillies for four years, beginning in 1915 when they won the National League pennant. His teams were 323-257, but his contract was not renewed after a sixth-place finish in 1918. Moran had a reputation for developing pitchers, including Grover Cleveland Alexander.[2] When he was hired to manage the Reds in 1919, he again produced a championship in his first season. His nine-year record as a manager was 748-586, with a .561 winning percentage, two National League pennants, a World Series championship, and four second-place finishes.

Cincinnati was expected to have a strong offense led by outfielders Edd Roush and Greasy Neale, third-baseman Heinie Groh, and Jake, who replaced the controversial Hal Chase, who was traded to the New York Giants. Chase had been accused but ultimately never proved of offering bribes to players to influence games on which he had wagered.[3] Outfielder Sherry Magee (1910 with Philadelphia), Jake (1913 and 1914), and Roush (1917) had won National League batting titles.

Moran strengthened his pitching staff with Slim Sallee, selected off waivers from the New York Giants on March 18, following an 8-8 season in 1918, and Ray Fisher, selected off waivers from the New York Yankees on March 15. He had served in the army during the 1918 season.

According to Jake, getting Kopf back to play shortstop was another key move.

"I want to claim my share of credit for the making of the Reds," Jake said after the 1919 season. "Not for anything I personally did at the bat or on first base, but for something I accomplished before the season opened. It was when Pat Moran and Garry Herrmann were worrying about the infield. Mr. Herrmann talked to me about Kopf, and asked me if I thought he'd help. I said that Kopf was the one man we needed, the one man who could solder up that infield so it would be airtight and dependable—and now I'm delighted over the results of the conversation."[4]

The Reds started the 1919 season with seven wins, stretching their win streak over two seasons to 13 games, and were 9-1 after 10. They were 12-13 during May and trailed the New York Giants by five games on June 5. The Reds went 22-6 in July and moved into first place to stay on July 30. They went 22-8 in August, including a 10-game winning streak, and 15-8 in September to finish the season 95-44, nine games ahead of the Giants.

Jake batted sixth and struggled at the start of the season. He had a few good games, including May 4, when he tripled with the bases loaded in the first inning and scored on a wild throw to lead the Reds over the Cubs, 8-1.

In his first game back in Brooklyn, May 13, he went 1-for-5. He had 19 putouts, one assist, and no errors and made numerous sensational picks at first base.[5] He was cheered by Brooklyn fans each time he batted. Brooklyn won, 4-3, in 11 innings. Jake went 2-for-19 in the four-game series, which the teams split.

He was also cheered by his wife and the wives of others on the team, who agreed to sit together, and each time Jake came to bat, they yelled, "Get a hit, Jake. Get a hit, Jake."[6]

On May 23, Jake was batting .193, and by early June, he considered quitting baseball. "I won't keep on this way," he said. "I'll make one effort to break away from this hoodoo that seems to have me handcuffed. I'll try all I can and see if I can't make good, all right. I'll keep right on and be happy. But if things continue as they have for three weeks, if I can't bat and if I can't field the way I should, I'll know the end is near. I'll know that I'm through as a big leaguer, and I won't take money from the Cincinnati club unless I can hold the pace I always held. It's either another stretch of success for Jake Daubert, or I leave the game forever."[7]

Moran didn't lose confidence in Jake and worked to boost his confidence.

"Jake came to Cincinnati this year from Brooklyn so anxious to deliver the goods that he overreached himself," Moran recalled near the end of the season. "His very determination to do his very best made him do his very worst. It caused him to be nervous at bat, and the result was that he failed to hit at all. That continued so long that it preyed upon his mind and affected his fielding.

"I had a heart-to-heart talk with Jake one day and told him he was attempting too much. I advised him to take things more easily, to realize that he was a born batter who was bound to strike his stride and to be content with batting in a perfectly normal way. I pointed out that his fielding was falling off for no other reason than that he was foolishly worrying about his hitting.

"Jake saw the value of those observations and stopped the worrying. He began his comeback against Brooklyn, and he has kept it up ever since. With the return to form in hitting went a brace in his work at first base. Now Jake is the same star he always was and is driving in his full share of runs every week."[8]

Jake also received a pep talk from Charles Maddock, a clerk at the Metropole Hotel in Cincinnati and one of the Reds' biggest fans. *The Cincinnati Post* shared the story of the exchange after the Reds returned from St. Louis to begin an 18-game home stand:

> When Daubert came back, he met Maddock.
> "Jake," Maddock said to him, "I want to talk to you."
> "You'll have to hurry," Daubert said grumpily, "for I'm going to leave soon."
> "You are going to do nothing of the sort," replied Maddock earnestly. "Why, Jake, there is not a better liked man on the team today than you. "I'll wager everything I own that when you go to bat today everyone will give you the cheer of your life."
> "Gee, Maddock," Daubert said, "I wonder if you're right."
> That afternoon when Daubert strode to the plate for the first time the whole stand "arose" and began to cheer. Daubert cracked out a single. He made three hits that day and has not stopped since.
> In the evening, he again saw Maddock, who hadn't been able to get to the park. "Maddock, I'm going to stay. You were right."[9]

Moran also made a move that helped Jake and the Reds. He put Jake back in his familiar second spot in the batting order on June 5. Jake went 0-for-2 that day in a 1-0 loss at St. Louis, but in the next three games, he went 6-for-11, all Cincinnati wins over Brooklyn. It was his former team's first trip of the season to Cincinnati, and the Reds swept the four-game series. Jake's fielding also improved. He made nine errors in the first 35 games, including two on June 4. He had only eight errors in the last 105 games.

Jake didn't forget what he considered unfair treatment by Ebbets. Baseball had a rule that prohibited anyone not directly involved with the game from sitting in the dugout. "Ebbets had a habit of sitting on the bench in his civilian clothes," Jake's son, George recalled. "He did that out in Cincinnati in 1919, the first time that Brooklyn played Cincinnati. My dad had the umpire chase him off the bench. So Charlie had to sit in the stands." [10]

Beginning July 1, Jake went 33-for-75 in 17 games for a .440 average with three doubles and four triples, raising his average to .304. He went 5-for-5 on July 28, raising his average to a season-high .308. During a 12-game hitting streak from August 7 to 16, he batted .340.

Jake finished the season at .276 and led the league with a career-high 39 sacrifices. More impressive, he wasn't slowed by his normal injuries and played every inning of all 140 games.[11]

Late in the season, Jake and former Brooklyn teammate Lew McCarty, now with the Giants, planned a hunting trip for the fall with an agreement that Jake would cover the expenses if the Reds won the National League pennant and McCarty would pay the bill if the Giants won the title.[12]

Jake again filed a suit against Brooklyn when he did not receive the money owed from the previous settlement. He was to receive $500 when he signed with Cincinnati, $500 on May 10, and $500 on June 10. As of August 29, he said the June payment was not made.[13]

The Reds clinched the National League pennant on September 16, beating the Giants 4-3. Center-fielder Edd Roush led the league with a .321 average, and third-baseman Heinie Groh hit .310. The starting pitchers were Slim Sallee, who was 21-7 with a 2.06 earned run average; Dutch Ruether, 19-6 and 1.82; Hod Eller, 19-9 and 2.39; Ray Fisher, 14-5 and 2.17; and Jimmy Ring, 10-9 and 2.26

Chicago won the American League pennant with an 88-52 record, 3 ½ games ahead of the Cleveland Indians, and was in first place every day except from June 23 to July 7. Outfielder Shoeless Joe Jackson at .351, second-baseman Eddie Collins at .319, and outfielder Nemo Leibold at .302 led the White Sox. Pitcher Eddie Cicotte, who was 29-7 with a 1.82 earned run average and 30 complete games, and Lefty Williams, 23-11, 2.64, and 27, led the pitching staff.

The White Sox team batting average was .287, and the Reds' .263. The Reds' pitching staff had a 2.23 ERA, and the White Sox 3.04.

"Those batting averages don't count," Jake said. "It is all different when you go into a world's series. You might hit .400 through the season and fall down hard in the series. But I don't think we have a man on the club who will blow up under the strain. Our boys seem to be sure about the outcome."[14]

1919 WORLD SERIES

The Chicago White Sox lost what became the most remembered World Series. Often overlooked or forgotten is the team that won that series—the Cincinnati Reds. What forever will remain unknown is whether the Reds would have won the championship if the White Sox hadn't conspired with gamblers to throw the series.

The 1919 White Sox are remembered as the most infamous team in baseball history. Many true baseball fans may have trouble naming other World Series winners, but most know who lost in 1919.

Gambling was a part of baseball almost since its beginning. There were numerous scandals and rumors of game fixing, but none compared to the 1919 Black Sox scandal because none were on a bigger stage and dealt with so harshly.

One of the earliest scandals was in 1877. National League president William Hulbert imposed lifetime bans on four members of the Louisville team—pitcher Jim Devlin, outfielder George Hall, shortstop Bill Craver, and utilityman Al Nichols—for throwing games.

In 1905 Philadelphia Athletics pitcher Rube Waddell, a future Hall-of-Famer, missed the World Series after a suspicious shoulder injury, and the New York Giants won behind Christy Mathewson's three shutouts. There were rumors that gamblers bribed Waddell to fake the injury.

Boston Red Sox pitcher Smokey Joe Wood told friends to bet on his team in 1912 when he was scheduled to pitch with the Red Sox ahead 3-1 in the best-of-seven series. But Boston owner James McAleer ordered manager Jake Stahl to start newcomer Buck O'Brien, who was 20-13 during the regular season. The Red Sox lost that game and the next one but came back to win in Game Eight (one ended in a tie) with two runs in the bottom of the 10th inning against Christy Mathewson. Wood was the winning pitcher with three innings in relief for his third series victory.[15]

There also were many accusations of players "easing up" to affect pennant races and batting titles. One of the players most often associated with gamblers was "Prince" Hal Chase, considered the greatest first baseman before Jake arrived in the majors. Chase was a moody player who frequently was accused of missing signs and failing to make catches on throws from other infielders. In 1916 with the Cincinnati Reds, Chase was suspended by manager Christy Mathewson for offering bribes to his teammates and opponents. But the league never punished Chase because Mathewson was in the military and unable to testify.[16]

Managers Ty Cobb of the Detroit Tigers and Tris Speaker of the Cleveland Indians, two of the biggest stars in the history of baseball, were suspected in a game-fixing scheme near the end of the 1919 season in an unsuccessful effort to help the Tigers claim third place in the American League. Pitchers Dutch Leonard of the Tigers and Wood of the Indians also were involved. Although the league took no action after several hearings, Cobb and Speaker resigned as managers and were released by their teams before the end of the year.[17]

The biggest scandal was about to unfold. Before the 1919 series, there were rumors of a possible fix in the World Series, and the stories that White Sox players received money from gamblers continued during and after the series. White Sox president Charlie Comiskey offered $20,000 for evidence that any of his players intentionally threw the World Series.

"There is always some scandal of some kind following a big sporting event like the world's series," he said. "These yarns are manufactured out of whole cloth and grow out of bitterness due to losing wagers.

"I believe my boys fought the battles of the recent world's series on the level, as they have always done, and I would be the first to want information to the contrary. I would give $20,000 to anyone unearthing any information to the effect."[18]

But the story intensified during the next year. A day after a newspaper in Philadelphia published a story with allegations by known gambler Billy Maharg that eight members of the White Sox were involved in fixing the series, Eddie Cicotte, Joe Jackson, and Lefty Williams testified before a Cook County grand jury on September 28, 1920, about their part in the fix. Comiskey immediately suspended the players.

The testimony of the three White Sox players surprised members of the Cincinnati Reds.

"I can't fully realize it even yet," Moran said. "Seems hardly possible, yet there is Cicotte's confession to go on, so what can we say? I'm sure none of my boys dreamed they were being handed any gifts in any of the games, for the Sox snarled and growled and fought back all the time. As to Cicotte's pitching, we simply thought him either greatly overrated or very weary from his hard season's work."[19]

Jake didn't suspect there was anything suspicious about Cicotte's pitching.

"I wasn't paying much attention in that first game to Schalk and his signals, so I don't know whether Cicotte crossed him or not," Jake said after the testimony was published. "I was too busy picking out good ones to hit at. In the excitement of such a game you'll hardly ever stop to study close points of pitching. If you see the kind of ball you like, you smash it. Cicotte didn't seem to have much perhaps. Had he been a National pitcher we had often met, we just remarked: 'They must have easy pitching in this American League,' and tore into him."[20]

On October 29, 1920, eight Chicago players and five gamblers were indicted by a Grand Jury of conspiracy to obtain money by false pretenses.[21] They were cleared in the court by a jury on August 2, 1921, but the next day new commissioner Judge Kenesaw Mountain Landis issued a lifetime banishment from major league baseball for the eight players—Jackson, Cicotte, Williams, Happy Felsch, Fred McMullin, Swede Risberg, Buck Weaver, and Chick Gandil, who had retired after the 1919 season. Jackson was one of the greatest hitters in baseball history, with a lifetime batting average of .356 and was a certain Hall-of-Famer. Cicotte was a strong candidate for the Hall.

* * *

Chicago was heavily favored to win the World Series. In a position-by-position preview, *The New York Times* gave the Reds the edge at first base (Jake over Chick Gandil), shortstop (Billy Kopf over Charley Risberg) and pitching in the best-of-nine series (Harry Sallee, Dutch Ruether, and Horace Eller over Eddie Cicotte, Claude Williams, and Dick Kerr):

> Pursuing the dope around the infield it is found that the Reds have the edge at first base. Jake Daubert and Chic Gandil are the rival guardians of the getaway station. There can be no question that, in spite of his years, Daubert is Gandil's peer afield. Jake can still cover a deal of ground, and there are few first basemen who can turn more wide throws into put outs than he. In batting Gandil has done a little better work with the stick this year, according to the figures, but the fact that Daubert has played in quite a few more games than Chick must be taken into consideration. He has made more hits and has scored more runs than Gandil, but the additional number of times at bat charged against him has made his percentage lower than that of his rival.[22]

A week before the World Series, the White Sox were 7 to 10 favorites, but just before Game One, there were rumors that Cicotte had a sore arm, dropping the best odds to 5 to 6. There was a rush to place money on the Reds.[23]

Game One
Cincinnati 9, Chicago 1
October 1, at Redland Field, Cincinnati
Time: 1:42, attendance: 30,511

Eddie Cicotte was an excellent control pitcher who hit only two batters in 306 2/3 innings during the regular season. His first pitch to Morrie Rath in the bottom of the first inning was a strike, but when his next pitch hit Rath in the back, it signaled the fix was on. It was the second most notable hit-by-pitch in the history of baseball, behind only Carl Mays' pitch that struck and killed Ray Chapman in 1920.

Jake followed with the Reds' first hit, a single to center field, moving Rath to third base. Rath scored on a sacrifice fly by Heinie Groh for a 1-0 lead. The White Sox, helped by shortstop Larry Kopf's error, tied it with an unearned run in the top of the second on an RBI single by Gandil, who had two of Chicago's six hits against Dutch Ruether.

Although unnoticed by most in attendance, the first signs of a fix came in the fourth inning. After Pat Duncan reached base on a one-out single, Kopf hit the ball back to Cicotte, who turned and threw low to second base to get the force on Duncan. But shortstop Swede Risberg double-clutched before throwing to first, and Kopf was safe by a half-step. The Reds followed with five straight hits and scored on an RBI single by Ivey Wingo, a two-run triple by Ruether, a double by Rath, and a single to right field by Jake. Cicotte was lifted after Jake's hit, which gave Cincinnati a 6-1 lead.

The Reds added two more in the seventh. Jake led off with a triple to right field against reliever Roy Wilkinson and scored on Groh's single to center. Groh reached third on a grounder when Gandil dropped the ball at first, then scored an unearned run on a fielder's choice. They finished the scoring in the eighth against reliever Grover Lowdermilk when Ruether's second triple drove in Greasy Neale, who led off with a single.

One batter later, with a full count, Jake was beaned by Lowdermilk, fell to the ground, and appeared knocked out. As players rushed to Jake, fans screamed and then were quiet for a few moments before he got to his feet and rubbed his head as he walked to first base.[24]

Jake remained in the game and played the rest of the series, but he was hitless in his next 14 at-bats, and the long-term effects of that hit and numerous others would have a devastating result.

Ring W. Lardner, a satirical and humorous sports columnist, wrote a macabre account of the incident:

> Gents—up to the 8th inning this P.M. we was all setting there wondering what to write about and I happened to be looking at Jake Daubert's picture in the souvenir program, and all of

a sudden Jake fell over and I thought he was dead, so I said to the boys, "Here is your story. Jacob E. Daubert was born in Shamokin, Pennsylvania, on the 17th of April 1886, and lives in Schuylkill, Pa., and began playing with the Kane, Pa., club in 1907. With Cleveland in 1908 and Toledo for two years. Joined the Brooklyn club in 1910, and remained there until this season. Then joined the Cincinnati Reds and fell dead in the 8th inning of the 1st game of the World Series."

So everybody got up and cheered me and said that was a very funny story, but all of a sudden again Jake stood up and looked at the different pts of the compass and walked to 1st base and wasn't dead at all, and everybody turned around and hissed me for not giving them a good story. Well, gents, I am not to blame because when a man has got a fast ball like Grover Lowdermilk, and hits a man like Jake in the temple, I generally always figure they are dead, and the fact that Jake got up and walked to 1st base is certainly not my fault, and I hope nobody will hold it vs. me.[25]

Jake's three hits in Game One equaled the hits he had in the entire 1916 World Series. Neale also had three hits for the Reds, and Ruether went 3-for-3 with two triples, a walk, and three RBIs. Ruether pitched a complete game and allowed six singles and no earned runs.

Before the game, Jake was presented with a large bouquet of roses from fans. When the Reds won, fans considered the flowers a good sign and presented bouquets to him before the next two games.

Jake in Game One
3-for-4, 1 R, 1 RBI, 1 HBP, 1 CS, 9 PO
First inning: Single to center field, moving Morrie Rath to third.
    Caught stealing, catcher to shortstop, for second out.
Third inning: Flyball to left field with a runner on second base for
    second out.
Fourth inning: Single to right field, Rath scores from second for a 6-1
    lead, moves to second base on the throw to home.

Seventh inning: Leadoff triple to right field, scores on single by Heinie Groh for a 7-1 lead.

Eighth inning: Hit in the head by a pitch from Grover Lowdermilk

Game Two
Cincinnati 4, Chicago 2
October 2, at Redland Field, Cincinnati
Time: 1:42, attendance: 29,698

"We've got the jump now, and we hope to keep on going," Jake said before Game Two. "I'll admit that I was tickled over my hitting. Hope to get three more today."[26]

That didn't happen, but Jake made two spectacular defensive plays and contributed a sacrifice in the fourth that led to the Reds' first run. Morrie Rath led off the inning with a walk—one of three in the inning by the normally accurate Lefty Williams—and moved to second when Jake bunted to the pitcher. After Heinie Groh walked, Edd Roush singled to center for the first run. Larry Kopf drove in two more with a triple to left. The Reds made it 4-0 in the sixth on a two-out single by Greasy Neale. Chicago scored two unearned runs against Slim Sallee in the seventh on singles by Swede Risberg and Ray Schalk, helped by right-fielder Neale's throwing error.

In three at-bats, Jake grounded out twice and popped out to second. He also committed an error in the eighth inning when he went into short right field to get the ball after Joe Jackson singled. Jake threw wildly to Sallee, who was covering first, allowing Jackson to advance to second, where he was stranded. Jake more than covered for that error with two excellent fielding plays in the fourth inning. With runners on second and third and one out, Chick Gandil hit a hard grounder to first. Jake made a perfect stop and threw home to get Buck Weaver by three yards for the second out.[27] Risberg came to bat, again with runners on second and third, and hit a popup into short right field, which Jake went back and caught for the final out.

The Reds had only four hits against Williams but took advantage of his wildness. He walked a career-high six in the game after walking only

58 in 297 innings during the regular season. All four Reds runs were scored by batters who reached base by walking. Sallee allowed ten hits, including three by Jackson, and no earned runs. The White Sox were 0-for-7 with runners in scoring position and left seven on base.

Jake in Game Two
0-for-3, 1 SH, 12 PO, 2 A
First inning: Groundout to shortstop for second out.
Fourth inning: Sacrifice bunt to pitcher, moving Morrie Rath to second, Rath scores on a single for a 1-0 lead.
Fifth inning: Popup to second base with runners on first and second for second out.
Seventh inning: Leadoff groundout to shortstop.

Game Three
Chicago 3, Cincinnati 0
October 3, at Comiskey Park, Chicago
Time: 1:30, attendance: 29,126

Eddie Cicotte and Lefty Williams were expected to play key roles in Chicago's hope of winning the World Series despite a thin pitching staff. But 5-foot-7 Dickey Kerr, a 26-year-old rookie, provided the bright spot. He pitched a three-hit shutout for Chicago's first win. He walked one—allowing four base-runners—and struck out four. The Reds did not have a runner advance past second base. Kerr retired the last 15 batters in order and got 15 outs on ground balls.

The White Sox scored two unearned runs in the second inning against spit-baller Ray Fisher on a single by Chick Gandil after Fisher's throwing error to second on Happy Felsch's sacrifice attempt put runners on second and third. They added a run in the fourth when Swede Risberg tripled to right field and scored on Ray Schalk's bunt single.

Jake made another great defensive play with runners on first and second and no outs in the third inning when he raced in and caught Jackson's popup on a bunt attempt. But he struggled at the plate, including striking out in the ninth inning.

The floral presentation didn't help in this game, but the Reds no longer needed it, thanks to help from Cicotte and Williams.

Jake in Game Three
0-for-4, 1 K, 14 PO, 1 A
First inning: Flyball to center field for second out.
Third inning: Grounded into force at second base for third out.
Sixth inning: Liner to left field for second out.
Ninth inning: Struck out for second out.

Game Four
Cincinnati 2, Chicago 0
October 4, at Comiskey Park, Chicago
Time: 1:37, attendance: 34,363

A day after Dickey Kerr pitched a three-hit shutout for the White Sox, 24-year-old Jimmy Ring, who was 10-9 with a 2.26 earned run average as a starter and reliever during the regular season, duplicated it for the Reds.

He was in trouble only twice. In the second, Joe Jackson led off with a fly ball to shallow center field that Edd Roush misjudged for a double, then moved to third on a sacrifice by Happy Felsch. After Chick Gandil popped up in front of the plate, Swede Risberg walked and stole second. Ray Schalk was intentionally walked, bringing Eddie Cicotte to the plate. Cicotte worked a full count and then hit a hard grounder to second, which Morrie Rath fielded and threw to Jake for the final out.

Chicago's only other serious threat was in the third when the White Sox had runners on first and third with two outs after a hit batter and an error by Rath at second. But Ring got Felsch to ground to third for the final out. After that, Ring settled in even though he allowed a runner in every inning after the fourth, when he retired the White Sox on just seven pitches.[28]

Cicotte started for the White Sox and was much better than in the first game. He mixed his fastball and sweeping curve[29] and faced the minimum batters in seven innings. His pitching showed no signs he was trying to lose the game. His fielding was a different story. With one out in the fifth inning, Pat Duncan hit a grounder up the middle, which Cicotte knocked down. But his wild throw to first allowed Duncan to reach second. The next batter, Larry Kopf, singled to left. Jackson fielded the ball and made a perfect throw to home, but Cicotte cut off the throw, allowing Duncan to score. Cicotte then threw wildly to second, allowing Kopf to reach second on Cicotte's second error of the inning. Greasy Neale followed with a double to left for the second run.

Jake struggled at the plate again. After Rath opened the game with a single, Jake grounded into a double play at second base. He was thrown out by the catcher on a bunt in the fourth, grounded out to second in the sixth, and flied out to left in the ninth.

Jake in Game Four
0-for-4, 9 PO, 1 A

First inning: Grounded into a double play to second base for second out.

Fourth inning: Groundout to the catcher on bunt attempt for second out.

Sixth inning: Grounder to second for second out.

Ninth inning: Flyball to left field for second out.

Game Five
Cincinnati 5, Chicago 0
October 6, at Comiskey Park, Chicago
Time: 1:45, attendance: 34,379

Rain pushed Game Five back a day. Even though it was sunny and the sky was clear on Monday, it was cold, and the field still was wet.[30] Moran elected to start 24-year-old shine-ball pitcher Hod Eller, who had won 19 games during the regular season, instead of first-game winner Dutch Ruether on five days' rest. Eller responded by pitching the third-straight three-hit shutout of the series. He struck out nine, including the side in the second and third innings, four on called third strikes. The six straight strikeouts were a World Series record.

Eller walked one, allowed only four baserunners, and shut down Chicago's two threats. In the first, Nemo Leibold walked on a full count, then Eller fell behind Eddie Collins 2-0. Jake went to the mound and settled down Eller, who then got Collins to ground to shortstop, moving Leibold to second. Eller knocked down Buck Weaver's infield single to put runners on first and third, but Joe Jackson followed with a high popup to third and Happy Felsch closed the inning with a flyball to left. Eller allowed only two more baserunners, the last a two-out triple in the ninth by Weaver, who was stranded when Jackson grounded to shortstop to end the game.

The Reds managed only four hits against Lefty Williams, who lost for the second time. Three of those came in the sixth inning when Cincinnati scored four runs. Eller opened with a double to left-center, advanced to third on center-fielder Felsch's wild throw back to the infield, and scored on a single to right by Morrie Rath. Jake's sacrifice bunt to third, his second of the game, moved Rath to second. After Heinie Groh walked on four pitches, Edd Roush hit a flyball to center that Felsch misplayed into a triple. Rath and Groh scored, the latter on a close play at the plate. Catcher Ray Schalk was ejected after protesting the call and bumping umpire Cy Rigler. Pat Duncan's sacrifice fly to left made it 4-0. The Reds added an unearned run in the ninth without a hit on an error, walk, sacrifice, and groundout.[31]

Although Jake was hitless again, he had two sacrifices, and his steady influence over Eller in the first inning helped set the tone for the rest of the game.

Jake in Game Five
0-for-2, 2 SH, 11 PO

First inning: Sacrifice bunt to catcher with no outs, moving Rath to second base.
Fourth inning: Leadoff flyball to center field.
Sixth inning: Sacrifice bunt to third base with no outs, moving Rath to second base.
Eighth inning: Flyball to center field for second out.

Game Six
Chicago 5, Cincinnati 4, 10 innings
October 7, at Redland Field, Cincinnati
Time: 2:06, attendance: 32,006

The World Series would have been over if the format hadn't been expanded to a best-of-nine from a best-of-seven. The Reds, leading 4-1, needed one more win. Chicago manager Kid Gleason was frustrated by his team's play and that Cincinnati had twice beaten his star pitchers, Eddie Cicotte and Lefty Williams, in back-to-back starts. He turned to young Dickey Kerr, who had shut down the Reds in Game Three.

"There's something the matter with my ball club, and I don't know what it is," Gleason wrote in a newspaper column. "But I feel that my gang will fight down to the last game. I'm going to send Dick Kerr to the slab tomorrow. Maybe if he wins, I shall send him back the next day, and if he wins that one, I might send him back again."[32]

Eventually, he and the rest of the baseball world would know what was wrong. But on this day, his team managed to live to play another day. Later there were reports that players who had conspired with gamblers to throw the series were unhappy that all their payments hadn't been received.[33] Perhaps that inspired them to play to win. Eight of Chicago's ten hits were by players involved in the fix: Buck Weaver (3), Joe Jackson (2), Happy Felsch (2), and Chick Gandil (1).

Kerr struggled from the start and gave up two runs in the third. Jake, who regained his batting eye, hit a one-out single to right field, stole second, and scored on Pat Duncan's double, which also plated Edd Roush, who had been hit by a pitch. The Reds scored two more in the fourth when Greasy Neale tripled and scored on Dutch Ruether's double, then Ruether scored on a throwing error by Swede Risberg, who was attempting to get Ruether at third on a fielder's choice grounder to shortstop.

Ruether, who had pitched so well in the first game, again was in control through the first four innings for the Reds. Cincinnati fans began to celebrate, some headed for the gates, and stakeholders began to pay off wagers.[34]

Before the game, the White Sox had scored only six runs in five games and only one earned run. Cincinnati pitchers had held Chicago scoreless for 26 straight innings before the White Sox scored on a sacrifice fly in the top of the fifth inning. The White Sox tied the score with three runs in the sixth, showing new life. Weaver doubled on a popup that fell between Duncan and Larry Kopf in left field and scored on a single by Jackson, who then scored on a double by Felsch, chasing Ruether. Jimmy Ring came on and got two outs on a popup to Jake and a groundout to shortstop that moved Felsch to third. Ray Schalk's single to left field tied the score at 4.

The Reds had a runner at second with one out in the seventh after Jake's sacrifice to the pitcher, but a double play ended the threat. In the eighth, they again had a runner in scoring position after two two-out singles, but the threat ended on a groundball. In the ninth, Jake singled to center with one out but was forced at second on a grounder to short by Heinie Groh, who then was caught stealing.

It remained tied until the White Sox scored in the top of the 10th, when Weaver doubled to left, moved to third on Jackson's bunt single, and scored on a single to center by Gandil, who was one of the ringleaders of the fix and had been 0-for-3 in the game. Kerr retired the Reds in order in the bottom of the inning.

Jake in Game Six
2-for-4, 1 R, 1 SB, 1 SH, 11 PO
First inning: Grounder to the pitcher for second out.
Third inning: Single to right field, steals second, scores on double to right field by Pat Duncan. Edd Roush also scores from first for a 2-0 lead.
Seventh inning: Sacrifice bunt to the pitcher with no outs, moving Rath to second base.
Ninth inning: Single to center with one out, forced at second on a grounder.

Game Seven
Chicago 4, Cincinnati 1
October 8, at Redland Field, Cincinnati
Time: 1:47, attendance: 13,923

With a 4-2 lead in the series, the Reds needed to win one of three games, but after blowing a four-run lead and losing Game Six, there may have been concern among fans that the momentum had shifted and only 13,923 attended the game at Redland Field. There also was confusion about where tickets were being sold on the morning of the game, and many fans who were required to buy tickets in a three-game block at the start of the series decided not to spend money for Game Seven.[35]

Eddie Cicotte was back on the mound for the White Sox and looked like the pitcher he was during the regular season, using his effective shine ball. He scattered seven hits, walked three, struck out four, and threw 80 of his 120 pitches for strikes.[36]

Joe Jackson drove in runs with singles in the first and fifth innings. Happy Felsch drove in two more in the fifth with a bases-loaded single, following errors on consecutive plays on ground balls by Heinie Groh at third and Morrie Rath at second. That ended the day for Reds starter Slim Sallee, who allowed nine hits in 4 1/3 innings.

Cincinnati got its only run when Groh doubled, moved to second on a groundout and scored on a single by Pat Duncan in the sixth. In the ninth, the Reds had on runners on first and second with two outs. Rath worked a 3-2 count and was looking for a walk to load the bases for Jake, who was waiting on deck. But Cicotte's next pitch was down the middle. Rath hit a liner to right field, which Felsch tracked down to end the game.[37]

Jake struggled again at the plate, going 0-for-4 with a strikeout. In the seventh, with runners on first and second and two outs, Jake hit a hard grounder to second, which Eddie Collins fumbled before throwing to first to get Jake for the third out. Jake lunged for the bag and kicked up a lot of dust, but he was called out on what Jake and many others considered a bad call that ended a Reds rally.[38]

The Reds committed four errors, including one on a catch by Jake in the first, but overall he played excellent defense. Jake made a spectacular play when he raced to the right field stands and caught Swede Risberg's foul over the heads of spectators in the fourth inning.[39] In the eighth, Jake made a great pick on a throw by Larry Kopf, who went into deep short to field a grounder.

A story in *The Brooklyn Daily Eagle* emphasized the importance of Jake's defense:

> Jake played a whale of a game in covering first. Koph and Groh threw him some balls that he had to reach after, like an India rubber man. One of his reaches was so remarkable that the fans rose up and gave him three rousing cheers. Gandil is a quick man on first base and handles high throws as well as Daubert, perhaps, but Jake is the champion reacher of this universe. What boarding house he was raised in we don't know, but if we had a son ambitious to become a first sacker, we would ask Jake where he got that uncanny knack of stretching himself. He could get two helpings of sugar in wartime.[40]

Jake in Game Seven
0-for-4, 1 K, 1 E, 10 PO, 1 A
First inning: Popup to second base for first out. He committed an error in the top of the inning on a catch.
Third inning: Ground out to the pitcher for the third out.
Sixth inning: Strikeout looking for the first out.
Seventh inning: Grounder to second base for the third out.

Game Eight
Cincinnati 10, Chicago 5
October 9, at Comiskey Park, Chicago
Time: 2:27, attendance: 32,930

After Eddie Cicotte's performance, Chicago had every reason to be confident, with Lefty Williams and Dickey Kerr scheduled to pitch the next two games. "My gang is back playing ball again," White Sox manager Kid Gleason said.[41]

His hopes disappeared early in Game Eight when the Reds sent nine men to the plate and scored four runs in the first inning. Morrie Rath popped up to deep short to open the game, but that was the only out Williams recorded. Jake started things with a single to center, moved to second on a single to right by Heinie Groh, and scored on a double to right by Edd Roush. Pat Duncan doubled for two more runs, and Williams' day was over after 16 pitches. Bill Rariden hit a line-drive single to right against Bill James for the fourth run, which was charged to Williams.

Stories circulated that the lives of Williams or his wife were threatened before the game. [42]

The White Sox tried to strike back in the bottom of the inning when Nemo Leibold opened with a single off Hod Eller and moved to third on a double by Eddie Collins. Jimmy Ring started to warm up in the bullpen,[43] but Eller settled down and got the next three outs on a called third strike to Buck Weaver, a popup behind third by Joe Jackson, and a strikeout by Happy Felsch.

The Reds made it 5-0 in the second when Groh singled and scored on a double by Roush. Chicago got a run in the third when Joe Jackson hit the only home run of series, a deep drive to right field, but Cincinnati's offense continued to attack. In the fourth, with runners on first and second, Jake singled to center, but Leibold threw home to get Elller, who was trying to score from second. They added a run in the fifth when Larry Kopf tripled and scored on Greasy Neale's single. In the sixth against reliever Roy Wilkinson, Roush drove in two with a single, and Duncan's base hit drove in Jake, who had reached base on a fielder's choice and moved to third on Roush's hit. They threatened in the seventh when Rath and Jake walked with two outs before Wilkinson got Groh on a fly ball to center. The Reds made in 10-1 in the eighth on Bill Rariden's RBI single after a hit batter and a walk.

Chicago cut the deficit in the eighth with four runs on four hits. Jackson drove in two with a double and Chick Gandil one with a triple.

The fourth run scored when Roush at first lost the ball in the sun, then dropped the ball for an error, allowing Gandil to score. They tried again in the ninth when they had runners on second and third with two outs, but Jackson hit a grounder to second, which Rath fielded and threw to Jake for the final out of the series.

Jake in Game Eight
2-for-4, 2 R, 1BB, 1 SH, 8 PO

First inning: Single to center with one out, moves to second on single, scores on the double by Edd Roush for a 1-0 lead.

Second inning: Flyball to left field for second out.

Fourth inning: Single to center field with one out and two on. Advances to second when Hod Eller is thrown out at home.

Sixth inning: Reaches first base on bunt error by catcher on fielder's choice, moves to third on single by Roush, scores on single by Pat Duncan for 9-1 lead.

Seventh inning: Walks with two outs.

Ninth inning: Sacrifice bunt to the pitcher with no outs, moving Rath to second base.

* * *

Despite his 0-for-14 streak after being beaned in Game One, Jake finished the series with a .241 batting average. He went 7-for-29 with a triple and struck out twice. Greasy Neale, at .357, led the Reds, who batted .255 as a team. The Cincinnati pitchers allowed only 12 earned runs in the eight games, led by Hod Eller (2-0, 2.00 ERA), Jimmy Ring (1-1, 0.64), Slim Sallee (1-1, 1.35), and Dick Ruether (1-0, 2.57)

Shoeless Joe Jackson batted .375 for Chicago, including three doubles and the only home run of the series. Buck Weaver batted .324, and Ray Schalk .304. Gandil hit .233. The team batting average was .224. Chicago's pitchers combined for a 3.68 ERA. Lefty Williams was 0-3 with a 6.61 ERA, and Eddie Cicotte was 1-2 and 2.91. The White Sox stretched the series to eight games mainly because of Dickey Kerr, who was 2-0 with a 1.42 ERA.

The 8 Black Sox	Series	Season
Shoeless Joe Jackson	.375 (12-32)	.351 (181-516)
Chick Gandil	.233 (7-30)	.290 (128-441)
Happy Felsch	.192 (5-26)	.275 (138-502)
Fred McMullin	.500 (1-2)	.294 (50-170)
Swede Risberg	.080 (2-25)	.256 (106-414)
Buck Weaver	.324 (11-34)	.296 (169-571)
Eddie Cicotte	1-2, 2.91	29-7, 1.82
Lefty Williams	0-3, 6.61	23-11, 2.64

Although the actions of the White Sox players overshadowed the Reds' World Series championship, Jake and his teammates believed they won on their merit.

"I was there; I saw them," Jake said. "We had the jump on the Sox in every game."[44]

Jake's son, George, recalled in 1989 what his father had said about the series in 1921.

"My dad was adamant about Buck Weaver and Joe Jackson," George said. "He said they could never have thrown a game. He couldn't understand why Jackson and Weaver were banned from baseball because their record in the World Series was such that it refuted everything that was said about throwing games. They played their hearts out in the World Series, and the record shows it. In his estimation, Jackson was the type of ballplayer who wouldn't know how to throw a ballgame. It would go so much against his grain that it would almost make him sick to think about it."[45]

For over a century, countless articles and books have been written about the scandal, including the legitimacy of the Reds' title.

"Popular beliefs and myths aside, I will never be convinced that suspicious play of a few White Sox players is just cause to completely ignore the superior playing abilities of the Reds as a team," William A. Cook wrote in his 2001 book, *The 1919 World Series: What Really Happened?* "With or without a conspiracy to throw games by a few of the White Sox players, an informed baseball fan, after looking at both the statistics and actual events of the series will come away as I did, convinced beyond a doubt that the Cincinnati Reds would have won the 1919 World Series without any help from their opponents. The record clearly shows the Cincinnati Reds were an excellent team capable of playing well with any club in either the National or American Leagues in 1919."[46]

Tris Speaker, manager of the Cleveland Indians, praised the Reds in a column he wrote for *The Plain Dealer*:

> I want to hand the Reds a few bouquets. They played eight games and they played great ball in all except one and one-half. They had excellent team work. Their fielding was better than I was given to expect. Their batting was timely. They failed to crack except in the two instances I have just referred to, during the last two games in Cincinnati. And to back all that up, they had an excellent pitching staff.[47]

Speaker had special praise for Jake:

> In picking the stars of the series I will take Jake Daubert of the Reds and Buck Weaver of the White Sox with Dick Kerr and Hod Eller carrying off the honors among the pitching. My selection of Daubert may occasion some surprise but I think I am supported by the actual play by play detail of the eight games. Not once when called upon to sacrifice did he fail. He was one of the hitting factors in three of the Red victories while his fielding around the first sack never has been surpassed in a world's series.[48]

Each Cincinnati player received a check for $5,225.33,[49] and the Chicago players got $3,254.36.[50]

The Reds arrived in Cincinnati on a special train from Chicago on the morning of October 10. They were greeted by fans and the ringing of fire bells and whistles from factories, locomotives, and river boats and were escorted to automobiles and taken to the B.M.C. Clubhouse for a special breakfast. Even heavy rain didn't dampen the spirits of the fans who lined the streets. Jake was quoted as saying the showers came from the Chicago fans, who burst into tears as the Reds left for home. School students were given the day off to enjoy the celebration, but the rain forced the cancellation of a public reception at Fountain Square in the center of the city, where thousands gathered.[51]

Several days later, Jake was given a special reception when he returned to Schuylkill Haven. He was honored with a parade and a banquet on October 14, when he was given a diamond ring and a gold watch. The banquet at Keystone Hall was attended by 275 and lasted from 8:30 p.m. until one the next morning. The event was supposed to be a surprise for Jake, but he learned about it in the afternoon when he received a letter from a Pottsville businessman who expressed his regrets that he could not attend. Among those attending were Jake's father and Pop Kelchner, the manager when Jake played for Kane at the start of his professional career.[52]

Edward Hall, a manager for one of the local teams that Jake played for at the beginning of his career, shared a story about Jake's character, which was reported by *The Call* of Schuylkill Haven:

> He related an instance of where Schuylkill Haven had been scheduled to play Auburn and it was known that Auburn had padded considerable for that certain game. Daubert came to him in the morning and stated he had a chance to earn $15 playing with Orwigsburg at Fleetwood that same afternoon compared to the $2.50 he would get for pitching for Schuylkill Haven. Mr. Hill said he told him he did not like to see him lose the $15 but he felt the Schuylkill Haven fans would much rather have him play in this town. That the team would be all broken up by his going and they stood chances of being defeated. That Mr. Daubert then said, "Well, you're the manager and what you say goes, regardless of whether they offer me $25 to play, I'll play with the boys."[53]

A few days later, Jake and his family left for eight weeks to vacation in New York and Vermont, where Gertrude visited friends, and Jake hunted big game in Vermont and birds in New York with his friend and former teammate Lew McCarty.[54]

WORLD SERIES CHAMPION AND THE BLACK SOX

Jake after his trade to Cincinnati in 1919. (Photo is in the public domain and acquired from the George Grantham Bain Collection at the Library of Congress)

Jake warms up during game for Cincinnati in 1919. (Photo is in the public domain and acquired from the Ernie Harwell Collection at the Detroit Public Library)

Jake at bat for Cincinnati in 1919. (From the collection of Jack Daubert)

1919 Cincinnati Reds. Jake is at left in the second row. (Photo is in the public domain and acquired from the Ernie Harwell Collection at the Detroit Public Library)

Members of the Cincinnati Reds raise the National League championship flag in 1919. (From the collection of Jack Daubert)

Page 1 of *The Cincinnati Enquirer* on October 10, 1919, after the Reds won the World Series.

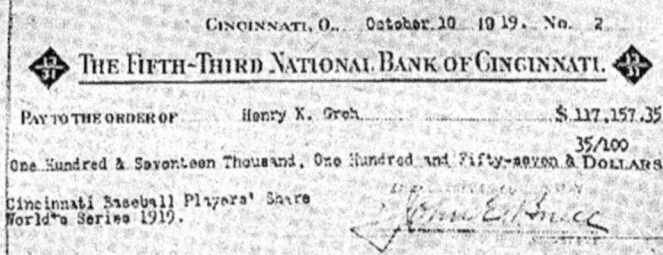

Heinie Groh, captain of the Reds, receives a check for $117,157.35 from John Bruce, secretary of the National Commission, for the players' share of the World Series receipts. Jake is standing at left along with Morrie Rath. (Photo from Page 1 of *The Post* of Cincinnati on October 10, 1919)

10

Not Ready to Quit

Every year during the second half of Jake's career, there were reports that his best days in baseball were behind him and he would retire soon. Every year Jake proved those reports wrong. He no longer needed to play baseball to support this family. His endorsements and businesses—especially his coal-dredging company—were successful.

Jake's approach to his family and finances hadn't changed from what F.C. Lane wrote in *Baseball Magazine* in 1912, soon after Jake burst onto the major league baseball scene:

> Daubert has but one worry and that is for the welfare of those dependent on him. When he worked in the mines, he was engaged in a dangerous occupation that was daily liable to lay him up with injuries. Baseball to the man that plays it for all that is in him is also a dangerous occupation. But Daubert does not on this account play any less speedy or determined a game. He shirks no risks which are properly his, but safeguards the future so far as he may by carefully saving his money as he goes along and heavily insuring himself against accidents.[1]

After the World Series championship, Jake could have left the game with financial security for his family and an impressive baseball legacy. He could have stayed in Schuylkill Haven year-round, run his businesses full-time, and spent more time with his wife and children living at

217 East Liberty Street. Instead, Jake boarded during the season at 307 Broadway in Cincinnati, near the present-day Reds ballpark. His injury-free 1919 season and the success of the Reds made it hard to walk away from the game he loved. And he still was playing the game at a high level.

During the next three years, Jake batted .316, with 47 triples and 61 doubles, and continued as one of the best defensive players in baseball. Leg and back injuries took a toll on Jake during the early part of his career, but in his last six seasons, he led the league in games played twice, playing in all 140 games in 1919 and all 156 in 1922.

Jake batted .304 in 1920, .306 in 1921, and .336 in 1922. He was among the league leaders in sacrifices, with 91 in those three seasons. In 1922 at age 38, he became the oldest to lead the National League in triples with 22 and hit a career-high 12 home runs. He continued as an elite fielder, leading the league's first basemen with a career-high .994 fielding percentage in 1922 and finishing second in 1923 (.993), third in 1921 (.993), and fifth in 1920 (.990). He led the league in putouts with 1,652 in 1922.

It wasn't all about the money for Jake, but he stood up for what he believed was fair. In late February, he delayed signing his 1920 contract, asking for more salary because of the addition of 14 games to the schedule.[2] About a week later, Jake, Edd Roush, and Hod Eller signed contracts and headed to spring training in Miami.[3]

There were other opportunities to make money in baseball by playing for industrial-plant teams, but he didn't want to play in what he considered a sideshow.

"I figure these factory teams a poor proposition for a man still able to stick in the majors," he said. "When a man joins a factory team, he gets out of the public eye no matter how good a player he is. But few persons care about him anymore. Ty Cobb might join a factory team tomorrow and continue playing as well as he could for the Tigers, but he wouldn't be Ty Cobb anymore. Industrial plants may rival even the majors in salaries, but they will never rival any branch of organized baseball in real baseball opportunities."[4]

As much as Jake loved the game, he knew his playing days wouldn't last forever. "Every time I see a new face on the club now, I look around to see if the fellow has a first baseman's glove," he said during spring training. "I know they'll be trying out first sackers by the carload lot from now on, 'cause I can't last forever."[5]

1920 SEASON

When Jake headed to spring training, he felt strong and looked forward to a good season. "If I felt old, creaky in the joints, or knew that I was slipping, I'd quit," he said. "I can quit any time I want, for I have plenty laid by, and I want to quit before I get to the place where I make a show of myself in big league company. I count on a good season partly because I feel much better than in several years and partly because, in my own opinion, I had a very bad season last summer. I think that this ball club won a pennant largely in spite of me, not on account of me—in other words. I didn't play my game, especially at the bat. There was an awful streak of hitless games, where I was really a handicap to the team. I hope to go along from the start this season without any more periods of misery to myself and the club, and I hope to surprise myself by coming back over the .300 line."[6]

Jake did surprise himself and others despite a scare during spring training. The injury jinx returned for Jake when he was hit on the back of his right hand on March 29 by the New York Yankees' George Mogridge and broke two bones. He returned home to Schuylkill Haven and was expected to miss at least a month, but when the season opened on April 14, Jake was in Cincinnati and in the lineup. He was 0-for-2 but walked three times, including the first inning when he moved to third on Heinie Groh's double and scored on Edd Roush's three-run homer. The Reds won, 7-3.

The injury and the ongoing pain didn't stop Jake. He went 13-for-32 with three sacrifices in the next eight games, including 4-for-5 with a walk in a 7-5 win over St. Louis on April 25 that moved the Reds into first place. Jake inserted a sponge in his glove to protect his injured right hand. He also started pulling the ball to right field.[7]

He didn't miss a game until May, when he was sidelined for two games with an ankle injury, the first games he missed since joining the Reds.

On June 22, he hit a homer leading off the 11th inning in the Reds' 3-1 win at Philadelphia. The next day he twisted his leg when his spikes caught on the bag while sliding into first base and missed the next five games[8] and three more in early July. He returned to the lineup full-time on July 6 and didn't miss another game until October 2, when he played in only one game of a triple-header.

Jake had five four-hit games and spent most of the season batting above .300. On July 11, he hit a walk-off three-run homer to right field in the ninth to beat the Boston Braves 6-3. He hit two triples in a loss to the Phillies on July 15.

The Reds were in the race for most of the year and in first place on September 6, but a 3-14 stretch dropped them 10 ½ back of the eventual champion Brooklyn Robins by September 25. They finished in third place at 82-71-1. Roush, at .339 and Jake, at .304, were the only players on the team above .300. Jimmy Ring, 17-16 and 3.54 ERA; Dutch Ruether, 16-12 and 2.47; and Hod Eller, 13-12 and 2.95, led the pitching staff.

In July, Jake told sportswriters that the 1921 season would be his last. "I am getting along in years," he said; "I have enough money to keep me comfortably, and I don't intend to remain in the game until I am shoved out."[9]

No young player had taken his place in 1920, and 1921 would not be the final season for Jake. But he already seemed to be planning for his days after baseball. In 1920, he organized and was the president of the Cox-Roosevelt League of Professional Baseball Players in support of the Democratic presidential ticket,[10] indicating that Jake might have a future in politics.

1921 SEASON

Jake returned his unsigned contract to the Reds because it did not include an increase. There were numerous reports that the Minersville baseball team, near his home in Schuylkill Haven, wanted Jake to become its manager, but Jake said he would not consider giving up his major league job to manage an independent team. Jake said he still expected to play for the Reds.

"There is no trouble between myself and the Cincinnati club," he said. "I am going to play first base for Cincinnati again this year. It has been my custom to leave for the south about March 12 each year, and my failure to sign my contract so far is due solely to the fact that there is no need of being in a hurry about it."[11]

But by March 11, nothing had changed, and Jake admitted that his major league career might be over.

"The best I got was the worst of it," Jake said. "I played for the Reds in 1919 when I was said to be through and only got a fair salary. I got into the game in 1920 when on many occasions I was in bad health and not fit to play but went in there just to steady the team. No return in a financial way is forthcoming, and I feel that I can do better by going into business, where I believe I can be successful."[12]

The nearly annual standoff ended on March 17, when the Reds announced that Jake would sign his contract and report to the team in 10 days.[13]

Jake reported to the Reds on April 7 in Indianapolis. He missed the entire training camp in Cisco, Texas, but when the season started on April 13 in Cincinnati against Pittsburgh, Jake was ready. The opening-day lineup was revamped from the previous year. Only Jake, left-fielder Pat Duncan, and catcher Ivey Wingo were the regulars back from 1920. Second-baseman Morrie Rath was traded to Seattle of the Pacific Coast League, and outfielder Greasy Neale was traded to the Philadelphia Phillies along with pitcher Jimmy Ring but rejoined the Reds in June after the Phillies released him. Shortstop Larry Kopf, third baseman Heinie Groh and center-fielder Edd Roush were holdouts. Roush signed at the end of April, Kopf in May, and Groh in June, but the Reds were 20 games back by the end of June. Jake filled in as captain of the team when Groh was out.

In the six years Jake played for Cincinnati, 1921 was the Reds' only losing season. They finished 70-83 and in sixth place, 24 games behind the league champion New York Giants. The team was hurt by numerous injuries. A 7-19 May dropped their record to 14-28, and they never recovered.

Five players hit over .300: Roush (.352), Groh (.331), Duncan (.308), Jake (.306), and outfielder Rube Bressler (.307). With the end of the Deadball Era, the pitching staff had a 3.46 earned run average, a decline from 2.90 in 1920 and more than a run worse than 2.23 in 1919. Rube Marquard (17-14, 3.39), Eppa Rixey (19-18, 2.78), and Dolf Luque (17-19, 3.38) led the team.

Jake had a 15-game hitting streak from July 27 to August 9, when he went 22-for-53, a .415 average, and raised his season average to .304. He finished strong, batting .395 in his last 20 games, including two when he went 4-for-4. He had a .993 fielding percentage, matching his best at that point in his career, and on April 25 had five assists in a game.

Several injuries again hampered Jake. He missed seven games in May because of another leg injury and two in August after he was hit on the right elbow by Brooklyn pitcher Burleigh Grimes. At the end of August, he left the team for four games to be with his wife, who had appendicitis.

Leg injuries—specifically what Jake called "charley horses"—affected him numerous times during his career. Late in the 1922 season, there was a debate about heel spikes being responsible for many injuries to players' knees, ankles, and feet from sliding and sudden stops when running.

"Infielders are constantly making short stops on all sorts of ground, dry and hard one day, soft and muddy the next," Jake said when asked for his opinion. "The heel spike is essential to them if they are to work at the best advantage, and I do not consider it a menace in running.

"What some genius should do is to invent a bandage or some other apparatus which will prevent charley-horse or the tearing of muscles from quick starting, not from stopping. It is the starting that has caused all of my troubles and which is responsible for the vast majority of cases of players being kept out of the game. The after effects of those injuries are more severe than the fans suppose. In the back of my right thigh is a hardened muscle, and there is another in the front of the right thigh. One player in this league has a muscle which tore apart and never could be sewed together. It sticks out the side of his leg in a lump, but strangely enough it does not interfere with his running. The evils of quick starting, not of too sudden stopping, are what drive many a fine fellow out of the game."[14]

1922 SEASON

Jake turned 38 early in the 1922 season. Soon after he arrived at training camp at Mineral Wells, Texas, on March 15, he was dealing with a sore back, but he didn't like when people referred to him as "old." Sportswriter Tom Swope wrote this story in *The Cincinnati Post* during spring training:

> At one of the numerous dinners tendered the Reds in Mineral Wells, the principal speaker of the evening—a Mineral Wells silver-tongued orator—sought to bestow unlimited praise on the Reds, collectively and individually. His object was to tell them how glad the citizens of the town had been to have them in their midst and to impress upon them they would be welcomed back next year.
>
> But there is one Red with whom a certain section of his speech did not make a great hit. In speaking of Jake Daubert, he referred to the Red first sacker as "that grand old character of the National game," etc.
>
> Jake's head came up with a jerk with the sentence, and it wasn't long afterward until the speaker again referred to "old Jake."
>
> Daubert is not a spring chicken anymore and does not attempt to pose as one. But he doesn't like to be called "old," and the "old" was about all he heard of the speech.[15]

The 1922 season was a rare time when leg issues didn't hamper Jake, and the result was one of his best years. He played in all 156 games and didn't miss an inning until September 18, when he left a game in the seventh inning in New York to catch a train so he could get home to Schuylkill Haven to take care of some business.[16]

Jake missed only 14 innings all season. He left in the bottom of the fourth inning of the second game of a doubleheader on September 21 at Boston. He had singled and tripled to drive in the Reds' runs in a 5-2 loss. On September 26, Philadelphia's Bill Hubbell hit him in the back of the head in the third inning. Jake fell to the ground and was surrounded by players from both teams. After a few minutes, Jake stood up and walked to first base, but he was so dizzy that he had to leave the game.[17] The Reds had the next three days off, and Jake returned to play the final three games against Pittsburgh.

Jake struggled at the start of the season, going hitless in 25 at-bats in the first seven games. He finally hit a ninth-inning double to start a career-best 22-game hitting streak, during which he batted .416 with two home runs, three doubles, three triples, and eight sacrifices, and raised his season average to .320.

The streak ended on May 15 against Brooklyn when Jake went 0-for-3 with a walk. Brooklyn president Charles Ebbets, Jake's former boss, had offered a hat to any of his pitchers who stopped Jake. He had to buy two hats. Leon Cadore held Jake to a flyball to right in the first and a walk in the third as part of a four-run inning. Al Mamaux got Jake on a groundout to second in the fourth and a flyball to right in the sixth.[18] The Reds won the game, 6-2.

Jake hit safely in the next six games and in 20 of the next 21. The 14-game hitting streak raised his season average to a season-high .368 on June 4, when he had the first of four four-hit games during the season. During a 44-game stretch that included the three hitting streaks, he batted .418 with two doubles, seven triples, two home runs, 18 walks, and nine sacrifices. In 199 plate appearances, Jake struck out one time. On August 27, he went 7-for-10 with two walks in a doubleheader sweep against Boston, including 5-for-5 in the opener.

Old Jake was showing no signs of slowing down. He batted .336 with a league-leading 22 triples and a career-high 12 home runs and matched his career high with 66 runs batted in. His 205 hits, 114 runs, 610 at-bats, and 700 plate appearances also were career highs. Jake had 31 sacrifices, walked 56 times and struck out only 21 times in the 700 plate appearances. He continued to play excellent defense and had a career-best .994 fielding percentage, which led all National League first basemen.

"It may seem like a strange statement, but I am convinced that my batting improvement is a matter of half an inch of wood," Jake said. "In other words, my bat strikes the ball with half an inch of added timber and consequent smashing power. I am hitting with the very center of the business portion of the bat—and last year, even though I was with the .300 hitters, I was grazing too many with the edge of the stick. I examined several old bats and found all sorts of imprints showing how often I had been meeting the ball with the edge of the wood, and a similar examination of this season's bats shows the imprints right in the middle."[19]

In the first game of a doubleheader at Boston on July 29, Jake recorded the 2,000th hit of his career. The single to center was against Mule Watson in the third inning, and the Reds won the game 5-4. He scored the 1,000th run of his career on September 23 in the fourth inning at Philadelphia. The Reds won the game, 5-4.

An unbylined article under an "All Sports" heading in *The Enquirer* of Cincinnati on June 18 provided an assessment of Jake:

> Red fans have learned to appreciate the valuable service to the club rendered by Jake Daubert, the veteran first baseman of the team. Jake is 37 years old, and there was some fear that he might not go along this year at top speed. There was a report that his legs were going back on him and that he was about through as an active performer. But there he is out there every day swatting the pill to great distance, running bases like a young colt, taking long slides and doing everything in his power to win the game. Jake is a fine example of a first-class hitter. He drives to all the fields and to great distances.
>
> Although he is a lefthand hitter, southpaw pitching does not bother him in the least, and many of his longest hits are made on the sidewheelers. Jake has never succumbed to the present passion for home runs, which is injuring the hitting of many players.
> He is up there every time trying to drive the ball safely, without regard to the distance of the boundary fence. He is especially reliable with runners on the bases.

> Though not so young as he used to be, Jake seems to have lost none of his speed. He runs bases with determination and takes everything that he reasonably can while on the paths. On the defensive side, Daubert is a tremendous assistance to the infield from his ability to handle all sorts of thrown balls. He has saved his teammates many and many an error by his ability and accuracy in digging low throws out of the dirt and spearing the high and wide one. But it is not only his mechanical skill which makes him such a good man for the club. He is a very earnest and conscientious worker, always in the game and setting a fine example to the younger players. He never shirks a duty and never misses play or practices. Always in the pink of condition, he leads the way on the field, and players who follow his industrious example will make no mistake. As captain of the team, Jake is in frequent consultation with Manager Moran as to the conduct of the club and the plays to be used on certain occasions, and the Red leader highly esteems his advice and cooperation.
>
> He is one of the grand old warriors of the pastime. Jake led the National League in batting in 1913, with an average of .350, and again the following year with a mark of .329. It is not likely that he can overtake Hornsby this season, but he will be right around there somewhere, and the best of it is that his hitting is not for the averages but for the good of the ball club at all times.[20]

The Reds continued to revamp their roster. Jake was named captain of the Reds after Heinie Groh was traded to the New York Giants at the end of 1921. In February, Larry Kopf was traded to the Boston Braves.

The team also started slowly, losing 10 of the first 11 games. On May 10, the Reds were 8-17 and in last place, 11 ½ games back of the first-place Giants. After that they went 78-51 (.589) and continued to climb in the standings. They finished 86-68, seven games behind the champion Giants, and closed the year with a doubleheader sweep over Pittsburgh to claim second place over the Pirates. In the first game, Jake worked a full count with two outs and the bases loaded in the bottom of the ninth. He laid off a curve ball from Wilbur Cooper that missed the outside of the plate by several inches, forcing in the run for the Reds' 5-4 win.[21]

Edd Roush held out until July. He batted .352 but played only 49 games. Four other players, in addition to Jake, batted over .300: outfielders George Harper (.340) and Pat Duncan (.328), third-baseman Babe Pinelli (.305), and catcher Bubbles Hargrave (.316). The pitching staff had a 3.53 earned run average and was led by Eppa Rixey (25-13, 3.53 ERA), Pete Donohue (18-9, 3.12), and Johnny Couch (16-9, 3.89).

After the season, Jake was named the first baseman on an all-star team selected by the National League umpires, who said his play "far surpassed the play of any other National League first sacker."[22]

Jake's remarkable season at age 37 was the subject of an unbylined commentary, headlined "Jake Daubert Earns Niche in Hall of Fame" in *The Binghamton Press* in January 1923:

> The career of the major league ball player seldom takes on extra steam after the 30-year mark. There are marvels of the game, of course, such ancient relics as Cyrus Young, Honus Wagner, Babe Adams, Napoleon Lajoie, Christy Mathewson, Eddie Plank and others who were exceptions to the rule. And again there is Jacob Ellsworth Daubert, born May 1, 1885, who, at the age of 37, had the second best season of his remarkable career.
>
> The "miracle player" of the National league today is Daubert. There is the baseball youth growing out of his teens who takes the kinks out of the bank rolls of the magnates. He is years away from the prime of his athletic life.
>
> But how many, after making the grade, hang around for 13 successive years, become wrinkled and gray and still are able to grapple successfully with Kid Youth and the game?
>
> They can be counted on the fingers of the hands. When it is the unanimous report that you are the best at your trade at the age of 37, that is something to brag about.
>
> For at that milestone the average big leaguer is down in the minors hanging on as a manager or back home at Main Street smoking the pipe and thinking of the good old days of years ago.

Since the official averages of the National League for the 1922 season have been released Daubert's figures have been the talk of the baseball sphere. Even the series of swatting records established by Rogers Hornsby pass from view in comparison with Daubert's fielding and batting performances. . . .

And don't forget that all of them . . . are almost young enough to sit on Jake's lap and squeal: "Daddy."

Daubert does not possess a single defect. There is the big lumberjack who, because he weighs in the neighborhood of 200 pounds, carries a mighty sock around the plate. But put him on first base and he stops the traffic from the rear. There are young phenoms who lack an asset—or so—a weak arm, but is fast; can run, but can't throw, etc., etc.

Naturally Daubert is proud of his record. But he doesn't boast about it. "I can see no reason why the life of a major league ball player should end around the early 30's," remarks Daubert. "A little common sense, ordinary judgment and condition are my three strong arguments.[23]

1923 SEASON

Jake traveled to New York on December 13, 1922, and met to discuss his contract with Reds president, August Herrmann, and other team officials attending the league meetings. Cincinnati offered Jake an increase over his 1922 salary, believed to be $8,000,[24] but it did not come close to Jake's request of "$13,000 for a one-year contract or $24,000 for a two-year contract," according to a letter he wrote to Herrmann on October 30. Neither Jake nor Herrmann disclosed the numbers, but the Reds also offered Jake an option for a two-year contract at a slightly lower amount—reported to be $10,000 per year.[25] Jake refused both offers but said he was willing to accept the team's terms and play until they found a suitable replacement for him.

"I do not wish to appear as a holdout," Jake said. "Nor have I any desire to hold up the club for an extravagant salary. But my business at home is such that I do not feel that I can work for the Reds or any other ball club for less money than I have asked.

"Last year, I played in every championship game for the Reds, but lost more money by not being at home to look after my coal washery than I received in salary from the club. My coal business has reached such proportions now that it needs my personal attention, so I am willing and even anxious to retire from baseball.

"Judging from what President Herrmann and Mr. Widrig said to me today, it looks as if there is a very small chance of our getting together. I told them that if they would not accept my proposal, it is up to them to secure another first baseman as soon as they can.

"Recognizing that competent men for the position do not grow on every bush and not wishing to leave the team in the lurch, I have offered to start the season with the Reds at the club's terms and remain until my successor can be found.

"Then I will go on the retired list and devote all of my time to my coal business, which is growing so rapidly it needs my personal attention."[26]

Two years earlier, there was a public notice in *The Call* of Schuylkill Haven that Jake and his partners, John Achenbach and H.R. Heim, scheduled a public sale to liquidate the "washery machinery and other property" of their River Coal Company of Schuylkill Haven on February 26, 1921.[27] But in 1923, Jake still was operating his washery and doing well, despite a drop in coal production in Schuylkill County, as reported on June 11, 1922, by *The Philadelphia Inquirer*:

> County officials, who visited the washeries on the Schuylkill River today state that most of the industries will soon be close, as too much sand and cinders are being washed down to make operation profitable.
>
> The washeries have been producing coal in this section the past two and a half months. It is said the closing down of the mines has cut off the supply of coal from the washeries, and instead of being as black as ink the Schuylkill river here for the first time in many years is absolutely clear. The washery owned by Jake Daubert, the baseball player, at Schuylkill Haven, is still obtaining plenty of coal from the river.[28]

GENTLEMAN JAKE

Jake still wanted to play baseball and agreed to stay in New York for an extra day and meet with team treasurer Louis Widrig, who told him: "Jake, we have offered you a sizable increase in your last year's contract and more money than you have ever received. I think that the club has been exceptionally fair, and I hope that you will see it in the same light. Of course, if you decide to remain in private life and retire from baseball, we will regret it, but will not oppose your decision."

Jake had not signed a contract when he left for home, but he agreed to think about it for a few days.[29] It wasn't until the beginning of March when the Reds announced that Jake had signed his contract and would report to training camp on March 11 in Orlando.[30] Terms of the contract were not listed, but it was believed to be for $11,000[31] for each of the next two seasons. His arrival was delayed, however, because of the flu, referred to as the grippe at that time,[32] and then pneumonia.[33]

After several weeks, Jake was improving but not fully recovered. "I have been out of bed just four days and seem to be getting stronger every day," he wrote in an April 2 letter to the sports editor of *The Cincinnati Post*. "I had a very serious siege of sickness, and it looked kind of bad for a little while. By the looks of my limbs, after the fever broke, I judged I must have weighed about 125 pounds, but if I continue to eat as I have been doing the past three or four days, I expect to be 25 pounds overweight when I join the team.

"I expect to join the team about the 14th or 15th unless I get stronger than expected, then, of course, I shall join the team sooner.

"I have not been out of the house as of yet. I may have an opportunity to do a little training here to try myself out before joining the team. Once I join the team I want to be in a position to do hard training, for I sure want to get back into the game."[34]

Jake finally arrived in Cincinnati on April 16 but still was weakened by his illness and had lost 12 pounds.[35] He pinch-hit on April 23 but didn't get into the lineup until April 28 after missing nine games. Jake obviously still was feeling the effects of his illness and struggled early. He was batting .143 on May 12. During the next month, Jake's batting improved but not to his liking, and he felt responsible for the Reds' early struggles.

"There's the reason," he said near the end of June. "See what I'm hitting? Not many points above .200. It was .228 the last time I looked at the figures. Can you figure it? I can't.

"I'm hitting the ball just as solidly as I did last season. I have the same swing, haven't changed my stance, pick on the curve and the fast one, but I'm lining to infielders and outfielders, hitting into double plays where last season I was getting them safe, advancing base runners and getting runs for the boys.

"I can go through the book and show where a hit or two in the pinch on my part would have won at least seven games that we have lost. What does this mean? Add seven victories to our pennant percentage, knock off seven defeats, and we'd be out in front of the Giants."[36]

A 17-game hitting streak at the beginning of July, during which Jake batted .303, raised his average to .245. But Jake's aggressive style of play and being underweight since the start of the season eventually took its toll, forcing him to miss nine games in late July because of a cold and exhaustion.[37] The rest seemed to help, and Jake responded by batting .400 during August, including three games when he went 4-for-5. From July 1 until the end of the season batted .341.

Jake finished the year with a .292 batting average in 125 games.

The Reds struggled at the start of the season and were 14-20 on May 28, in seventh place, 12 ½ games behind the first-place and eventual league champion New York Giants. There were rumors that Pat Moran would be fired as manager, and again Jake was mentioned as a possible replacement. At one point, Jake called his teammates together, told them he didn't want to be the manager, and encouraged them to support Moran.[38]

The Reds went 18-7 in May and continued to climb in the standings. They had nine-game winning streaks in June and August and were in second place for most of the season after July 10. The closest they got to the Giants was two games back on July 18. The Reds finished at 91-63, again in second place, 4 ½ behind the Giants.

Jake was in charge of the team for six games in August when Moran left after his father died. The Reds won all six, part of their second nine-game winning streak, and Jake went 18-for-29 (.621) with two doubles, two triples, a home run, and nine RBIs. He injured his foot when he was spiked in a collision at first base on September 8 and missed ten games, but again he filled in as manager for several games when Moran was called home because of his wife's illness.

Edd Roush, who held out again and missed the first 13 games, led the team with a .351 batting average. Outfielder Pat Duncan hit .327, and catcher Bubbles Hargrave .323. The pitching staff had a 3.21 earned run average, led by Dolf Luque (27-8, 1.93), Eppa Rixey (20-15, 2.80), and Pete Donohue (21-15, 3.38).

Jake was very busy during the offseason, organizing and participating in blue-rock and live-bird shoots throughout the region and running his businesses in Schuylkill Haven.

In December, Jake reportedly was offered the job of manager of the St. Paul Saints of the American Association. "Daubert is under contract to the Cincinnati club for another year, and I doubt if the St. Paul club could recompense us for his services," August Herrmann, president of the Reds, said. "Furthermore, I do not believe that Daubert would care to go to a minor league club. It is my belief that when Daubert ends his major league career, he will retire from baseball."[39] When Jake was contacted several days later, he said he knew nothing about the offer and called the reports "Stove league dope."[40]

Photo of Jake at his coal washery was part of the package donated to the Hall of Fame by Jake's son, George. The Hall of Fame description: "He stands in a shed, wearing a heavy, woolen shirt, buttoned up to his neck and thick work overalls, stained from coal and dirt. Snow still sticks to his black boots, laced up halfway to his knees. He holds an iron rod over a fire. An anvil, shiny from years of wear, sits in the foreground. Handwritten on the back of the photograph is 'Jake Daubert at Coal Washery.' " (Photo is part of the collections of the Daubert family and the Hall of Fame and is used with permission)

Jake was named captain of the Reds prior to the 1922 season. (Photo is in the public domain and acquired from the National Baseball Hall of Fame)

Jake had one of his best seasons in 1922 at age 38, when he batted .336 with 22 triples and played in all 156 games. (Photos are in the public domain and acquired from the George Grantham Bain Collection at the Library of Congress)

Jake played excellent defense throughout his career and had a career-best .944 fielding percentage in 1922 to lead all first-basemen. (Photo is in the public domain and acquired from the Ernie Harwell Collection at the Detroit Public Library)

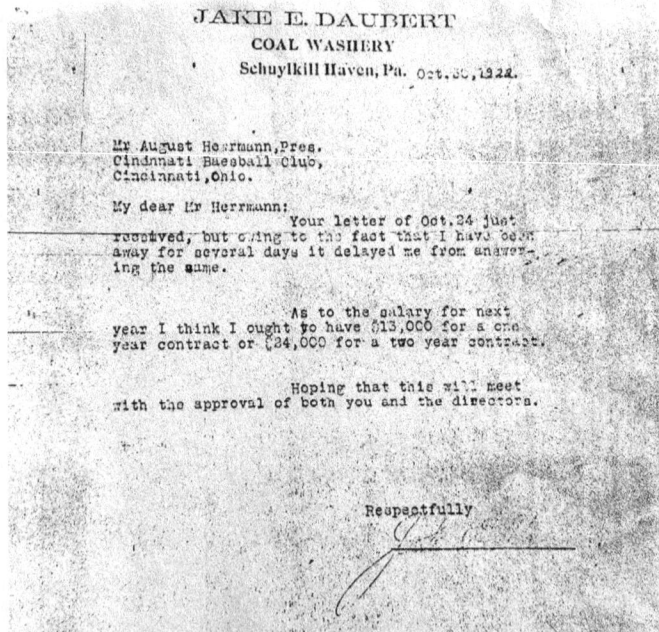

After the 1922 season, Jake returned his unsigned contract along with a letter to the Reds requesting a salary increase. (From the collection of Jill Daubert Malone)

Jake got off to a slow start in 1923 because of the flu and pneumonia, but he recovered to finish with a .292 batting average. (Photo is in the public domain and acquired from the Ernie Harwell Collection at the Detroit Public Library)

11

"Not a Staller"

Before the 1924 season, Jake received an impressive but unofficial honor when he was named the best first baseball of the past 30 years in a team selected by Honus Wagner, the star shortstop of the Pittsburgh Pirates and a member of the first Hall of Fame class in 1936.

"After going over them all, studying their hitting and fielding ability, their aggressiveness, love of the game and teamwork, here is my selection for the all-star National League team of the past thirty years," Wagner wrote. In addition to Jake, he selected Fred Clarke, manager and left field; Hughey Jennings, captain and shortstop; Napoleon Lajoie, second base; Jimmy Collins, third base; Jesse Burkett, center field; Willie Keeler, right field; Joe Kelley, extra outfielder; Rogers Hornsby, extra infielder; Johnny Kling, Roger Bresnahan, and George Gibson, catchers; and Christy Mathewson, Mordecai Brown, Grover Cleveland Alexander, Deacon Phillippi, and Babe Adams, pitchers. Wagner didn't include himself, who many consider the greatest shortstop in major league history.

"Jake Daubert, Fred Clarke, Jesse Burkette and Willie Keeler could hit left-handed pitching just as well as right-handed pitching," Wagner wrote. "I would certainly feel sorry for any pitcher who had to face such a ball club with the lively ball now in use. The hit-and-run play would be pie for these birds. The lively ball would rarely ever get stopped in the infield. They would run the bases almost as they pleased.

"Before anybody starts in to criticize my selection, I wish they would sit down and compare the brains of those players with others they have in mind. Every one of them was noted for aggressiveness and a desire to win that kept them fighting until the last man was out in the ninth."

Wagner noted that Jake never got his due. "Jake Daubert, my first baseman, is a better man than he ever got credit for being. He is a wonder on shifting his feet when forced to catch wild throws. Handling the feet is more important in a first baseman than his hands. Most anybody can catch the ball. The feet must put him in position to do so and also to get him out of the way of the base runner. Jake is very good on low throws."[1]

Jake, who turned 40 on April 17, expected the 1924 season would be his last year as a baseball player. No one anticipated how final the season would be. And no one could have imagined the season would be bookended by the deaths of the Reds' two leaders.

Manager Pa Moran and some players left for training camp in Orlando on March 1. When the Reds held their first practice on March 4, Moran was sick in bed with a severe attack of gastritis,[2] and coach Jack Hendricks led the team. Moran was taken to the Orange County Hospital, Orlando, the next day, because of stomach and kidney issues.[3] A day later, on March 7, he was reported to be unconscious and died at 6 p.m. His wife and acting manager Hendricks were by his side.[4] Moran, a heavy drinker, died at age 48 from Bright's Disease, a kidney ailment.[5]

When he learned about Moran's death, Jake was preparing to leave for spring training. "I have been associated with him at Cincinnati since 1919, and it was always a pleasure to play for him," Jake said before breaking into tears.[6]

Moran's death was difficult for Jake. "I didn't want to come down here after good old Pat died," Jake said after arriving in Orlando. "I don't feel like playing ball with him gone. But we must carry on for his memory, so I'll do the best I can this year without him."[7]

In August, a bronze plaque was dedicated in Moran's memory at Redland Field, and Jake, wearing his uniform and with his voice choked with tears, gave an impressive tribute. "Goodbye, Pat, we miss you very much," Jake said.[8]

The Reds were 425-329 (.564) during Moran's five years as manager. He also managed the Philadelphia Phillies to a 323-257 (.557) record in four years and won the National League pennant in 1915. In nine years, his teams were 748-586 (.561)

Again Jake was rumored to be the next manager of the Reds, and many of the players, sportswriters, and fans favored Jake, who was interested in the job. Team officials reportedly favored Hendricks, whose only experience as a major league manager was in 1918 when he led the St. Louis Cardinals to a 51-78 last-place finish. He had recently joined the Reds as a coach and had spent most of his career as a minor league manager, including nine years leading the Indianapolis Indians of the American Association.

Hendricks met with Jake when the first baseman arrived in Orlando. "I have not been signed up as yet, but if I am signed when Mr. Widrig appears tomorrow, I want to know if my appointment will be satisfactory to you," Hendricks said.

"Absolutely," Jake responded. "I am not saying that I would not take the position if it was offered to me, but I will be for you from the first game to the last."[9]

Hendricks was signed to manage the team two days later. Jake may have been disappointed, but it was not his nature to create division on the team. He encouraged his teammates to support the new manager. Hendricks realized Jake's importance to the team and retained him as captain, in addition to assigning him to oversee and evaluate the rookies on the team.[10]

Jake and other team leaders rallied behind Hendricks. "I have not yet been misinformed by any one of the Reds on any point," Hendricks said. "Any time I ask one of them about anything, I can rely on getting an honest answer. I have checked up often enough to know I cannot be too positive in saying this."[11]

The Enquirer of Cincinnati provided a preseason assessment of Jake in an "All Sports" column, an unbylined feature:

> Captain Jake Daubert does not need any particular encomiums, for the fans, during the five years he has been with the Reds, have learned to recognize him as one of the ablest, most courageous and most ambitious players who ever wore the Red uniform.

"NOT A STALLER"

They will appreciate his worth all the more this year, for Jake is now going at tremendous speed, and playing as good ball as he ever did in his long and honorable career.

Last spring he was afflicted with a severe attack of the grippe all through March, and was unable to go to the training camp or get in any preliminary practice before the start of the regular season. Yet he reported here for the opener and went right into the game and stuck there without a break. Weakened by his illness, and not having had the advantage of training, Jake hit very lightly for the first few weeks of the season, though he was trying as hard as ever for the good of the club.

This year the veteran was at the camp as early as any of the other regulars, and he has toiled and practiced and played with all the enthusiasm of a youngster. He was the first of the heavy batters on the club to reach his hitting form,, and he has been clouting the ball all over the lot in the practice games, as well as playing his customary brilliant game on the bag, where he has no superior in the country today. Daubert is an ideal type of ball player in every way. Mechanically, his work is of the highest class.

There has never been a better first baseman over a long term of years than this Pennsylvania Dutchman. He is a basket for all sorts of throws, taking them on either side, high or low, with equal skill and accuracy. He is a boon to his infielders, whom he saves from many an error through his uncanny ability in handling wide hurls of every description. At the bat, he is a natural left-hand hitter who is never bothered by southpaws, but is always likely to come through with a long shot against any kind of pitching.

He is at his best in a pinch, and he is always working for the good of the club as a whole rather than for his individual record. He has played many a game with his legs bound up like those of a race horse, but the fans would never have suspected it from the speed and agility with which he circled the bases and fielded his position. Many considered Jake as the logical successor of Pat Moran as manager of the club, and he would have accepted the position if it had been offered to him, but when Jack Hendricks was appointed Daubert went to him at once, congratulated him heartily and pledged his earnest support, which he has given and is giving freely and conscientiously, and will continue to do so.

There are no sour grapes in Jake's cup. He is as fine a character off the field as he is a player on the diamond, and he will always be a distinct credit to the Reds, the National League and to the national pastime.[12]

The Reds were expected to contend for the 1924 league championship, mainly because their star hitters, Edd Roush and Jake, were signed for the start of the season. Cincinnati had purchased star pitcher Carl Mays from the Yankees on December 11, 1923. Mays was a 20-game winner four times, including twice with the Boston Red Sox. With New York, he was 26-11 in 1920 and 27-9 in 1921.

In the opener against Pittsburgh, Jake went 1-for-3. He drove in a run in the fourth inning with a single and walked to load the bases with one out in the bottom of the ninth before Roush's sacrifice fly won it 6-5.

Jake struggled after that, going hitless in the next six games. He ended an 0-for-24 streak on April 24, going 3-for-5, including a first-inning double in Cincinnati's 5-4 win over the Pittsburgh Pirates. But on April 26, after ten games, Jake was batting .105. He didn't strike out in his first 49 plate appearances, but he had only three hits and scored one run in those ten games. Jake suggested that he be benched, but Hendricks refused, showing his confidence in Jake.[13]

On May 3, Jake went 4-for-4 to raise his average above .200 and continued a gradual improvement. But Jake struggled and missed games again because of injuries. On May 28 at St. Louis, he was hit in the head with a pitched ball by Allen Sothoron in the first inning of the first game of a doubleheader. Jake tried to duck out of the way of an inside fastball but was struck above the right temple and fell to the ground. He left the field with help from two teammates, and after getting to the clubhouse, the pain was severe, and he went to the hospital, where it was determined he suffered a concussion but no skull fracture.[14]

Jake was discouraged by his slow start, and after the beaning, some of his close friends on the team said he might retire rather than return to the team.¹⁵ Jake returned home to Schuylkill Haven for several days, then wired *The Cincinnati Post* that he would rejoin the team in Boston.

"I will play as long as they desire me and as long as I can be of any use to the club," he said after he rejoined the team.¹⁶ But Jake went 0-for-5 in the game, feeling dizzy and having a bad headache. He again returned home to rest.¹⁷

When Jake left the team, there were rumors he was annoyed that he had not been named manager.

"Nothing hurts me so much as this idle talk about my desiring to be manager of the team," he said. "The same thing was started last year on one of our eastern trips when one irresponsible individual broke out with a story that I was slated to succeed Pat Moran. I nailed that yarn instantly, and I want to do the same about this one. I am for Hendricks, heart and soul, and so are the other players on the team. There is nothing but harmony in the club, and we are all trying our best to win for Jack and the club."¹⁸

Jake's injury was more serious than originally believed, and he missed the next 18 games. The beaning was reported as the eighth of his career, but Jake still planned to return, and Hendricks was anxious to have him back with the team.

"I don't think Jake's injury is a permanent one," Hendricks said. "I was at his home in Schuylkill Haven all of Monday night and had a long talk with him. He is suffering from terrific headaches and dizzy spells. But I think Jake will be with us again before long.

"Of course, it was tough on Jake and us. I need his advice and playing services badly. Jeff Tesreau winged him (several years ago), and (Grover) Lowdermilk also hit him during the world's series in 1919, but I think this last crack was the worst of all."¹⁹

Jake rejoined the team in Brooklyn on June 17 but wasn't ready to get back in the lineup. He coached first base.

"It was just three weeks ago that I was beaned," Jake said. "It was in St. Louis, and Allen Sothoron was pitching. No, the ball did not curve unexpectedly; it was just a fast straight one right at me. I simply didn't get out of the way of it in time, and the ball struck me in the back of the head. That's all. Such things are likely to happen to anyone. I've been hit in the head a number of times, but this was one of the worst cases I've had. In fact, it is the worst case, by a big margin.

"Ever since the accident I've been troubled with severe headaches. I tried to play, in fact, did play one game of our series in Boston, but I was so weak and giddy immediately afterward that I was forced to lie down. I then decided to take no chances with my condition and to give myself a good rest.

"Since then, the severity of the headaches has gradually diminished. I am still troubled; my head pained me a little after today's easy workout, but the pain is getting less and less; I may be able to play in a day or two, but I doubt that I'll be able to get into the series with Brooklyn."

There were stories that Jake's eyesight may have been affected by the beaning and possibly could end his playing career. "I don't know how those reports originated," he said. "My eyesight hasn't been affected a bit by the beaning. Of course, when I happen to bend over and then straighten up things seem to go black before my eyes, but that's merely the effect of the headaches and general giddiness. I'm sure that no permanent harm will result."[20]

Although he denied permanent damage to his eyesight, when he rejoined the team, he admitted the seriousness of the beaning.

"Either I am getting old, or a few rivets have worked loose in my skull, or Sothoron put more steam on that ball than I thought.," he said. "Anyway, this eighth experience of mine was the worst of the lot. For several hours I couldn't see. And when my sight did return, it kept coming and going like switching an electric light on and off. Besides, blood oozed out of my ears, and I developed a first-class headache that lasted for three weeks. I tried various remedies, but the thing that seemed to produce the best results was a simple massage."[21]

Jake was back in the lineup for a doubleheader against St. Louis on June 25. He went 1-for-5 in the first game, which the Cardinals won, 3-2. In the second game, Jake was 2-for-3 with a walk and a sacrifice. In the ninth inning, Jake won the game with a walk-off double to center after Carl Mays doubled and Curt Walker was intentionally walked to get to Jake. The hit came against Sothoron, who had beaned him almost a month earlier. Another irony in the game was that the winning pitcher was Mays, who was with the Yankees when he threw the pitch in 1920 that killed Cleveland Indians shortstop Ray Chapman, the only player in major league history to be killed by a pitched ball.

The Reds were impacted by injuries that sidelined numerous other players, including Roush, who missed 32 games because of leg problems. They won seven of the first nine games and were in first place on May 13, 1 ½ games ahead of the New York Giants but then went 21-34, fell into fifth place at 36-41, and were 14 games back on July 8.

"With all of our regulars back in the game, we should pick up considerably and probably finish in the first division," Jake said in June while he was out after being beaned. "But the injury jinx that has followed us since the start of the season has just about ruined our chance to win the pennant this season. I don't see how they can stop us from winding up among the first four, but as for copping the flag—well, our prospects look pretty dark. Our early season injuries have given us a tremendous handicap to overcome.

"The way our players were getting hurt for a while there was something awful. Why, there hasn't been a regular player on the team who hasn't been out of the game for a time with something the matter with him. I've never seen anything like it in my previous experience.

"There's an odd coincidence connected with my accident. Just before the start of the game Jack Hendricks announced to the boys that he had an ambulance backed up against the gate for the next player to be injured. And then, in the first half of the first inning, in my first time at bat, I got mine. Of course, Jack was kidding, but his words seemed prophetic afterward."[22]

Cincinnati was 33-20 during the last two months, including a six-game winning streak in early August. The Reds finished 83-70 and in fourth place, ten games back of the champion Giants. Roush led the team with a .348 average. Mays went 20-9 with a 3.15 earned run average to lead the pitchers, who combined for a 3.12 ERA.

Jake's headaches persisted, and he missed 12 more games in late June and early July. He went 18-for-49 (.367) during a 12-game hitting streak in the middle of July to raise his average to .249. He missed eight games at the end of July because of a torn ligament in his side.[23] Jake returned to the lineup on August 1, hit safely in 22 of the next 25 games, including another 12-game hitting streak, and had seven doubles and three triples. He batted .373 during that stretch to raise his average to a season-high .289 on August 26, when he went 3-for-5 with a triple, two doubles, and two runs batted in. He finished at .281 in a career-low 102 games.

Rumors continued that Jake would retire at the end of the season, especially after Hendricks' contract was extended for another season, but that was not his plan in mid-August.

"I will not quit the game until the game quits me," he said. "All reports to the effect that I am dissatisfied with existing conditions are wrong, and so are reports that I must leave the game to attend to my business affairs. I shall stay on duty until I can no longer keep pace with the pastime—and, the way I am feeling nowadays, that may not be for sundry years to come.

"I owe all I have to the game. The game gave me the money on which my business enterprises were founded; the game has been good to me, and I owe it to baseball to stick with it, irrespective of all other things, as long as I can play my role in the baseball drama. I'd like to establish a record for long service in the big league, but that can hardly be accomplished now. No man is likely to ever approach Anson's record for continuous campaigns."[24]

Cap Anson was a first baseman who played 27 consecutive seasons from 1871-1897, mostly with the Chicago Cubs and retired at age 45.

"When the time comes that baseball doesn't want me, I'll step aside, but I hope that time will not come for several years," Jake said. "Right now, I am in great shape, fully recovered from my early injuries of the season, and I think my recent batting marks speak for themselves. I believe I am good for a long time yet to come, and so I'll stick right here."[25]

There were reports that Jake might be traded after the season, and Brooklyn and Pittsburgh were among the teams listed. "Bosh, rot," Hendricks said. "There are at least five National League clubs which would be tickled to death to have Daubert play first base for them next season, and one of them is the Cincinnati club."[26] Other reports had Jake heading to Portland, Oregon, to manage the Pacific Coast League team[27] or to Reading, Pennsylvania, to be player-manager and part-owner of the International League team.[28]

He apparently was interested in the Reading job, but in late September, he announced it would not happen. "I cannot get out of the National League; therefore, I will not be at Reading next year," he said in a brief explanation.[29]

Jake missed eight games in September, including the season's last six games. He became ill in New York during the Reds' last trip east in mid-September. He missed a game at Brooklyn on the 14th and the second game of a doubleheader at the New York Giants on the 18th. At one point, Hendricks reportedly sent Jake home to Schuylkill Haven to rest, but Jake rejoined the team in Philadelphia and played on September 19 and 20 against his doctor's advice. He later told Dr. Harry Hines, the Reds' team physician, he thought it might be his last major league game and didn't want "people to think Jake Daubert was a staller."[30]

On September 20, Jake played his last game, ironically at the Baker Bowl in Philadelphia, where he had played his first game 14 years, five months, and seven days earlier. He went 2-for-5, scored a run, drove in one, and committed a fielding error in the Reds' 9-6 win over the Phillies. It was the 20th win of the season for Mays. In the first inning, Jake singled against Bill Hubbell, went to third on a double by Roush, and scored on a groundout. In the second, he hit a two-out single to drive in a run. His last at-bat was an unreported out on a batted ball in the ninth against Lefty Weinert. Jake made up for his error with a great play in the fourth. With two outs and runners on first and second, Cy Williams hit a hard liner toward right field. Jake dove for the ball and knocked it down, then picked it up and beat Williams to the first-base bag for the final out of the inning.

Jake returned home to Schuylkill Haven to rest, but against the advice of his physician, he returned to Cincinnati for the last game of the season on September 28 and the start of the Reds' annual barnstorming tour.

"I tried to keep him at home," Gertrude said two weeks later. "He knew he should remain at home. But he wouldn't stay. He came to Cincinnati because he didn't want anyone to think he was stalling about being sick and ducking those last few games."[31]

When the tour began on September 30, Jake was not with the team. He reportedly was suffering from gallstones and didn't want to share in the profits of the tour if he couldn't play.[32] He also was not sleeping and had lost almost 20 pounds.[33]

Jake's condition was much more serious. He complained of severe pain in his left side for several weeks, and on October 2, Reds team physician Dr. Harry Hines performed surgery at Good Samaritan Hospital in Cincinnati to remove Jake's appendix and drain his gallbladder. No gallstones were found, and Jake was expected to recover fully.[34] Gertrude arrived in Cincinnati to be with Jake until they could return to Schuylkill Haven.

Three days later, Jake was reported in very critical condition and near death because of complications from the surgery. On October 8, Gertrude wired their children, George and Louise, to take the next train from Harrisburg to Cincinnati.[35] Dr. Hines performed a blood transfusion, but it didn't help.

Jacob Ellsworth Daubert died at 4 a.m. on Thursday, October 9, 1924, in Good Samaritan Hospital in Cincinnati. He was 40 years old and is believed to be the oldest major league player to die while still active.[36]

The cause on his death certificate was acute gastric dilation and acute appendicitis. Dr. Hines also listed the cause of death as "exhaustion, resulting from indigestion, which was induced by a diseased gallbladder and appendix." He said the May 28 beaning also contributed to Jake's death.

"Jake never was able to rest properly after that injury," Dr. Hines said. "He could not relax and get the sleep a man must have to retain his vitality. Even after the operation, when he was exceedingly weak, he could not sleep. He tried to rest and could not. The strain of being constantly awake and conscious of the sufferings caused by his disordered stomach gradually sapped his life."[37]

There were conflicting reports about who was with Jake when he died. *The Cincinnati Post* reported:

> Mrs. Daubert, after a brief rest, was called to his bedside at 2 a.m. and remained in constant attendance until five minutes before death took the "Grand Old Man of the National League." She

collapsed a few minutes before Jake died and had to be given medical attention.[38]

According to *The Post*, Jake's son, teammate Lew Fonseca, and friend Fred Bain were there when he died, and his daughter and brother, Irvin, arrived soon after his passing.

Fonseca contacted Roush, who was leading the Reds' barnstorming tour. The players unanimously agreed to cancel the rest of the trip and said they couldn't think of putting on their uniforms with Jake dead. They returned to Cincinnati that night.[39]

Before Game Six of the World Series on October 9, players from the New York Giants and Washington Nationals gathered at home plate to pay tribute to Jake's memory. Fans stood in silence for more than the requested minute.[40]

"I can't say much, too depressed," said August Herrmann, president of the Reds. "This is a shock that has almost stunned me, although I had been warned that Jake was in a critical condition. I can say this much however: I have, in the course of my baseball years, had hundreds of great ball players on our club, but never was there a finer character, a grander personality than Jake Daubert.

"He was a power for good. The game is better for his participation, and the game is dealt a heavy blow by his departure. Maybe I can talk more freely when I have had a little time to recover from the shock."[41]

"Jake Daubert never had a superior on or off the field," manager Jack Hendricks said. "In the game he was both an ideal player and a brilliant leader. He knew baseball backward. Outside the game, he was a cultured gentleman. I have visited at his home and found him a wonderful host and the most respected citizen in his community. One thing sure, Jake Daubert never had an enemy, and everyone who ever met him was his friend for life. The more I saw of him, the more I admired him. Nobody can replace him. Men of Jake Daubert's stamp only happen once in a generation."[42]

Jake's body lay in state at the Mack Johnson mortuary until 8 p.m. October 10, and services were held by the Masons and Elks of which Jake was a member. His body was then put on a train to Schuylkill Haven, accompanied by his family, for services and burial.⁴³ Thousands of people greeted the train in Pottsville on October 11 and attended a viewing at the Daubert home on Liberty Street in Schuylkill Haven on October 12.⁴⁴

Services were conducted the next day at the Daubert home by Rev. E.S. Noll of the Reformed Church of Schuylkill Haven and Rev. L.M. Fetterolf of the First Reformed Church of Pottsville. More than 100 automobiles accompanied the hearse to Pottsville, where Jake was buried in Charles Baber Cemetery. The Masonic Lodge of Schuylkill Haven conducted services at the grave. Pallbearers were former teammate Lew McCarty; Reds teammates Pat Duncan, Carl Mays, Edd Roush, and Eppa Rixey; manager Jack Hendricks; and Howard Yoder and Raymond Brubaker of the local gun club where Jake was a member.⁴⁵

"The funeral of Jacob Daubert, our worthy and esteemed townsman, held Monday was without doubt the largest of any similar sad event ever held in Schuylkill Haven," according to *The Call* of Schuylkill Haven. The weekly newspaper reported there were 81 floral tributes, and Jake was dressed "in a blue pin-striped suit and rested in a handsome metallic casket, covered with grey broad cloth, with full glass lid."⁴⁶

The Call also reported: "A pathetic figure indeed, in addition to the sorrowing widow and grief-stricken children, on the saddest day and the most sorrowful event in their lives, was the bent figure of the eight-two year old father, who with drawn and tear-stained countenance, was very noticeable in the slow and doleful procession following the flower-draped casket."

There were numerous tributes praising Jake, including this one by sportswriter Tom Swope in *The Cincinnati Post*

> Baseball fans, players, officials and writers the country over are genuinely grieved over the death here early Thursday morning of Jake Daubert, one of the grandest men ever connected with the national game.
>
> The better one knew Jake the more he admired and loved the man. He had no enemies. Players on opposing teams were his friends the same as those who were more closely associated with him on his own club.

He was looked up to by all the big leaguers as a leader among ball players.

He was a clear and straight thinker. A man who lived cleanly and played every game honestly. His was not given to playing jokes or tricks. He never disputed an umpire's decision just to be kicking. When he kicked he did so because he thought the umpire had erred. And the umpires respected Jake as much as did anyone.

Next to baseball Jake loved trapshooting better than any other sport. Just as he was a leader on the diamond so was he a leader at the traps.

And in the business world Jake also was quite a figure. He had prepared for a comfortable future when his baseball days were over by establishing a well-paying business at Schuylkill Haven, Pa., which, in recent years, was making him as much or more money than baseball.

Jake was perhaps as good a friend as the writer ever had in baseball circles, and words fail when we try to express our sorrow over his death.[47]

W.A. Phelon wrote a tribute in the *Cincinnati Times-Star* that was shared in *The Call* of Schuylkill Haven, including these excerpts:

The story of Jake Daubert's life is a glowing page for the strong youth of America to copy. . . .

Daubert played the game in clean and sportsmanlike fashion. He was never accused of spiking or other roughness, and no shady tactics ever appealed to him.

Needless to say, he was the soul of baseball honor, and no breath of scandal ever touched his name. Away from the diamond he was as great in other lines of sport and ranked high as a marksman, taking place with the best target-shooters of the land. . . .

The personal character of Jake Daubert was magnificent, clear of life and language, a family man of the finest American type, he was a splendid example to the younger players and the youngsters found him their best friend. He was always ready to advise and counsel a juvenile, and he strove to help not hinder the rising stars.

Be it added also that Jake Daubert was no "blue law" fanatic and no reforming pharisee. "If a drink will help you, take it," was ever Daubert's word.

"Just use and don't abuse the good things of life and you will be all the happier."

Daubert was a wonderful conversationalist. He was well posted on topics both of sport and ordinary life. He could talk for hours and every sentence was a jewel. He never used profanity, seemed almost devoid of even current slang, and his keen intelligence made it a pleasure to chat with him after the game was over.[48]

Jake's hometown newspaper, *The Call,* published this editorial:

In Tears They Laid Him Away

It was a sad and sorrowing concourse of friends, with bowed and bared heads that on Monday paid tribute and a mark of respect to one whom they had on numerous occasions greeted with shouts, hurrahs and all the pent up enthusiasm of interested spectators on the field of sport. It was a different tribute on this day. All was silent and faces were set. Tears found their way into many eyes.

It was the last opportunity to honor the Victor of many a stiffly contested ball game; to honor one who played that national game in a clear cut, gentlemanly way and won for himself by his so doing and his kind, considerate and honorable dealings with his fellowmen, the close and appreciative friendship of legions. It was the funeral of Jacob Daubert.

Only once in decades can a small community, or a so-called country town, boast of having one of its residents a character of national repute as was Daubert. Only once in a decade does a man reach such a high goal of splendid attainments and keep true

"NOT A STALLER"

to those inmost traits of character, clean and unsullied, that bind man to man, and invite friends for a lifetime of earnest, sincere, unbroken, mutual loyalty and devotion. That man was Jacob Daubert.

It was a big, but, oh, such a sad day for Schuylkill Haven, when in tears and sorrow they laid him away in the tomb. But in that day and this period of mourning, a keen satisfaction is ours in the knowledge that the community is not alone in sharing a sorrow in the passing of one of her citizens, but that that sorrow is shared by many other communities and legions of friends throughout the land.

And then too his death has more than any other circumstance or condition, proven that in that particular vocation which he followed, one which is the highest of our national sports, success is obtainable and friends may be made and retained by hewing close to the mark set in honesty of purpose and modesty of effort.

No finer tribute can we pay than in repeating from the words spoken at his funeral bier: "A man who by honest effort gained for himself a national reputation; A man who grew great by clean living and solid merit, hard work and diligent effort; A man who played faithfully and honestly America's greatest game, a game in which clean living and skill will inevitably lead to distinction."

Such was "Jake" Daubert. His passing is mourned deeply by the community in which he resided, and his memory will ever be recalled with fondest recollections and deepest sorrow.[49]

In July of 1925, Jake's widow, Gertrude, filed an application with the Industrial Commission of Ohio seeking $6,500 for his death, claiming that the beaning on May 28, 1924, caused sleeplessness and loss of vitality, resulting in his death.[50]

In September, Jake's body was exhumed, and an autopsy was performed at Fountain Springs Hospital in Schuylkill County for insurance claims to determine if the beaning during the 1924 season contributed to his death.⁵¹ The autopsy, performed on September 21 by Dr. R.D. Spencer, showed no sign of a skull fracture.⁵²

Gertrude's claim with the Industrial Commission was refused on December 19, 1928. She appealed and was denied again on July 12, 1929. She filed a suit against the Cincinnati Baseball Club Company on August 10, 1929, seeking compensation for the injury.⁵³ The court dismissed the case on October 21, 1931.⁵⁴

The first Jake Daubert Memorial Shoot was held on April 18, 1925, in Shoemakersville, 18 miles southeast of Schuylkill Haven, with a trophy to be held by the winner until the next year's event.⁵⁵

Jake's father died on November 4, 1928, from miners' asthma at 89. He had worked in the mines for 57 years. The *Pottsville Republican* wrote about his influence on Jake:

> Many times Daubert gave credit to his aged father for his success. Many times he told of how his father had preached to him on fair play. Many times he spoke of the spirit that his father instilled into him.⁵⁶

Jake's wife, Gertrude, remained in the Schuylkill Haven house until 1940, when she moved to Allentown to live with her daughter, Louise.

On July 28, 1966, Jake was inducted into the Cincinnati Reds Hall of Fame following a campaign by his wife and daughter.⁵⁷

"He belongs in the Hall of Fame," Gertrude said. "I wanted to see him there before I die, and I'm 82 now. Next, I want to see him inducted in the Hall of Fame at Cooperstown, N.Y."⁵⁸

Gertrude died on November 18, 1967, at Osteopathic Hospital, Allentown. She is buried in the Daubert plot in the Charles Baber Cemetery in Pottsville, along with Jake.

Louise died in 1970.

Jake was inducted into the Brooklyn Dodgers Hall of Fame in 1990.

George, who lived most of his life in Schuylkill Haven, died July 11, 2000, in North Palm Beach, Florida, at 94. He had waged an unsuccessful campaign to have his father inducted into the National Baseball

Hall of Fame, including written communication with the Hall's Veterans Committee during the last year of his life.

Although the cause of Jake's death was listed as acute gastric dilation and acute appendicitis on the death certificate, years later, his son, George, suffered from the same symptoms and was diagnosed with hereditary spherocytosis. According to the Cleveland Clinic: "Hereditary spherocytic anemia is a rare disorder of the surface layer (membrane) of red blood cells. It leads to red blood cells that are shaped like spheres and premature breakdown of red blood cells." The condition also is known as Minkowski-Chauffard disease. Those with the disease often develop an enlarged spleen, jaundice, and gallstones. There is no cure, but treatment may include removal of the spleen and gallbladder.

Some of Jake's descendants, including two of his great-grandchildren, Jack Daubert and Jill Daubert Malone, also have the disease and were treated by surgery to remove their spleen and gallbladder.

Modern medicine probably would have saved Jake's life. With his passion, dedication, and drive as a player, he likely would have been just as successful as a manager. It's hard to imagine what Jake Daubert would have accomplished in another 40 years.

By all accounts, Jake never allowed his success to affect his values negatively. He remained popular and respected by those around him—family, friends, teammates, and fans. They admired the gentlemanly way he acted. They appreciated the dedication and hard work he invested in becoming successful in baseball and in business. And he never forgot where he came from and how fortunate he was to escape Pennsylvania's dark and dangerous coal mines to play America's pastime at the highest level.

As his great-grandson, Jack Daubert, proudly shares: "He was the true embodiment of the American dream."

1924 Cincinnati Reds. Jake is third from the right in the front row. (From the collection of Jack Daubert)

Portrait of Jake at the National Baseball Hall of Fame. (Photo is in the public domain and acquired from the National Baseball Hall of Fame)

"NOT A STALLER"

Newspaper headlines announce Jake's death.

GENTLEMAN JAKE

Jake Daubert death certificate.

The headstone on Jake's grave. (Photo by Harry J. Deitz Jr.)

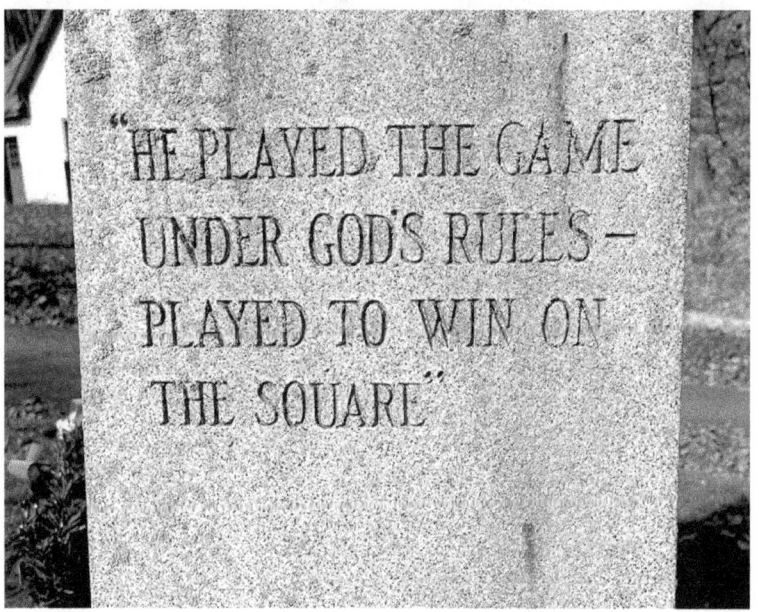

Jake was inducted into the Cincinnati Reds Hall of Fame in 1966. From left are Billy Myers, 1940 shortstop; Don Bollock of the Cincinnati Chamber of Commerce; Jake's grandson, Jacob Ellsworth Daubert; and Mike McCormick, 1940-41 center fielder. (From the collection of Jack Daubert)

12

Memories and Memorabilia

Jake replayed every game
"He lived baseball," Jake's son, George, said in a 1989 interview with the *New York Post* when he was 80. "After every game, he played the damn game over six times. He was a student of the game. He would study the game. When dad was playing, he carried a little black book, and he would write in there the eccentric movements of a pitcher. If he was going to throw a fastball, he may do some little thing to tip him off. He watched those little things.

"In those days, nobody said, 'Now this is the way you slide into the bag, this is the way you throw, this is the way you run, this is the way you hit.' Nobody told you anything. You went to spring training, and it was everybody for himself."[1]

He claimed family from France
Genealogy research by Dr. Ann Yezerski for this book shows Jake's family came to the United States from Germany. But in 1919, Jake claimed his family was from France. It's likely that it was in response to anti-German sentiment in the years after World War I. The article:

> Jake Says He Is French
> It is not generally known that Jake Daubert, now with the Reds, should properly spell his name d'Aubert. "My family," Jake explains, "are from a little city just a few miles west of the

209

German boundary, and named for them—a name it has borne for 500 years or more—D'Aubertville. Some of them, adventuring the way Frenchmen did 200 years ago, came over here and, after England permanently ousted France from the colonial regions, settled down. In other words, we are not Germans, as so many people think, but French of an old, old stock, and we still have a flock of relatives in the ancient city."[2]

Auberville is a small community in the Normandy region of northwestern France, almost 400 miles west of Germany.

"Although Daubert (D'Aubert) can be a French name, my research shows that the ancestry of Jake Daubert is German and was actually Taubert," Ann explained. "However, his direct lineage, as far back as I have it now, goes to Peter Daubert (Jake's 4th great grandparent) in 1719, born in Emmaus, Pa. Peter's son, also named Peter, was in the Revolutionary War and served at the Battle of Fort Washington (near Philly). Jake's great-grandfather, Johannes Heinrich Daubert (notice the German, but he went by Henry), died in Schuylkill County in Pine Grove.

"Jake may have claimed France since that was the better answer during the World Wars. However, French inhabitants of the Coal Regions are extremely rare, and German immigrants are the soul of colonial Pennsylvania."

Jewelry, flowers, and automobiles

Jake received many special items in recognition of his baseball accomplishments. Numerous times he was presented large bouquets of flowers prior to games. In 1913 he was given a gold bat by fans. After winning the batting title in 1913, Jake was selected as the Chalmers Award winner, an early version of the most valuable player award in the National League, and was given a Chalmers automobile. He also received watches as gifts.

Among the interesting items he received were diamond-studded pins, which were presented to players before championship rings became popular. In addition to the pin with 16 diamonds he received from teammates when he led them on a barnstorming tour of Cuba after the 1913 season, he and his teammates were given special pins after winning the National League pennant in 1916 and the World Series in 1919. Many of those are considered rare, but Jake's championship pins from the World Series are still in his family. His great-grandson, Jack Daubert, purchased them when they were auctioned by the Robert Edward Auction in 2011.

"I didn't want it outside the family," Jack said.

The 1919 pin was awarded to members of the Reds team and according to the publicity for the auction house, it is one of only four known to exist still: "The front of the 14K gold pin features a single diamond set in the center of a baseball-diamond motif. Lettered in relief around the diamond motif is "World's Champions 1919." Jake's name is engraved on the back. It sold for $82,250.

It was sold by Joan Heimbach, one of three children of Jake and Gertrude's daughter Louise. She provided this information about the pin:

> My name is Joan Daubert Becker. I am the granddaughter of Jacob E. Daubert, first baseman for the Cincinnati Reds. Though my grandfather died before I was born, my grandmother Gertrude Daubert, kept his memory alive. I loved hearing stories of how he used to go hunting with Ty Cobb. Casey Stengel would send my grandmother tickets (box seat) every year. My godmother was the wife of the Reds' manager. Once in a while, "ma" would bring out the 1919 World Series pin. On the back it read "Jacob E. Daubert." In my child's mind, I thought it was pretty, but didn't understand its significance until many years later. I knew my grandfather had played in a World Series, but didn't know how infamous the 1919 Black Sox series was! I do remember my grandmother saying that "they" (the Reds) didn't get the respect they were due. Right before my grandmother died, she handed down the 1919 Player's pin to me for safekeeping. I've had the pin ever since, from 1962 until the present. I hope its new owner cherishes it as much as I have.[3]

"I couldn't let that leave the family, and that's why I spent so much on it," Jack explained. "It's not like I could go to Joan and talk her out of selling it because she had already committed to selling it (through the auction house). I kept bidding against somebody else, and he ran it up so high."

Jack also purchased Jake's 1916 pin that was presented to members of the Brooklyn Robins. The pin was sold by James Gregg, Jake's great-grandson and son of Joan's sister Jeda.

The front of the circular 14K gold pin has a floral design and a scroll with the engraving "Brooklyn National League Champions 1916." J. E. Daubert is engraved on the back. There also is a small hole at the top that likely was drilled so the pin could be worn as a pendant. It sold for $10,575.[4]

Small first baseman's glove
Jake played most of his career with a small glove at first base, which made his excellent defensive work even more impressive. It wasn't until his last year, 1924, that Jake switched to a slightly larger glove.[5]

Lucky rabbit's foot
Like many ballplayers, Jake was superstitious. He always rubbed a rabbit's foot across the front of his shirt before he left the clubhouse.[6]

Jake's other businesses
Jake's main business outside of baseball was a coal washery near his home at 217 East Liberty Street in Schuylkill Haven. He also ran a successful coal dredging business, collecting coal from the Schuylkill River that washed downstream from the mines, then separating the coal from the impurities.

He was a partner for several years in the Daubert and Baker Coal and Ice Company, was part owner of the Euclid Theater at 23 East Main Street in Schuylkill Haven, and reportedly owned a billiard parlor in Llewellyn early in his baseball career.

Jake made money from endorsements, including for baseball bats, shotguns, cars, watches, and cigars.

Patented his bat
After Jake batted .350 and won the batting title in 1913, he had the bat model he used patented. The bat had a larger-than-normal handle to

reduce slipping. According to a report in *The Brooklyn Daily Eagle:* "A manufacturer rushed an emissary to Jake with the offer of a royalty for his invention, and Jake accepted. He got a nice piece of money while his fame lasted."[7]

Jake reportedly used a bat that was 34.5 inches long, weighed 32 ounces, and was made of Ash.

No crooked digits

Jake had his share of injuries during his 15-year major league career. Ironically, for the first baseman, broken fingers were not among them. According to a story in *The Scranton Republican:*

> Nearly every ball player at some time during his career has had one of his fingers broken and many of them have two and three crooked digits. Daubert has been playing ball for eleven years, and is now in his ninth year as a Robin, but he had never had one of his fingers broken. This is all the more remarkable when it is considered that during each game, he has about ten chances. Figuring that he has averaged 125 games for the last twelve seasons and accepted about ten chances in each game, Jake's total number of grounders and thrown balls he has handled without having one of his fingers broken total about 14,000.[8]

Smallest head in majors

According to Clarence Lavery, manager of the Cincinnati branch of A. G. Spalding & Brothers in 1924, Jake's cap was the smallest in the league.

"Jake has the smallest head of all the big league players I ever outfitted," Lavery said. "His head is so small the cutters at our factory refuse to believe the measurements I send in, and each year they ship me caps for Daubert that are so large it is necessary for me to take them to a cap factory here and have them ripped apart, cut down and resewed.

"I have talked to other men in our firm and from them found out no other big leaguer uses a cap as small as Daubert."[9]

Started chewing late

The 1920 season was the first year Jake chewed tobacco while playing baseball.

"I used to chew gum," he said, "but during the winter, I got to chewing tobacco around my coal barge and home, and I find it more satisfactory than gum.

"I tried many kinds of tobacco, several plugs and several scraps, and they all burned my mouth. I was about to give it up, when I tried a sack of *** and found it just what I had been looking for."

The brand of tobacco was omitted from the article at the manufacturer's request.[10]

Jake in the Masons

Jake and his friend and teammate Lew McCarty became Third Degree Masons on February 29, 1916. The ceremony was conducted in Brooklyn, with 400 attending.[11]

Jake timeline

April 17, 1884	Born in Shamokin to Jacob and Sarah (Hoy) Daubert
August 27, 1884	Half-brother Clifford died in mine explosion in Shamokin
1890	Family moved to Llewellyn area
1896	Began work at Blackwood Colliery, East of Tremont, age 11
March 23, 1897	Mother Sarah died
September 5, 1903	At 19, married Gertrude Viola Acaley
March 13, 1904	Daughter Louise Arietta born in Llewellyn
September 20, 1905	Son George Jacob born in Llewellyn
1906	Signed by Kane, Interstate League
1907	Played for Kane
1907	Played for Marion, Ohio-Pennsylvania League
1908	Played for Nashville in Southern Association
1909	Played for Toledo, American Association
1909	Played for Memphis, Southern Association
September 1, 1909	Drafted by Brooklyn

Memories and Memorabilia

April 14, 1910	Debut with Brooklyn Superbas
April 26, 1910	Living on Willing Street, Llewellyn
1912	Living at 339 Washington Ave., Brooklyn
1913	Won National League batting title and MVP award
1914	Won National League batting title
1913-1915	Living at 721 Coney Island Ave., Brooklyn
March 2, 1916	Half-brother Calvin died in mine cave-in near Tremont
1916	Brooklyn lost in World Series
1917	Living at 217 E. Liberty, Schuylkill Haven
February 1, 1919	Traded to Cincinnati Reds
1919	Cincinnati won World Series
1920-24	Boarder during season at 307 Broadway, Cincinnati
September 20, 1924	Played last game
October 9, 1924	Died in Cincinnati, Ohio

Jake's 1916 National League championship pin. (From the collection of Jack Daubert)

Jake's 1919 World Series championship pin. (From the collection of Jack Daubert)

Medallion recognizing Jake's batting titles and MVP award. (From the collection of Jack Daubert)

Jake was presented with bouquets of flowers prior to special games. (From the collection of Jack Daubert)

Jake's first-baseman's glove in 1922.

Jake Daubert cigar box and cigar band. (From the collection of Jill Daubert Malone)

Jake's autograph.

13

In Others' Words

Red Dooin, manager of the Phillies:

"Who's the fastest man in the league getting down to first base? Why, I should say Jake Daubert, and won't stop to deliberate at all. It isn't generally thought that Daubert is such a very fast man. But he's a big fellow and, like other big fellows, doesn't get credit for speed because he doesn't appear to be moving his legs so fast on the way down to first. But after watching him all but beat out fast bounder-batted balls straight at infielders and cleanly handled by them, there isn't much question left about his speed."[1]

George Cutshaw, Brooklyn second baseman in 1914 after the Robins' barnstorming team defeated Minersville, 5-0.

"You folks around here do not realize what a wonderful ball player and field general Jake Daubert is. Over in Brooklyn and in every other town in the league, the fans think he is the best first sacker in the business and they all like him on the job for us. There is a reason for this, too, Jake led the league in hitting for two seasons now and he is known and feared by every twirler in the league. Through him we have defeated many teams that had us licked all through the game and if everything was left to him in Brooklyn, we would have a pennant this season, as we had the team to do it with and all we needed was the entire generalship of Jake. As a gentleman Jake is a first class one and he is liked by every man on the club. He gets more out of the fellows than any other man on the club, and the fellows like to hear a comment from him because it is always so politely given. I tell you the bunch in this locality have something to be proud of in the person of Jake Daubert."[2]

Grantland Rice, famous sportswriter, in 1914:
"Jake Daubert is rapidly developing into the Ty Cobb of the National League. Jake has now led his circuit two years in succession. Wagner is the only other National leaguer outside of Daubert who has held the crest two successive seasons. Jake is a first-class hitter, and, like Cobb, is fast enough to add many an infield tap to his base hit column. The day of the old-fashioned slugger leading his league is now about over. Fast sprinters like Cobb and Daubert carry too thick an edge to be beaten out by those who lose all their infield taps."[3]

The Junior Eagle was a special children's section produced by *The Brooklyn Daily Eagle* in the 1910s. It was 12 pages on Sundays and a half page on weekdays. Boys and girls were invited to contribute original stories, photographs, and sketches.

On May 20, 1917, the following was published:

A Fine Quality

Did you ever find yourself in a situation where you knew it would hurt you to tell the truth? Surely you did. The way you met the situation is a good mark of your character.

Jake Daubert, Brooklyn's famous first baseman, was in this position. He was at bat. The umpire called two strikes and two balls. The fifth ball was pitched. The umpire called it a ball. Few paid any attention to it. But Jake and a few others knew that it had not been a ball. It had been a strike. He could have "gotten away with it." Did he?

No, he did not. He explained matters in their proper light.

Isn't that a fine example of making up your mind to be truthful and honest and sticking to it? It certainly takes a lot of good, sturdy quality in the makeup of a man, or boy or girl for that matter, to act as Jake did.[4]

Player comments about Jake after 1912 season

Johnny Evers, Chicago Cubs second baseman:

"Jake Daubert is the best first baseman in the business. Our own man, Saier, is coming strong and will bear watching next season. I do not think anybody at present is the equal of Frank Chance when he was in his prime though I will have to admit that Daubert has played a consistently brilliant game which certainly gives him a high ranking at his position."

Frank Chance, Chicago Cubs first baseman:

"There is no better first baseman in the game right now than Jake Daubert. Ed Konetchy is very good. There is not so much to choose between them. Merkle is also good. Our man, Saier, is a comer, but, of course, he is still too inexperienced to be ready to grab off chief honors. From what I can hear of Chase and his decline from form, I do not think there is any better man than Daubert."

Armando Marsans, Cincinnati Reds outfielder:

"Jake Daubert is a great first baseman. You know I used to play first base myself a little and I liked it. I have watched Jake Daubert play and he is a nice fellow and a great player. I think he is as good as there is."

Edward Reulbach, Chicago Cubs pitcher:

"The palm for the greatest first baseman in my opinion lies between Ed Konetchy and Jake Daubert. Both are great first basemen in every sense of the word and both are fine fellows as well. Personally, I do not think there is much to choose between them, but if there is, there might be a shade of difference in favor of the Brooklyn player."

James Lavender, Chicago Cubs pitcher:

"I am a pitcher and naturally not so much interested in first base as some players might be, but I have noticed the work of Jake Daubert particularly, and in the games he has played against us I must say he has always been a star. This is my first year in the league, and my opinion will not be worth so much as the opinions of other players with more experience, but I think Daubert is about the best first baseman that I have ever seen."[5]

Milt Stock, Phillies third baseman:
"Jake Daubert was the greatest bunter I ever saw. In his prime he could bunt almost at will. I don't know exactly what he did to the ball, but he seemed to put reverse English on it some way so that it would stop just where he wanted it to stop.

John McGraw, long-time manager of the New York Giants:
"We all liked Jake. He was a clean hard fighter on the ball field, but just as clean and a great companion in private life."[6]

Al Ritter, clubhouse manager at Redland Field.
From *The Cincinnati Post:*

> Bohne and Daubert "Most Particular"
>
> No one gets a closer insight into the character of the various Reds than Al Ritter, clubhouse man at Redland Field.
>
> Ritter's job is to keep the clubhouse and the belongings of the various Reds in order, and all members of the team unite in saying he is the most efficient man in this respect they ever have seen around a ballpark.
>
> Of the Reds, Ritter says Jake Daubert and Sammy Bohne are the most particular about their stuff. They require that everything be orderly and even give instructions as to how their undershirts should be dried.[7]

F.C. Lane, Editor of *Baseball Magazine* in 1914:
"Why take Jake Daubert as a type of batting success? If you are trying to learn at firsthand how championships are won, why not consider Ty Cobb, who has worn the batting crown for years? or Napoleon Lajoie, who has won so many laurels they fairly clutter up the walls of his trophy room? or that resolute old warrior, Hans Wagner, and his 'Seventeen Seasons' Success?

"We admit the batting greatness of these men. We know of the wonderful records they have made. And if our theme had been merely one of the batting championships, we would have consulted them as experts of the highest ability. But our theme is not merely one of batting championships. It is at once narrower and broader. It is the story of what one man accomplished in the face of obstacles that were all but insuperable; one man, a slender athlete with a losing club, who was considered a good fielder but never a brilliant batter. It is the story of this man, who thought in his own heart that when he exceeded the .250 mark he was doing really better than he had any right to expect; but who, nevertheless, patiently, persistently, though most of his best effort went unrewarded, almost unobserved, struggled on, scaled the heights which looked so inaccessible, nor paused even with an assured position beyond the three hundred mark which he himself deemed beyond his strength; but kept right on until, after disappointments and discouragements you will never know, he at length found himself on the very pinnacle, above all other batters of his league, the undisputed champion."[8]

14

Jake's Own Words

Jake was one of the most prominent baseball players during the Deadball Era. Writers went to him for his intelligent and well-spoken comments in a self-effacing manner. Here are some thoughts shared by Jake, most of them from several in-depth articles written by F.C. Lane for *Baseball Magazine:*

How first base is played
From 1911

I don't suppose I can tell anybody how to play first base. It is one thing to get in and play the game according to my own ideas, and a different thing to set myself up as an authority.

A youngster who wants to play first base—or anywhere else on the team—must have the natural ability. He must be able to play the mechanical part of baseball with ease.

A first baseman should be a left-hander.

This is not conceit because I am left-handed, but it is a clearly apparent fact that a left-handed man can handle first base more successfully than a right-hander. He has the entire infield "before" him, so to speak, and does not have to make the turns that a right-handed player is often compelled to make. Of course, there have been some brilliant first basemen who were right-handed, but they were brilliant in spite of this fact and not because of it.

A first baseman must always make a specialty of handling thrown balls, He must be able to accept the throw of other players without regard to the man who may be coming down the first base line from the plate at top speed. At the same time he must take the throw in such a way that he will be able to touch the bag and yet keep clear of the runner.

The youngster can learn the peculiarities of players opposing him by close observation. Nearly every batter has some manner of betraying himself. Few use the same style of bunting and hitting,

I have found it good policy to play "deep" when there is a pitcher working who can be depended on to get to first ahead of a runner. Once I heard a manager say to a recruit who made a spectacular one-handed stab: "Use both your hands—I signed 'em both." I should advise a first baseman to use both his hands in taking throws until he has become absolutely sure. A wide throw that gets away may mean a lost game.

If you want to succeed at baseball learn every detail of the game. It is a never-ceasing source of new problems, new situations, new conditions. The process of figuring out a play should become second nature to the player.[1]

Advice for the base-stealer
From 1912
- Learn to slide from either side of the base.
- Train for a steal as you would train for a short dash.
- Never be afraid to hit the dirt.
- Always watch the pitcher.
- A good start is half.[2]

Advice for the batter
From 1912
- Never strike before the ball leaves the pitcher's hands.
- Always keep your eye fixed on the ball.
- There is no rule for standing at the plate for every good player has his own way of standing.[3]

Advice on fielding
From 1912
- Always figure out plays in advance.
- Learn to catch a ball with ease.
- Learn to catch equally well from either side.
- Learn to catch a high ball as easily as a grounder.
- Above all, remember what to do with the ball when you get it.[4]

Rules for beginners
From 1912
- A star player must have natural ability in the first place. Natural ability, however, is not enough.
- A star player must above all things have ambition.
- Unless he strives constantly to succeed, he will not succeed.
- But ambition is not enough either, for it must go hand in hand with hard work.
- Baseball is no place for a lazy man.
- No player ever yet achieved prominence without the hardest kind of hard work.
- Work is the key note of all baseball success.[5]

Keys to hitting .300
From 1914

Any ball player would rather be a good batter than anything else.

I used to dream about hitting .300 in the Majors, but I never expected to get there.

Two seasons I hit for .307, but I couldn't believe I deserved that average.

I felt sure it was far beyond my natural gait and counted myself very lucky to reach the mark once.

I figured I was a .250 hitter, and that whatever success I might have would be due to fielding.

It is true that I hit last year for .350, just an even 100 points higher than I thought two seasons ago was my natural speed.

Boosting a batting average 100 points looks like a hard task.

I believe three things accounted for my success last year: first, luck; second, the knowledge experience had given me; third, simply trying to do my best at all times.

Some batters are natural hitters like Hans Wagner and Joe Jackson. These men are born batters, and don't seem to need much experience.[6]

Experience is a key
From 1914

I think a man must have some natural ability as a batter to start with, but the rest depends upon the use he makes of it.

Whatever their ability, most batters need experience. I know I would never have gone very far without it.

Most young players fail to hit through their own imagination. They think the pitcher is a good deal more wonderful than he is and underrate their own importance.

The first time I faced a big league pitcher in a box, he looked as big as a house.

A batter wouldn't go very far without confidence. When I was batting .266 for Brooklyn I lacked confidence. Now I have it. By confidence I do not mean certainty I will make a safe hit every time I face a pitcher, but certainty that I can hit the ball.

Pitchers, however famous, are human beings like the rest of us.

It doesn't take much physical strength to be a .300 hitter. All ball players are in athletic trim, but, if a .300 hitter needed any great weight or muscle, I would never have made good myself.[7]

Chop hitter vs. slugger
From 1914

It doesn't take much strength to drive a ball out of the infield.

The slugging batter puts his strength into extra bases, rather than extra hits.

The slugger can drive the ball farther on account of his strength than the man who lacks his muscle, but he can't drive it safe any oftener.

I never was a slugger myself, for I haven't the strength or that style of batting which the sluggers almost always use.

I am a chop hitter rather than a slugger.

You can tell by looking at a batter whether he is a natural chop hitter or a slugger.

Sam Crawford is a typical slugger with broad shoulders and great physical strength.

Joe Jackson is a slugger, though he looks rather slender. He is of that deceiving wiry build, and has a good deal of strength in his shoulders and arms.

Frank Baker doesn't look very strong, but he is big-boned, and his wrists unusually developed.[8]

Importance of speed
From 1914

Cactus Cravath, Heinie Zimmerman, and Chief Meyers are all typical sluggers.

An ideal example of a chop hitter, quick, nervous, active, is John Evers.

Some players can slug or chop at a ball with equal skill. Ty Cobb is the greatest of batters largely on this account.

The fielders never know where to play for him. The man who always slugs is at a disadvantage if the fielders can lay for his hits.

Speed is as useful to the batter as to the base stealer.

When a slow runner gets to first on a hit he has earned his passage.

A fast man gets to first on a play that will be an infield out to the slow runner.

The value of speed in batting is this: The sprinter beats out the slow runner in a dash from home plate to first base by about a stride. The fast man drives a ball to shortstop and beats out the throw by a foot. The slow runner drives the ball to shortstop in exactly the same way, but is caught at first. Result, fast man makes a single, slow man is out. Result, the value of speed, or, as I would put it, some men bat .300 with their legs as well as their arms.[9]

Importance of quick start
From 1914

A quick start in the sprint to first is half the race.

Speed helps the slugger to make long hits, but it doesn't help his batting average any.

The official scorer makes no more count of a four-base hit than a scratch single.

The secret of batting is in the eye. A good batting eye means more than good eyesight.

The .200 hitter may see just as far and just as well as a .300 hitter, but he doesn't make any use of it in batting.

A crack shot can hit a bird on the wing because his eye and finger on the trigger act together.

The amateur hunter can see the bird as well as the expert, but his finger on the trigger is perhaps a fraction of a second too late.

The good batter is like the good marksman. His wrists and shoulders act with his eye.

Most batters always keep their eye on the ball.

Good batters can generally hit the ball without watching it all the time.

I do not think that a batter, however good, can hit a sharp breaking curve unless he has his eye on it all the time.[10]

Luck plays a part
From 1914

I lay a good deal of my success to luck.

I have beat out more infield hits this year than ever before.

An infield hit is a failure on the batter's part. He swings at the ball and almost misses it, but beats the throw to first by a combination of luck and speed.

Place hitting is the rarest thing in baseball. Once or twice a season a batter may be able to drive the ball just where he wants it to go. As a general thing, all he can do is to send it either to right or left.

The batter who hits a ball hard has done all any man can do. If it goes into a fielder's hands, it isn't his fault.

The difference between a grounder and a fly ball is the difference of an inch or less in the elevation of the bat.

No batter can swing at a twisted curve and judge his swing that fine.

No batter can tell as a sure thing whether he will hit a grounder or a fly ball.

I never tried to outguess the pitcher. Some players may be able to do so, but I have no such ability.

If I depended on outguessing the pitcher I would not hit over .200.[11]

Marquard was tough

"The hardest pitcher in the world for me to face is Rube Marquard, at least that has been my experience this year," Jake said in 1912. "I think that the pace Marquard is traveling now is about the best in the league. As for the American league, I have never faced Walter Johnson, though I have heard a great deal about him, and the majority of opinions I hear expressed seem to agree that he is about the best in the business."[12]

Four years later he listed the toughest pitchers for him:
    Grover Alexander, Philadelphia Phillies
    Jim Vaughn, Chicago Cubs
    Al Mamaux, Pittsburgh Pirates
    Fred Toney, Cincinnati Reds
    Harry Sallee, St. Louis Cardinals
    Jeff Tesreau, New York Giants[13]

Jake's humor

On days when games were rained out, sometimes players would gather and tell stories. The following example from *The Brooklyn Times in 1914* shows Jake's humorous story-telling during a conversation with third-baseman Red Smith and Stephen and Ed McKeever, co-owners of the Brooklyn team with Charles Ebbets. They shared the story of "One Armed" O'Hara, who they said was a pitcher for the Irishtown Invincibles.

> "He was the greatest hurler I ever saw," Stephen said, "and if he was alive today I'd sign him for our team. O'Hara could pitch,

field his position and bat like a fiend. Although he only had one arm he could drive the ball further than Wheat. If you don't believe me just ask any of the old timers who were raised in Irishtown and they will tell you about him."

"Aw, this fellow wasn't in it with a guy that played in the Appalachian League," Red Smith said. "It was my first year in professional baseball, and I was a teammate of his. His name was O'Shaughnessy, and he had only one leg. He was a right fielder, and could cover more ground than anyone I ever knew. And you should have seen this fellow run the bases. Why, it was nothing for him to purloin second, third and home."

"What became of him, Red?" (catcher) Lew McCarty asked.

"Well, I'll tell you," Smith replied. "We were in the midst of a 0 to 0 game one day, which had gone into the eighteenth inning. O'Shaughnessy, the first man up, doubled to center, the next man fanned, so 'One Leg' dashed for the far bag. He hit the dust in the prettiest hook slide imaginable, and was safe, but at a cost. His plates became entangled in the bag strap, and the good limb was broken just about the knee. The bones were shattered, amputation was necessary, and, of course, that ended his days of usefulness. If it hadn't been for this, he would be playing in the big leagues."

"Oh, those two bushers couldn't hold a candle to the ball player I chummed with back in the days when I was a breaker boy," Jake said. "He was an armless wonder, named 'Scurgy' O'Keefe, and played shortstop on the miners' club down in Llewellyn, Pa. He worked in the coal mine during the week, so Sunday was the only chance to play ball. He never got any practice, and for that matter, neither did I. I was just learning to play the first bag, and this fellow helped me a lot."

"If he was armless how could he throw?" a writer asked.

"Why, I told you he played shortstop," Jake said. "When a ball was hit to him he'd kick it on a line to any part of the diamond. That's where I learned to handle bad throws."

"You win, Jake." Ed McKeever said. "I'll never sing the praises of 'One Armed' O'Hara again."[14]

Jake's system
From 1916

What system do I follow in batting?

Why, I haven't any system at the plate. I know some players when batting try to figure out what the pitcher has in mind, but I never follow that plan.

All the energy that I might put into this misreading stunt seems better place to me when it's in my wrists or shoulders where I can get at it handy whenever I want to use it in a hurry.

If I had depended on my ability to hypnotize the pitcher I would have been lucky to bat above the .200 mark.[15]

His greatest play
From 1916

When a ball player is asked to describe the greatest play, he is up a stump. He cannot recall the greatest play he ever made because he does not know what is meant by the term "greatest." If he is pressed on the subject, he will recall the play that interested him the most, and which was not always the most difficult. I recall the play that interested me most, because it was the only triple play I was ever in, and it was the only one I ever saw.

Some men are lucky in seeing strange freaks in baseball, as well as other walks of life, and others never seem to be around when the curiosities happen. It is a fact that I never saw a triple play in the major leagues, and I never saw but one in the minors, and took part in that.

I was with Memphis in the Southern Association at the time, which was in 1909, the year I was drafted to play with Brooklyn in 1910, and three years after the beginning of my career as a professional. I was playing first base, and there were runners on first and second.

The man on first started to run, with the pitcher's arm on the hit-and-run play. I yelled, "There he goes!" as a warning to the other players. Of course, the man on second also started for third. Just as I yelled, the batter swung on the ball and knocked a line drive straight into my hands. I threw to second, doubling up the man who had been on that base, and the ball was returned to me at first base, tripling up the man who had been on first.

The whole thing came to pass so quickly that all hands were astonished.[16]

Advice for older players
From 1923
- Proper food and sufficient sleep are most essential for every athlete. Eight hours of sleep is just about right, but more seldom does any harm. It is when the player gets less that he suffers.
- Don't be a pessimist. Look on the bright side. If you can't boost, keep quiet. The knocker never gets anywhere on a ball club.
- Take the game seriously, but try not to worry over its disappointing features, for in baseball you are a hero one day and a dub the next. You must take the bitter with the sweet.
- Keep your wits about you. Try to outguess the other fellow by figuring ahead. Have your play mapped out and then try to execute it.[17]

15

By the Numbers

Sizing up Jake
    5-10 ½ 160 pounds
    Bats left, throws left

Special awards
    1913 National League batting title
    1913 National League MVP
    1914 National League batting title
    Cincinnati Reds Hall of Fame
    Brooklyn Dodgers Hall of Fame

Jake's career stats highlights

BA	.303
OBP	.360
SLG	.401
OPS	.760
OPS+	117
WAR	39.4
Fielding	.991

    Batted .305 against LHP
    Batted .298 against RHP

Jake went 5-for-5 in a game four times:
May 22, 1912
August 15, 1912
July 28, 1919
August 27, 1922

31 times he had four hits in a game.

22-game hitting streak

Jake's longest hitting streak was 22 games from April 21 to May 14, 1922. He went 32-for-77, a .416 batting average, with three doubles, three triples, two home runs, 25 runs scored, and eight sacrifices. He struck out once in 101 plate appearances. After that streak ended, he hit in the next six games, going 12-for-26 (.462) and followed that with a 14-game streak, going 27-for-60 (.450). During those 44 games, he batted .418 and struck out once in 199 plate appearances.

Record for sacrifices

Jake still holds the National League record for sacrifice bunts. His 392 sacrifices in 15 years is second only to Eddie Collins of the American League, who had 512 in 25 years.

Excellent contact hitter

Jake struck out only 489 times in 8,749 plate appearances—1 in every 17.9 plate appearances. In 1922 he struck out only 21 times in 700 plate appearances.

Excellent fielder

Jake committed only 181 errors in 20,943 chances, a .991 lifetime fielding percentage. In 1924, when he was 40, he had .990 fielding percentage.

Year-by-year stats

YEAR	GP	PA	AB	R	H	2B	3B	HR	RBI	SB	CS	BB	SO	BA	OBP	SLG	OPS	HBP	SH
Brooklyn Superbas/Robins/Dodgers																			
1910	144	635	552	67	146	15	15	8	50	23	0	47	53	.264	.328	.389	.717	5	31
1911	149	652	573	89	176	17	8	5	45	32	0	51	56	.307	.366	.391	.757	2	26
1912	145	627	559	81	172	19	16	3	66	29	0	48	45	.308	.369	.415	.784	6	14
1913	139	572	509	76	178	17	7	2	52	25	0	44	40	.350	.405	.423	.829	3	17
1914	126	542	474	89	156	17	7	6	45	25	0	30	34	.329	.375	.432	.808	5	33
1915	150	641	544	62	164	21	8	2	47	11	13	57	48	.301	.369	.381	.749	1	39
1916	127	555	478	75	151	16	7	3	33	21	7	38	39	.316	.371	.397	.769	4	35
1917	125	550	468	59	122	4	4	2	30	11	3	51	30	.261	.341	.299	.640	6	25
1918	108	445	396	50	122	12	15	2	47	10	0	27	18	.308	.360	.429	.789	5	17
Cincinnati Reds																			
1919	140	613	537	79	148	10	12	2	44	11	0	35	23	.276	.322	.350	.672	2	39
1920	142	630	553	97	168	28	13	4	48	11	13	47	29	.304	.362	.423	.785	3	27
1921	136	576	516	69	158	18	12	2	64	12	6	24	16	.306	.341	.399	.740	3	33
1922	156	700	610	114	205	15	22	12	66	14	47	56	21	.336	.395	.492	.886	3	31
1923	125	556	500	63	146	27	10	2	54	11	12	40	20	.292	.349	.398	.747	4	12
1924	102	448	405	47	114	14	9	1	31	5	10	28	17	.281	.331	.368	.699	2	13
Total	2014	8742	7673	1117	2326	250	165	56	722	251	78	623	489	.303	.360	.401	.760	54	392
Post Season																			
1916	4	19	17	1	3	0	1	0	0	0	0	2	3	.176	.263	.294	.557	0	0
1919	8	36	29	4	7	0	0	0	1	1	1	1	2	.241	.290	.310	.601	1	5

All statistics from Retrosheet.org and baseball-reference.com

A steady starter

Jake played in 2,014 games: 2,001 at first base and 13 as a pinch-hitter. He was 1-for-12 with a walk as a pinch-hitter during his career.

Jake vs. pitchers

Pitcher	At-bats	Pct.
Chief Bender	3-8	.375
Harry Coveleski	1-3	.333 (double)
Eppa Rixey	27-82	.329
Rube Marquard	31-100	.310
Allen Sothoron	4-13	.308
Christy Mathewson	25-82	.305
Burleigh Grimes	31-104	.298
Pete Alexander	11-56	.267
Cy Young	1-4	.250
Mordecai Brown	1-14	.071
Jack Quinn	0-4	.000

Most strikeouts

Pitcher	Ks	At-bats
Hippo Vaughn	22	29-127
Wilbur Cooper	19	41-175

Hit by pitches

Jake was hit by pitches 54 times. The most were by Joe Oeschger and Jeff Tesreau, three each.

A league leader

In addition to leading the National League in batting in 1913 and 1914, Jake led the league in sacrifice hits in 1919 and 10 times was in the top 10.

He led the league in games played in 1919 and 1922.

He led the league in triples in 1918 and 1922.

He led the league in fielding percentage among first basemen three times and was in the top five for 14 years.

JAKE IN THE NATIONAL LEAGUE TOP 10

Batting average

Year	Avg.	Rank
1911	.307	8
1913	.350	1
1914	.329	1
1915	.301	5
1916	.316	2
1918	.308	5
1922	.336	10

Sacrifice hits

Year	No.	Rank
1910	31	4
1911	26	7
1914	33	2
1915	39	2
1916	35	2
1917	25	6
1919	39	1
1920	27	9
1921	33	4
1922	31	3
Career	392	2

Games played

Year	No.	Rank
1919	140	1
1922	156	1

Triples

Year	No.	Rank
1910	15	5
1912	16	4
1918	15	1
1919	12	3
1920	13	8
1922	22	1

Singles

Year	No.	Rank
1911	146	1
1912	134	5
1913	152	1
1914	126	2
1915	133	2
1916	125	5
1919	124	7
1922	156	6

Fielding percentage

Year	Pct.	Rank
1910	.989	2
1911	.989	3
1912	.993	1
1913	.991	2
1914	.993	2
1915	.993	2
1916	.993	1
1917	.991	2
1918	.991	2
1919	.989	3
1920	.990	5
1921	.993	3
1922	.994	1
1923	.993	2

Jake's teams

Year	Team	Record	Place	Back	Pennant	Attendance
1910	Brooklyn	64-90	6th	40	Chicago Cubs	279,321
1911	Brooklyn	64-86	7th	33.5	New York Giants	269,000
1912	Brooklyn	58-95	7th	46	New York Giants	243,000
1913	Brooklyn	65-84	6th	34.5	New York Giants	347,000
1914	Brooklyn	75-79	5th	19.5	Boston Braves	122,671

1915	Brooklyn	80-72	3rd	13	Philadelphia Phillies	297,766
1916	Brooklyn	94-60	1st	---	Brooklyn Robins	447,747
1917	Brooklyn	70-81	7th	26.5	New York Giants	221,619
1918	Brooklyn	57-69	5th	25.5	Chicago Cubs	83,831
1919	Cincinnati	96-44	1st	---	Cincinnati Reds	532,501
1920	Cincinnati	82-71-1	3rd	10.5	Brooklyn Robins	568,107
1921	Cincinnati	70-83	6th	24	New York Giants	311,227
1922	Cincinnati	86-68-2	2nd	7	New York Giants	493,754
1923	Cincinnati	91-63	2nd	4.5	New York Giants	575,063
1924	Cincinnati	83-70	4th	10	New York Giants	473,707

Jake's games played

Jake played in 89.4 % of his team's games:

Year	Jake	Team
1910	144	154
1911	149	150
1912	145	153
1913	139	149
1914	126	154
1915	150	152
1916	127	154
1917	125	151
1918	108	126
1919	140	140
1920	142	154
1921	136	153
1922	156	156
1923	125	154
1924	102	153
Totals	2,014	2,253
Avg.	134	150

Jake's ejections

Date	Umpire	Reason
5-21-1913	Bill Klem	Called third strike
6-16-1914	Ernie Quigley	Umpire positioning
9-04-1914	Ernie Quigley	Call at 1B
9-14-1914	Bill Klem	Called third strike
4-26-1915	Lord Byron	Condition of ball
9-04-1915	Lord Byron	Called third strike
7-19-1916 (2)	Mal Eason	Called third strike
9-21-22 (2)	Barry McCormick	Call at 2B

Jake's salaries[1]

1910	$2,000
1911	
1912	$3,500
1913	$4,500
1914	$4,500
1915	$4,500
1916	$9,000
1917	$9,000
1918	$9,000
1919	$5,759
1920	$7,000
1921	$7,000
1922	$8,500
1923	$11,000
1924	$11,000

Jake Daubert vs. Hal Chase

	Jake	Hal
Years	15	15
Games	2,014	1,919
BA	.303	.291
Field %	.991	.979
Field % 1B	.991	.980
Errors	181	423
Errors 1B	181	402
Hits	2,326	2,158
Runs	1,117	980
Doubles	250	322
Triples	165	124
Home runs	56	57
BB	623	276
SO	489	660
RBIs	722	941
SB	251	363
SH	392	216
OBP	.360	.319
WAR	39.4	22.9
World Series	1-1	0-0

Afterword

No Call From the Hall

Among the signs of being the greatest is becoming the standard by which others are judged. At the beginning of Jake's professional career, he often was compared to Hal Chase, the excellent fielding first baseman who first played for the New York Yankees. A few years later, Jake was the standard by which other first basemen were compared.

Chase played from 1905-1919 with five teams, the first nine seasons with the New York Yankees. His career included two years in the Federal League. He had a career batting average of .291 and won the National League batting title with a .339 average in 1916. He had a .980 lifetime fielding percentage at first base.

Chase was known as Prince Hal and was considered a disruptive player. He also was regarded as one of the most corrupt players in baseball and was accused but never convicted of influencing the outcome of games in which he had placed bets.

Jake's .303 batting average and .991 lifetime fielding percentage far surpassed Chase.

Outfielder Edd Roush is the only member of the 1919 World Series champion Cincinnati Reds in the Hall of Fame. He was voted in by the Veterans Committee in 1962. Roush batted .323 in 18 years, including 12 with Cincinnati. He won batting titles in 1917 (.341) and 1919 (.321) and led the league in doubles in 1923 (41) and triples in 1924 (21).

Three players from the 1916 Brooklyn Robins are in the Hall of Fame: outfielder Zack Wheat, pitcher Rube Marquard, and Casey Stengel for his later career as a manager. Wilbert Robinson was inducted into the Hall of Fame in 1945 as a manager by the Old-Timers Committee.

Wheat played 18 of his 19 years with Brooklyn and batted .317. He won the batting title in 1918 with a .335 average. Wheat was voted into the Hall in 1959 by the Veterans Committee.

AFTERWORD

Marquard played six of his 18 years with Brooklyn and eight with the New York Giants. He had a 201-177 record and 3.08 earned run average. Marquard had three 20-win seasons, the best in 1911 when he was 24-7 with a 2.50 ERA and led the league in strikeouts with 237, which was 62 more than his next best of 175 in 1912 when he was 26-11. The Veterans Committee voted him into the Hall in 1971.

Stengel batted .284 in 14 years as a player, including six years with Brooklyn. He was inducted into the Hall of Fame as a manager in 1966 by the Veterans Committee. He had a 1,905-1,842 record in 25 years as a manager for the Brooklyn Dodgers (1934-1936), Boston Bees and Braves (1938-1943), New York Yankees (1949-1960), and New York Mets (1962-1965). He is best known for his 12 years as Yankees manager when they won seven World Series championships and 10 American League titles, compiling a 1,149-696 record.

Does Jake Daubert deserve to join them in the Hall of Fame? His candidacy, like many others, is one of considerable debate.

He was, without question, one of the stars during his 15-year career. Jake's credentials don't match those of Ty Cobb, who was a member of the first Hall of Fame class in 1936, but during much of Jake's career, he received comparable headlines to Cobb and was regarded as one of the most respected and feared batters.

He won two batting titles and a most valuable player award.

He had a career batting average of .303.

He had 2,326 hits and scored 1,117 runs.

He was the premier bunter of his era.

He remains the National League leader in career sacrifices with 392.

He struck out only 489 times in 8,749 career plate appearances.

He was among the best fielding first basemen of the Deadball Era when defense was the primary importance of that position. His .991 lifetime fielding percentage is even more impressive when the small gloves of that time are considered.

He was one of the early leaders for players' rights, ultimately leading to the baseball union, the Major League Baseball Players Association. Some writers have speculated that Jake's union activism may have hampered his chances of being elected to the Hall of Fame.

He was not a home run hitter, which became a standard for first basemen after the Deadball Era, but he was the epitome of small ball that was the standard offense during the Deadball Era.

As intelligent, well-spoken, talented, and respected as Jake was, he was not as flashy as others during his era. And he refused to brag about his talent or considerable accomplishments. All of that may have hampered Jake's support in the Hall of Fame voting when he never received more than two votes.

I contacted several baseball writers and historians who have written about the Deadball Era. Here are their assessments about Jake's Hall of Fame consideration:

William A. Cook wrote the book *The 1919 World Series: What Really Happened?* in 2001. He believes the Cincinnati Reds were an excellent team that would have won the 1919 World Series without any help from the White Sox players.[1]

> Jake is one of those forgotten players that belongs in the Hall of Fame. He played 15 years in the majors, won two batting titles playing for Brooklyn and finished his career with a .303 batting average and 2,326 hits. Those stats alone certainly stand up against other first basemen in the HOF such as Gil Hodges. He also won the Chalmers award in 1913, the forerunner of today's MVP award.
>
> Jake was important to me when I was writing my controversial book a couple of decades ago because he was one of many Cincinnati Reds that strongly reinforced my thesis that the Reds were going to defeat the White Sox in the 1919 World Series no matter how it was played, fair, fixed or otherwise, because they were a better team. Since I wrote the book and fended off a lot of critics, I have now silenced them by applying metrics to my thesis, and Jake Daubert is just one of the players who proves my point. For the 1919 season White Sox first baseman Chick Gandil had a BA of .290, OBP .325, DLG. .383, OPS .709. Daubert while he hit for an average of .276, had had a OBP of

AFTERWORD

.362, SLG. .423, OPS .785. Who's kidding who? Jake Daubert was a better player than Gandil. This was true for most of the Reds and some of their pitchers too. Of course, Shoeless Joe Jackson led everybody. Although both Daubert and Gandil had a poor World Series in 1919, Daubert outhit Gandil in batting average .241 to.233. Daubert also had two stolen bases, Gandil 1.

Tom Zappala wrote the book *The Cracker Jack Collection . . . Baseball's Prized Player,* about the Cracker Jack baseball card sets released in 1914 and 1915. Jake was among those featured in the book, which notes: "It is hard to fathom why Jake Daubert has been bypassed by the Hall of Fame."[2]

Tom shared the following for this book:

> There is no doubt in my mind that Jake Daubert should be in the Hall of Fame. Considered by many to be the best fielding first baseman of the Deadball Era, Daubert also won two batting titles to go along with his .303 batting average, 2,326 hits and led the league on three different occasions in fielding percentage over his 15-year career.
>
> Compared to the first basemen currently in the Hall, Daubert had a higher lifetime batting average than 10 of them, had a higher OBP than five, and banged out more hits than 12 . If you compare Jake Daubert's overall statistics with the likes of Frank Chance, Gil Hodges (taking the power numbers and putting them aside), George Kelly, and Ben Taylor, there is certainly an argument for Jake Daubert to be in Cooperstown.

John McMurray is chairman of SABR's Deadball Era committee. He wrote the following for this book:

> Jake Daubert was an excellent and often superb player. Still, in spite of being a two-time batting champion, a sharp fielder, and among the best first basemen of his era, Daubert faces a steep climb to make it to the Hall of Fame. First, Daubert does not fit

the mold of the traditional Hall of Fame first baseman, which, especially in recent decades, has been seen through a modern lens of the power-hitting slugger. Daubert's career as a high-average, line-drive hitting contact hitter with a dynamic but relatively short peak puts him closer in the mind's eye to John Olerud or to Mark Grace, namely very good players who fall short of the Hall of Fame threshold. Daubert as a fielder may have been his era's equal of Don Mattingly or Keith Hernandez, but defensive prowess at first base rarely does a Hall of Famer make.

Other issues complicate Daubert's case. In six Hall of Fame votes held between 1937 and 1955, Daubert never won more than two percent of the vote. Stuffy McInnis, whose offensive statistics closely parallel those of Daubert, has received comparably slim support for the Hall of Fame. It is true that several players—from Jack Chesbro to Buck Ewing to Jesse Burkett—all made the Hall of Fame after very low initial vote totals. Yet Daubert's contemporaries never saw fit to elect him, and Daubert has not come close to election in nearly a century of Hall of Fame voting. So it is a relatively heavy lift to suggest that Daubert should make the Hall of Fame now, even with advanced metrics.

Daubert too may not be the most deserving Deadball Era player not in the Hall of Fame. Bill Dahlen, Sherry Magee, and Jimmy Sheckard—probably in that order—all have strong cases. Some also argue that the time is past to put long-ago players into the Hall of Fame, considering the relative scarcity of players in the Hall of Fame from more recent decades. That perception, surely, will work against Daubert's candidacy. Had he not died young and his career ended prematurely after only 15 seasons, Daubert's Hall of Fame case would be more solid.

On the margins, celebrity and visibility may also matter. Daubert lacked a particular transcendent moment on the field, which has often been central to some players' Hall of Fame cases. Quotable as he was, Daubert's vigor and personality today do not resonate in the public memory the way which the personalities of the top stars of that period still do. Daubert, in spite of his

AFTERWORD

outspokenness and his well-chronicled leadership abilities, has been relegated to the relative anonymity often afforded to steadily consistent players in that pre-video highlights time. When one does not meet the traditional statistical benchmarks, individual defining moments, especially in the World Series, appear to matter more for the Hall of Fame, often at the expense of consistent excellence.

Daubert's best Hall of Fame chance, it would seem, would come from thinking outside of the box. Daubert offers something no other player does when one considers his groundbreaking work in players' rights combined with his distinguished playing career as a high-average first baseman given that few of those are in the Hall of Fame. The record he still holds for sacrifice hits speaks to Daubert's unselfishness as a player and how he contributed to his team's success within the parameters of how the game was played at the time. Together, those might be the most prominent arguments in favor of inducting Daubert into the Hall of Fame.

There can be no doubt that Daubert at his best between 1911 through 1914 was legitimately one of the elite players in the game. That Daubert finished his career with a higher fielding percentage than Hal Chase and was arguably a better overall player than Chase (who was considered a standard at the position prior to Chase's scandals) speaks to the notion that Daubert may have been both overlooked and significantly underrated. Even if Daubert's Hall of Fame candidacy falls short, his legacy as a top hitter, elite fielder, and tireless worker for the rights of players will remain. Daubert was a player of consequence and one who deserves to be remembered more fully for his many accomplishments and for his distinctive imprint on baseball during the Deadball Era.

Jake's son, George, spent the latter years of his life working to get his father into the Hall of Fame. He died in 2000.

"It's just one of those things," George said about his father's exclusion from the Hall of Fame. "There are other ballplayers that belong in there and aren't. And there are some in there that don't belong."[3]

Endnotes

Preface
1. *West Schuylkill Press*, "How First Base Is Played," Tremont, Pennsylvania, June 10, 1911. p. 3.
2. *The Kentucky Post*, Covington, Kentucky, "Cincinnatus Column" October 9, 1924, p. 7.

Chapter 1
1. www.shamokincreek.org.
2. USGenWeb Archives, Northumberland County Area History, Shamokin.
3. Department of Commerce and Labor, Bureau of the Census report, 1910.
4. Shamokincity.org, "Shamokin and Coal Township History."
5. *The Lancaster Intelligencer*, August 27, 1884, p.1.
6. *West Schuylkill Press*, Tremont, July 19, 1890, p. 1.
7. *Baseball Magazine*, "Jake Daubert, the Hal Chase of the National League," by F.C. Lane July 1912.
8. Department of Commerce and Labor, Bureau of the Census report, 1910.
9. "Department of the Interior, Bureau of Mines report, "Coal-mine fatalities in the United States 1870-1914," p. 281.
10. Ibid., p. 286.
11. phmc.pa.gov/Archives/Research-Online/Pages/Molly-Maguires.
12. *The Lancaster Intelligencer*, Lancaster, Pa., August 27, 1884, p. 1.
13. *Harrisburg Telegraph*, Harrisburg, Pa., March 3, 1916, p. 2.
14. *The Wilkes-Barre Record*, Wilkes-Barre, Pa., September 24, 1912, p. 17.
15. *Baseball Magazine*, "Jake Daubert, the Hal Chase of the National League" by F.C. Lane, "July 1912, p. 45.
16. *The New Era*, Lancaster, Pa. September 11, 1918, p. 6.
17. *Baseball Magazine*, "Jake Daubert, the Hal Chase of the National League," by F.C. Lane, July 1912, p. 46.
18. *Miners Journal*, Pottsville, Pa. August 11, 1902, p. 4.
19. *Miners Journal*, Pottsville, Pa., August 21, 1902, p. 4; *The Philadelphia Inquirer*, August 21, 1902, p. 11.
20. *The Chicago Eagle*, July 29, 1922, p. 3.
21. *The Philadelphia Inquirer*, September 14, 1902, p. 11.
22. *The Boston Globe*, August 1, 1924, p. 7.
23. *The Daily Republican*, Monongahela, Pa., "Clever First Base Player: Jake Daubert of Brooklyn Nationals, One of Season's 'Finds,' Tells of Early Start," September 16, 1910, p. 3.
24. *The Plain Dealer*, Cleveland, February 9, 1908, p. 16.
25. *The Daily Republican*, Monongahela, Pa., "Clever First Base Player: Jake Daubert of Brooklyn Nationals, One of Season's 'Finds,' Tells of Early Start," September 16, 1910, p. 3.
26. *The Plain Dealer*, Cleveland, February 9, 1908, p. 16.
27. *The Boston Globe*, August 1, 1924, p. 7.
28. Ibid.

Chapter 2
1. *The Daily Republican*, Monongahela, Pa., "Clever First Base Player: Jake Daubert of Brooklyn Nationals, One of Season's 'Finds,' Tells of Early Start," September 16, 1910, p. 3.
2. SABR's Spring 2012 *Baseball Research Journal*, "Gentleman Jake, The Giant-Killer, and the Kane Mountaineers" by Ed Rose.
3. *The Pittsburgh Daily Post*, June 22, 1924, p. 26.
4. www.Kaneboro.org.

ENDNOTES

5. SABR's Spring 2012 *Baseball Research Journal,* "Pop Kelchner, Gentleman Jake, The Giant-Killer, and the Kane Mountaineers" by Ed Rose.
6. www.albright.edu/about-albright/collegehistory.
7. SABR's Spring 2012 *Baseball Research Journal,* "Gentleman Jake, The Giant-Killer, and the Kane Mountaineers" by Ed Rose.
8. Ibid., quoting "Joe McCarthy: Architect of the Yankee Dynasty" by Alan Levy.
9. Ibid.
10. *The Plain Dealer,* Cleveland, "Daubert Saves Marion Team From Failure," January 28, 1912, p. 2C.
11. *The Marion Star,* Marion, Ohio, August 7, 1907, p. 6.
12. *Baseball Magazine,* "Jake Daubert, the Hal Chase of the National League" by F.C. Lane, July 1912, p. 47.
13. *The Marion Star,* Marion, Ohio, August 16, 1907, p. 6.
14. *Pottsville Republican,* Pottsville, Pa., August 22, 1907, p. 1.
15. *Morning Tribune,* Altoona, Pa., July 29, 1911, p. 10.
16. *The Marion Daily Mirror,* Marion, Ohio, November 11, 1907, p. 7.
17. *The Plain Dealer,* Cleveland, February 9, 1908, p. 16.
18. *The Pittsburgh Sunday Post,* June 22, 1924, p. 26.
19. www.baseball-reference.com.
20. George Stovall SABR bio by Stephen Constanelos.
21. *The Plain Dealer,* Cleveland, "Confidential Stories About Ball Players," August 8, 1920, p. 82.
22. *Baseball Magazine,* "Jake Daubert, the Hal Chase of the National League" by F.C. Lane, July 1912, p. 47.
23. *The Plain Dealer,* Cleveland, August 3, 1908, Page 6, quoting article by Rice in the *Nashville Tennessean.*
24. *Baseball Magazine,* "Jake Daubert, the Hal Chase of the National League" by F.C. Lane, July 1912, p. 47.
25. *The Pittsburgh Sunday Post,* June 22, 1924, p. 26.
26. *The Daily Republican,* Monongahela, Pa., "Clever First Base Player: Jake Daubert of Brooklyn Nationals, One of Season's 'Finds,' Tells of Early Start," September 16, 1910, p. 3.

Chapter 3

1. www.mlb.com, "The long road to the LA Dodgers' naming" by Ken Gurnick, December 1, 2021; *The New York Times,* "Willard Mullin Dies" by William N. Wallace, December 22, 1978.
2. www.baseball-reference.com.
3. Ibid.
4. *New-York Tribune,* February 26, 1910, p. 5.
5. Baseball-reference.com and 1942 TSN Guide 163.
6. *The Daily Standard Union,* Brooklyn, February 16, 1910, p. 10.
7. *The Brooklyn Citizen,* March 3, 1910, p. 6.
8. *The Brooklyn Daily Eagle,* March 28, 1910, p. 26.
9. *Los Angeles Times,* "Daubert Chased Home-Run King Off the Job," Harry A. Williams, December 6, 1915, p. 19.
10. Ibid.
11. www.Baseball-reference.com.
12. *The Brooklyn Citizen,* August 8, 1910, p. 4.
13. *The Plain Dealer,* Cleveland, February 12, 1911, p. 16.
14. *The Philadelphia Inquirer,* November 20, 1910, p. 4.
15. *Buffalo Evening News,* May 11, 1911, p 14.
16. *The Cincinnati Post,* Cincinnati, Ohio, May 22, 1911, p. 2.
17. *The Brooklyn Citizen,* May 28, 1911, p. 5.
18. *The Brooklyn Daily Eagle,* May 28, 1911, p. 58.
19. *The Brooklyn Times,* May 29, 1911, p. 5.
20. *The Brooklyn Daily Eagle,* "Daubert to Lead New Superba Line-Up in 1912 Campaign," January 16, 1912, p. 22.
21. *The Brooklyn Citizen,* January 21, 1912, p. 5.
22. SABR bio project, "Zack Wheat" by Eric Enders.
23. *The Brooklyn Daily Eagle,* "Jake Daubert Still Ailing," April 30, 1912, p. 22.
24. *The Brooklyn Citizen,* April 24, 1912, p. 4.
25. *Sun and New York Press,* New York, "Is It Daubert or Dahlen?" August 11, 1912, p. 14.

26. *The Pittsburgh Gazette Times,* August 17, 1912, p. 9.
27. *The Brooklyn Times,* "Daubert Most Popular Player on Brooklyns," October 1, 1912, p. 3.
28. *The Call,* Schuylkill Haven, Pa., "Locals Defeated by Brooklyn," Oct 18, 1912, p. 1.
29. *The Evening World,* New York, "Ball Players Organize to Protect Themselves," October 21, 1912, p. 12.
30. *The Brooklyn Times,* December 11, 1912, p. 10.
31. *The Sun,* New York, "Dahlen to Lead Dodgers," November 10, 1912, p. 17.
32. www.Baseball-reference.com, citing research by Doug Pappas, Society for American Baseball Research, and Dr. Michael Haupert.
33. *The Brooklyn Times,* "Jake Daubert and Five of the Veteran Giants Sail Today for New Orleans," February 22, 1911, p. 5.

Chapter 4

1. *Buffalo Evening News,* Buffalo, New York, "Minute-Men of Baseball—Jake Daubert," by Ripley, July 29, 1912, p. 10.
2. *Deadball Stars of the National League,* "Jacob Ellsworth Daubert," by Jim Sandoval, p. 294.
3. *Altoona Tribune,* Altoona, Pa., "Daubert Lives as Greatest Bunter in National Game" by King Features Syndicate, Inc., October 23, 1924, p. 13.
4. *The Columbus Dispatch,* "Jake Daubert Saves Fielders Many Errors," March 29, 1913, p. 6.
5. *Baseball Magazine,* "Jake Daubert—a Self-Made Success" by F.C. Lane, February 1914, p. 34.
6. *Baseball Magazine,* "Jake Daubert, the Hal Chase of the National League," by F.C. Lane, July 1912, p. 49.
7. New York Tribune, "Daubert Receives the Prize Auto," October 8, 1913, p. 8.
8. *Baseball Magazine,* "Jake Daubert, the Hal Chase of the National League," by F.C. Lane, July 1912, p. 44.
9. *Los Angeles Times,* "Daubert Chased Home-Run King Off the Job," by Harry A. Williams, December 6, 1915, p. 19.
10. *Baseball Magazine,* "Jake Daubert, the Hal Chase of the National League," by F.C. Lane, July 1912 p. 47.
11. Ibid., p. 50.
12. *Baseball Magazine,* "Jake Daubert—a Self-Made Success" by F.C. Lane, February 1914, p. 33.
13. Ibid., p. 36.
14. Ibid., p. 43.
15. Ibid., p. 43-44.
16. Society for American Baseball Research, F.C. Lane profile.
17. *Baseball Magazine,* "Jake Daubert—a Self-Made Success" by F.C. Lane, February 1914, p. 38.
18. Ibid., p. 37.
19. Ibid., p. 37-38.
20. Ibid., p. 40-42.
21. www.baseball-almanac.com, "Jake Daubert home runs."
22. *Baseball Magazine,* "How a Ballplayer Grips His Bat" by F.C. Lane, September 1917, p. 481.
23. *Baseball Magazine,* "Jake Daubert—a Self-Made Success" by F.C. Lane, February 1914, p. 44-46.
24. National Baseball Hall of Fame, "Chalmers Award Honored Baseball's Best" by Craig Muder.
25. Society for American Baseball Research, "Jake Daubert bio."
26. *Baseball Magazine,* "The All America Baseball Club" by F.C. Lane, December 1913, p. 34.
27. *The Brooklyn Daily Eagle,* April 6, 1913, pp. 1, 5.
28. www.ballparksofbaseball.com.
29. *The Brooklyn Daily Times.,* "Brooklyn Opens the Big Race," April 9, 1913, p. 1.
30. *The Daily Standard Union,* Brooklyn, "Brooklyn Start With a Defeat in Pennant Race," April 10, 1913, p. 12.
31. *New-York Tribune,* "Jake Daubert to Talk to 'Fans' in Tribune," September 29, 1913, p. 10.
32. *New-York Tribune,* October 9, 1913, p. 12.
33. Ibid., October 12, 1913, p. 14.
34. *The Standard,* Lykens, Pa., October 17, 1913, p. 1.
35. Society for American Baseball Research, "Bill Dahlen bio" by David Krell.
36. *New-York Tribune,* "Ebbets Dedicates Robinson, too," November 21, 1913, p. 10.
37. *New-York Tribune,* December 3, 1913, p. 11.
38. *The Brooklyn Daily Eagle,* Brooklyn, New York, December 9, 1913, p. 20.

ENDNOTES

39. *Superstars and Screwballs: 100 Years of Brooklyn Baseball* by Richard Goldstein, Dutton Adult, 1991.
40. *The Daily Standard Union,* Brooklyn, December 23, 1913, p. 11.
41. *Baseball Magazine,* "Jake Daubert—a Self-Made Success" by F.C. Lane, February 1914, p. 46.

Chapter 5

1. *The Daily Standard Union,* Brooklyn, December 13, 1913, p. 8.
2. Society for American Baseball Research, "Joe Tinker bio" by Bob Webster.
3. Ibid., "Was the Federal League a Major League" by Emil Rothe.
4. *The Plain Dealer,* Cleveland, January 7, 1914, p. 7.
5. *The Brooklyn Daily Eagle,* "Jake Daubert May Jump to Federals; Has a Big Offer," January 10, 1914, p. 1.
6. Ibid., "Gilmore Says Keep Hands Off Daubert, p. 12.
7. *The Brooklyn Citizen,* January 10, 1914, p. 4.
8. *The Brooklyn Daily Eagle,* "Daubert Sees Light; Says Now He'll Stick," January 10, 1914, p. 1.
9. *The Brooklyn Daily Times,* "Daubert's Wife Wants Him to Join Federals," January 10, 1914, p. 1.
10. *New-York Daily Tribune,* January 11, 1914, p. 14.
11. *The Brooklyn Daily Times,* "Mrs. Daubert Excused," January 12, 1914, p. 1.
12. *The Brooklyn Times,* "Jake Daubert's Loyalty to Receive Its Reward," January 13, 1914, p. 10.
13. *The Brooklyn Daily Eagle,* "Daubert Signs Five-Year Contract," May 25, 1914, p. 18.
14. Society for American Baseball Research, "Was the Federal League a Major League?" by Emil Rothe, 1981.
15. Historic Baseball, historicbaseball.com, "Renegade league battled with Al, NL for fans."
16. *The Brooklyn Daily Times,* "Daubert nearly missed the game," April 14, 1914, p. 1.
17. *The Brooklyn times,* "Capt. Daubert Out of Oakland Management," April 25, 1914, p. 8.
18. *The Brooklyn Daily Eagle,* "Jake Daubert Guilty," May 6, 1914, p. 2.
19. Ibid., "Gov. Smith Signs Sunday Ball Bill and Movie Shows," April 19, 1919, p. 2.
20. *Baseball Magazine,* "Jake Daubert—a Self-Made Success" by F.C. Lane, February 1914, p. 36; and www.baseball-almanac.com.
21. *The Brooklyn Daily Eagle,* Monday, July 6, p. 1.
22. *The Brooklyn Times,* August 15, 1914, p. 10.
23. *The Brooklyn Daily Eagle,* "Daubert Sent Home to Save His Leg," August 21, 1914, p. 16.
24. *The Pittsburgh Press,* October 30, 1914, p. 36.
25. *The Brooklyn Daily Eagle,* "Daily Freak Is Costly; Umpire Fires Daubert," June 17, 1914, p. 22.
26. *New-York Daily Tribune,* "Inside Baseball Sends Daubert,, Egan and Robbie to Bench," September 5, 1914, p. 11.
27. *The Buffalo News,* "Daubert May Manage Brooklyn Nationals," June 18, 1914, p. 1; and *The Pittsburgh Press,* "Jake Daubert May Manage Superbas," June 19, 1914, p. 33.
28. *The Daily Standard Union,* Brooklyn, "Jake Daubert Is Not Slated for Manager," June 19, 1914, p. 12.
29. *The Brooklyn Daily Eagle,* "C. Ebbets Denies Management Yard," June 19, 1914, p. 20.
30. *The Brooklyn Times,* "Daubert Did Not Want Robby's Job," June 29, 1914, p. 4.
31. *The Brooklyn Citizen,* "Jake Daubert Sore Over Yarn He Is After Robbie's Job," August 11, 1914, p. 4.
32. *The Pittsburgh Press,* "Dodgers' Manager Opposed," October 30, 1914, p. 36.
33. *The Daily Standard Union,* Brooklyn, "Reulbach Sees Ebbets; Fails to Sign Contract," January 19, 1915, p. 8.
33. *New Castle Herald,* New Castle, Pennsylvania, May 29, 1914.

Chapter 6

1. *New York Tribune,* September 3, 1915, p. 14.
2. *Superstars and Screwballs: 100 Years of Brooklyn baseball* by Richard Goldstein, Penguin Books USA Inc., 1991, p. 109. Used with permission of the author.
3. *The Brooklyn Daily Eagle,* "Daubert to Raise Hogs," April 1, 1915, p. 16.
4. *The Brooklyn Daily Times,* "Jake Daubert Will Leave Brooklyn Flat," March 23, 1916, p. 8.
5. *Pottsville Daily Republican,* Pottsville, Pa., "$12,000 Home for Jake Daubert," June 23, 1916, p. 6.
6. *The Call,* Schuylkill Haven, Pa., "Jake Daubert to Move Here," March 9, 1917, p. 5.
7. *The Brooklyn Times,* April 9, 1915, p. 10.

8. *The Brooklyn Daily Eagle,* July 29, 1915, p. 14.
9. Ibid., "Jake Daubert Fined $50 for Run-In With Byron," September 13, 1915, p. 8.
10. Ibid., May 14, 1915, p. 16.
11. Ibid., "Here's Jake Daubert at Bat In Contest for Alderman," September 2, 1915, p. 1.
12. *The Daily Standard Union,* Brooklyn, September 2, 1915, p. 4.
13. *The Brooklyn Daily Eagle,* "The Fraternity and the Feds," September 18, 1915, p. 18.
14. Ibid., "Players Fraternity Starts Campaign for Faster Games," September 20, 1915, p. 20.
15. Ibid.

Chapter 7

1. *Mount Carmel Item,* Mount Carmel, Pa., "Jake Daubert's brother killed," March 3,, 1916, p. 3.
2. *Pottsville Republican,* Pottsville, Pa., April 18, 1916, p. 4.
3. *The Brooklyn Daily Eagle,* March 16, 1916, p. 16.
4. *The Standard Union,* Brooklyn, August 6, 1916, p. 10.
5. *The Brooklyn Daily Eagle,* "Daubert With the Team," August 21, 1916, p. 18.
6. *The Brooklyn Daily Times,* "Merkle Will Help Robins," August 26, 1916, p. 8.
7. *Pottsville Republican,* Pottsville, Pa., "Daubert Home Is Heart Broken," September 4, 1916, p. 2.
8. Ibid., September 6, 1916, p. 2.
9. *The Times Leader,* Wilkes-Barre, "Jake Daubert Is Certain Robins Will Win Pennant," September 20, 1916, p. 9.
10. *The Pittsburgh Post,* "Big Scandal Marks Close of Hot Race," October 4, 1916, p. 10.
11. *The Brooklyn Daily Times* October 4, 1916, p. 4.
12. *The Daily Standard Union,* Brooklyn, "Champion Superbas Get Great Send-Off," October 6, 1916, p. 12.
13. *Baseball Magazine,* "How the National League Champions Delivered in the Big Series" by William Phelon, December 1916.
14. *The Brooklyn Daily Eagle,* "Brooklyn's Royal Rooters Accompany Team to Boston," October 7, 1916, p. 8.
15. *The Sun,* New York, October 8, 1916, p. 17.
16. *The Standard Union,* Brooklyn, "Robins' Game Fight Fall Trifle Short of Victory," October 8, 1916, p. 1.
17. *The Brooklyn Daily Eagle,* "Daubert, out at First by Inches, All but Tied Game," October 8, 1916, p. 1.
18. Ibid.
19. *New York Tribune,* "New Ticket Scandal Causes Stir in Hub," October 9, 1916, p. 12.
20. *Baseball Magazine,* "How the National League Champions Delivered in the Big Series" by William Phelon, December 1916.
21. *The Brooklyn Daily Eagle,* "Team Still Has a Big Appetite," October 10,1916, p. 15.
22. Ibid., "Superbas Defeat Red Sox on Their Merits," October 11, 1916, p. 24.
23. Ibid., "Bald-Headed Man Helps Daubert Bat," October 11, 1916, p. 24.
24. *Mount Carmel Item,* "Prizes for Daubert," October 11, 1916, p. 4.
25. *The Brooklyn Daily Eagle,* "Robins Camp Full of Optimism Now," October 11, 1916, p. 21
26. baseball-reference.com, "Platoon Splits."
27. *Baseball Magazine,* "How the National League Champions Favored in the Big Series" by William Phelon, December 1916.
28. Ibid.
29. *Baseball Magazine,* "What players thought of the series," December 1916.
30. Ibid.
31. *The Brooklyn Daily Eagle,* "1916 World's Series Broke All Records," October 13, 1916, p. 18.

Chapter 8

1. *The Reading News-Times,* Reading, Pa., "Ice Plant Deal," January 24, 1917, p. 12.
2. *The Evening News,* Wilkes-Barre, Pa., "Jake Daubert Saves Family From Death," January 16, 1917, p. 9.
3. *The Buffalo Enquirer,* "Sports Topics," January 26, 1917, p. 10.
4. *Elmira Star-Gazette,* New York, "Baseball Men Tell Salaries of Their Stars," January 22, 1917, p. 8.
5. *The Brooklyn Daily Times,* "Brooklyn Club Not Recruiting College and Semi-Pro Players," January 23, 1917, p. 8.

Endnotes

6. *Rochester Democrat and Chronicle,* "Players' Fraternity Non Est.," July 13, 1917, p. 20.
7. *The Brooklyn Daily Times,* "Jake Daubert Hurt," June 26, 1917, p. 6.
8. *The Brooklyn Daily Eagle,* "Jake Daubert Is No Longer an Iceman," September 18, 1917, p. 24.
9. *The Call,* Schuylkill Haven, Pa., "Jake Daubert to Conduct Euclid Theatre," October 19, 1917, p. 6.
10. *Deadball Stars of the National League,* "Jacob Ellsworth Daubert," by Jim Sandoval, p. 294.
11. *Baseball Magazine,* "When They Say 'You're Slipping'," October 1917.
12. National Baseball Hall of Fame, "One Account of War" by Matt Kelly.
13. *The Pittsburgh Press,* "No Baseball Salaries for Players in Service," February 1, 1918, p. 29.
14. *The Brooklyn Daily Eagle,* "Jake Daubert Promotes Baseball Ambulance Fund," July 9, 1918, p. 16.
15. Centers for Disease Control and Prevention: cdc.gov/flu/pandemic-resources/1918-commemoration/1918-pandemic-history.
16. *The Pittsburgh Press,* "Mamaux Signs Contract," February 14, 1918, p. 28.
17. *The Standard,* Lykens, Pa., "Jake Daubert Heads Coal Dredging Company," March 22, 1918, p. 1.
18. *The Brooklyn Daily Times,* "Daubert Takes to Dancing As a Means of Testing Leg," March 19, 1918, p. 10.
19. *The Brooklyn Daily Eagle,* "Chuck Ward Off to the Army and Robbie Is Sore Beset," March 29, 1918, p. 22.
20. *The Brooklyn Citizen,* "Through The Sportiscope," May 4, 1918, p. 5.
21. Ibid., "Baker Ruling Will Not Close Parks of Big Leagues," July 20, 1918, p. 5.
22. *The Brooklyn Citizen,* "Daubert Trade Talk Is News to Robbie and Ebbets Field," March 27, 1918, p. 5.
23. *The Brooklyn Daily Eagle,* May 15, 1918, p. 16.
24. Ibid., "Daubert Hitting Well," May 29, 1918, p. 8.
25. Ibid., "Daubert's Claim for Salary Is Rejected by Commission," October 6, 1918, p. 33.
26. Baseball Reference, "National Commission."
27. *The Brooklyn Daily Eagle,* "Daubert's Claim for Salary Is Rejected by Commission," October 6, 1918, p. 33.
28. *The Brooklyn Daily Times,* "National Commission Throws Out Peckinpaugh's Claim," November 8, 1918, p. 4.
29. *The Sun,* New York, December 11, 1918, p. 13.
30. *The Philadelphia Inquirer,* "Jake Daubert Will Have to Sign Contract Offered Him or Quit," December 5, 1918, p. 12.
31. *The Sun,* New York, December 11, 1918, p. 13.
32. *The Brooklyn Daily Times,* "Daubert Hopes to Play Here," December 11, 1918, p. 8.
33. *New York Tribune,* "Jake Daubert Goes to Giants for Walter Holke and Pitcher George Smith," December 12, 1918, p. 13.
34. *The Brooklyn Daily Times,* "Daubert Not Traded to Giants Says C.H. Ebbets," December 12, 1918, p. 8.
35. Ibid., "Ebbets Thinks the Swap Will Be Made," December 13, 1918, p. 10.
36. *Evening Public Ledger,* Philadelphia, "Phils May Get Daubert," December 18, 1918, p. 16.
37. *The Brooklyn Daily Times,* "Jake Daubert Holds Up Trade," February 9, 1919, p. 12.
38. Ibid., "Brooklyn Club Settles Jake Daubert's Suit; Going to the Reds," March 3, 1919, p. 1
39. *The Philadelphia Inquirer,* March 7, 1919, p. 14.

Chapter 9

1. Society for American Baseball Research, "Christy Mathewson" by Eddie Frierson.
2. Ibid., "Pat Moran" by Daniel R. Levitt.
3. Ibid., "Hal Chase" by Martin Kohout.
4. *New Castle News,* " 'Never Can Tell,' Says Jake Daubert," October 21, 1919, p. 8.
5. *The Brooklyn Daily Eagle,* "Daubert Still Has That Reach," May 14, 1919, p. 18.
6. *The Cincinnati Post,* "Jake's Case Is Not Hopeless," April 21, 1922, p. 16.
7. *The Repository,* Canton, Ohio, "Jinx After Jake Daubert of Reds; Maybe He'll Quit," June 6, 1919, p. 31.
8. *The Brooklyn Daily Eagle,* "Moran Sets Jake Daubert Straight," September 22, 1919, p. 18.
9. *The Cincinnati Post,* "Maddock Helps Reds Win," September 1, 1919, p. 7.
10. *Superstars and Screwballs: 100 Years of Brooklyn baseball* by Richard Goldstein, Penguin Books USA Inc., 1991, p. 131. Used with permission of the author.

11. *The Enquirer,* Cincinnati,, "Notes of the Game," September 29, 1919, p. 10.
12. *Elmira Star-Gazette,* New York, August 27, 1919, p. 8.
13. *The Cincinnati Post,* "Daubert Again Sues," August 30, 1919, p. 3.
14. *The New York Times,* "Confidence of Reds a Valuable Asset," September 30, 1919, p. 22.
15. The National Pastime Museum, "Gambling in the Deadball Era" by Jacob Pomrenke, May 27, 2013.
16. Ibid., "The Whitewashing of Hal Chase" by Jacob Pomrenke, May 27, 2013.
17. *Chicago Tribune,* "Cobb and Speaker Got Themselves Into a Real Fix" by Jerome Holtzman, May 21, 1989.
18. *The Pittsburg Press,* "Comiskey Offers Reward for Proof of Treachery," October 11, 1919, p. 18.
19. *The Brooklyn Daily Eagle,* "Reds Amazed at Confessions; Thought They Won on Merit," September 30, 1920, p. 22.
20. Ibid.
21. Society for American Baseball Research, "The Black Sox Scandal" by Bill Lamb.
22. *The New York Times,* "Series Contenders Rate Nearly Equal," September 21, 1919, p. 115.
23. Ibid., "Gothamites Dig Up Some Bets on Reds," October 1, 1919, p. 13.
24. *The Pittsburgh Gazette Times,* "Jake Daubert Almost Furnishes Real Serious Story," October 2, 1919, p. 15.
25. *The Binghamton Press,* New York, "Gleason's Strategy Went Amuck When Jake Daubert Refused to Die, According to Ring Lardner," October 2, 1919, p. 18.
26. *The Mansfield News,* Mansfield, Ohio, "Reds and Sox Again Contend," October 2, 1919, p. 4.
27. *New York Daily Tribune,* October 3, 1919, p. 15.
28. Society for American Baseball Research, "October 4, 1919: Ring's pitching, Cicotte's errors lead Reds over White Sox in Game 4" by Mike Lynch.
29. Ibid.
30. Ibid., "October 6, 1919: Hod Eller scatters three this, fans nine to lead Reds in Game 5" by Mike Lynch.
31. Ibid.
32. *The St. Louis Star,* " 'Something Is Wrong; I Do Not Know What It Is,' Says Gleason," October 7, 1919, p. 14.
33. Society for American Baseball Research, "October 7, 1919: Rookie Dickey Kerr keeps White Sox alive in Game 6" by Jacob Pomrenke.
34. *The Chicago Daily Tribune,* "Lead of 4 Runs Is Overcome to Beat Reds," October 8, 1919, p. 17.
35. Society for American Baseball Research, "October 8, 1919; Eddie Cicotte returns to form in Game 7" by Jacob Pomrenke.
36. Ibid.
37. *The Gazette Times,* Pittsburgh, "White Sox Beat Reds in Seventh Contest," October 9, 1919, p. 2.
38. *The Dayton Daily News,* "Close Ruling Breaks Up Rally By Redlegs," October 9, 1919, p. 14.
39. *The Plain Dealer,* Cleveland, October 9, 1919, p. 18.
40. *The Brooklyn Daily Eagle,* October 9, 1919, p. 20.
41. *The Chicago Daily Tribune,* "Not Same Team, Says Gleason," October 9, 1919, p. 21.
42. Society for American Baseball Research, "October 9, 1919: Cincinnati Reds beat the Black Sox to win first World Series championship" by Mike Lynch.
43. Ibid.
44. Baseballhistorycomesalive.com, "Deep Dive Into the Black Sox Scandal" by Gary Livacari, October 12, 2022, quoting from *Burying the Black Sox* by Gene Carney, 2006.
45. *Sunday Post-Star,* Glens Falls, New York, "Black Sox scandal memories still alive" by The Associated Press, July 2, 1989, p. 28.
46. *The 1919 World Series: What Really Happened?* by William A. Cook, McFarland & Company, Inc., Publishers, 2001, Reprinted with permission of the author.
47. *The Plain Dealer,* Cleveland, "Speaker Says Cincinnati Deserves Title," October 10, 1919, p. 22.
48. Ibid.
49. *The Cincinnati Post,* "Each Regular Gets $5225," October 10, 1919, p. 1.
50. *The Lancaster Daily Eagle,* Lancaster, Ohio, "Cincinnati Players' Share of World's Series Receipts," October 10, 1919, p. 1.

ENDNOTES

51. *The Enquirer,* Cincinnati, "Red Victors Return," October 11, 1919, p. 8.
52. *The Call,* Schuylkill Haven, Pa., "World's Greatest 1st Baseman Banqueted," October 17, 1919, p. 1.
53. Ibid, p. 3.
54. Ibid., December 19, 1919, p. 1.

Chapter 10

1. *Baseball Magazine,* "Jake Daubert, the Hal Chase of the National League," by F.C. Lane, July 1912, p. 49-50.
2. *Harrisburg Telegraph,* "Jake Daubert Holds Out For Increased Salary," March 1, 1920, p. 10.
3. *The Cincinnati Post,* "Roush, Eller, Daubert Agree, But Groh—?" March 6, 1920, p. 1.
4. *The Evening News,* Harrisburg, Pa., "Jake Daubert," April 7,, 1920, p. 11.
5. *The Cincinnati Post,* "Sees End of Career," March 19, 1920, p. 18.
6. *Buffalo Evening News,* "Karpe's Comment on Sport Toptics," April 5, 1920, p. 14.
7. *The Brooklyn Daily Eagle,* "Daubert Changes Batting Style," May 20, 1920, p. 24.
8. *The Cincinnati Post,* "Daubert Lames Self," June 24, 1920, p. 16.
9. *The Pittsburgh Press,* "One More Year for Jake," July 28, 1920, p. 32.
10. *The Cincinnati Post,* "Ballplayers to Aid Cox," July 19, 1920, p. 1.
11. Ibid., "Jake Daubert Announces He will Play First Base for Reds Again This Year," February 25, 1921, p. 16.
12. *Pottsville Republican,* Pottsville, Pa., "Jake Daubert May Be Out of Major League," March 11, 1921, p. 14.
13. *Dayton Daily News,* "Jake Daubert Will Sign With Redlegs," March 17, 1921, p. 1.
14. *The Brooklyn Daily Eagle,* "Superba Players Not Keen on Plan to Eliminate Heel Spikes in Baseball," August 24, 1922, p. 44.
15. *The Cincinnati Post,* "Eloquence Lost on Jake," March 28, 1922, p. 8.
16. *The Enquirer,* Cincinnati, "Notes of the Game," September 19, 1922, p. 11.
17. *The Dayton Daily News,* Dayton, Ohio, "Reds Through With Quakers," September 27, 1922, p. 20.
18. *The Record-American,* Mahanoy City, Pa., "Speaking of Hitters, How 'Bout Jake?" June 13, 1922, p. 5.
19. *The Pittsburgh Press,* "Baseball Gossip," June 18, 1922, p. 23.
20. *The Enquirer,* Cincinnati, June 18, 1922, p. 51.
21. Ibid., "All Sorts," November 12, 1922, p. 97.
22. *The Brooklyn Citizen,* "Umpires Pick All-Star N.L. Team," October 18, 1922, p. 4.
23. *The Binghamton Press,* Binghamton, New York, "Jake Daubert Earns Niche in Hall of Fame," January 3, 1923, p. 16.
24. baseball-reference.com and Michael Haupert research of Hall of Fame contracts.
25. *The Dayton Dailey News,* Dayton, Ohio, "Daubert Still Out of Cincinnati Red Fold," December 16, 1922, p. 12.
26. *The Enquirer,* Cincinnati, "Red Chiefs Fails To Reach Salary agreement With Daubert," December 14, 1922, 12.
27. *The Call,* Schuylkill Haven, Pa., February 25, 1921, p. 6.
28. *The Philadelphia Inquirer,* "Will Close Washeries," June 11, 1922, p. 18.
29. *The Enquirer,* Cincinnati,, "Jake Daubert Got 'Back To Mines' Without Signing," December 16, 1922, p. 12.
30. *The Cincinnati Post,* "Daubert Signs His Contract," March 5, 1923, p. 1.
31. baseball-reference.com and Michael Haupert research of Hall of Fame contracts.
32. *The Cincinnati Post,* "Daubert Is Sick," March 10, 1923, p. 3.
33. *Dayton Daily News,* Dayton, Ohio, "Daubert Very Sick," March 16, 1923, p. 1.
34. *The Cincinnati Post,* "Daubert Expects to Be Overweight When He Joins Reds," April 5, 1923, p. 14.
35. *The Enquirer,* Cincinnati, "Reds To Open Season Minus Services of Roush and Daubert," April 17, 1923, p. 9.
36. *The Pittsburgh Press,* "If Reds Fail To Win, Jake Daubert Will Shoulder The Blame," July 15, 1923, p. 12.
37. *The Enquirer,* Cincinnati, "Bressler Plays First in Place of Daubert," July 19, 1923, p. 9.
38. *The Philadelphia Inquirer,* "The Old Sport's Musings," July 23, 1923, p. 10.
39. *The Brooklyn Daily Eagle,* "Daubert Has Another Year With the Reds," December 4, 1923, p. 24.
40. *The Plain Speaker,* Hazleton, Pa., "Nothing to Report Says Jake Daubert," December 10, 1923, p. 10.

Chapter 11

1. *The Dayton Herald,* Dayton, Ohio, North American Newspaper Alliance, "Jake Daubert, of Reds, Is Placed at First Base on All-Star National Team of Past 30 Years, Selected by Wagner," January 15, 1924, p. 19.
2. Ibid., "Pat Moran on Sick List," March 4, 1924, p. 1.
3. *The Cincinnati Post,* "Special Treatments Help Pat Moran," March 6, 1924, p. 16.
4. *The Enquirer,* Cincinnati, "Final Out Is Called on Moran," March 8, 1924, p. 1.
5. Society for American Baseball Research, "Pat Moran" by Daniel R. Levitt.
6. *The Enquirer,* Cincinnati, "Tears Dim His Eyes," March 8, 1924, p. 9.
7. *The Cincinnati Post,* "Jake Daubert Dies After Heroic Fight," October 9, 1924, p. 1.
8. Ibid.
9. *The Enquirer,* Cincinnati,, "Jake Daubert Assures Manager Jack Hendricks of His Hearty Cooperation For Coming Year," March 13, 1924, p. 12.
10. *Mount Carmel Item,* Mount Carmel, Pa., "Daubert in Charge of the Rookies," March 22, 1924, p. 4.
11. *The Cincinnati Post,* "Players Believe They Have Whale of a Chance to Win Pennant and There Is Harmony," April 3, 1924, p. 14.
12. *The Enquirer,* Cincinnati, "All Sports," April 13, 1924, p. 40.
13. Ibid., "Notes of the Game," April 28, 1924, p. 11.
14. Ibid., "Jake Daubert Hit by Pitched Ball," May 29, 1924, p. 13.
15. *The Dayton Herald,* "Rumored That Jake Daubert May Not Return to Redlegs," June 2, 1924, p. 11.
16. *The Enquirer,* Cincinnati, "Notes of the Game," June 4, 1924, p. 11.
17. *The Cincinnati Post,* "Jake Again Goes Home," June 5, 1924, p. 10.
18. *The Dayton Daily News,* "Gossip in Sport World," June 6, 1924, p. 38.
19. *The Call,* Schuylkill Haven, Pa., June 13, 1924, p. 4.
20. *The Brooklyn Daily Eagle,* "Daubert Expects Soon To Resume Playing for Reds," June 18, 1924, p. 24.
21. *Deadball Stars of the National League,* "Jacob Ellsworth Daubert," by Jim Sandoval, p. 295.
22. *The Brooklyn Daily Eagle,* "Daubert Expects Soon To Resume Playing for Reds," June 18, 1924, p. 24.
23. *The Enquirer,* Cincinnati, "Notes of the Game," July 27, 1924, p. 24.
24. *The Sunday Times-Signal,* Zanesville, Ohio, "Jake Daubert Spikes Reports He Is Ready to Retire From Baseball," August 24, 1924, p. 9.
25. Ibid.
26. *The Cincinnati Post,* "This Is Station Swope Broadcasting," September 5, 1924, p. 13.
27. Ibid.
28. *The Philadelphia Inquirer,* "Daubert May Manage Reading as Owner," September 22, 1924, p. 19.
29. *Reading Times,* Reading, Pa., "Jake Daubert Will Not Be Keys' Pilot," September 29, 1924, p. 3.
30. *The Daily News-Tribune,* Greenville, Ohio, "Jake Daubert Dies Following Valiant Battle," October 10, 1924, p. 5.
31. *The Cincinnati Post,* "This Is Station Swope Broadcasting," October 10, 1924, p. 22.
32. *The Enquirer,* Cincinnati, "Barnstorming Begins," September 30, 1924, p. 10.
33. Ibid., "Condition of Daubert Is Grave," October 8, 1924, p. 10.
34. *The Cincinnati Post,* "Daubert Rally Follows Double Operation on Captain of Reds," October 2, 1924, p. 12.
35. *Pottsville Republican,* Pottsville, Pa., "Call Family of Daubert," October 8, 1924, p. 10.
36. baseball-reference.com, "List of major league players who died while still playing"; and Wikipedia.com, "List of baseball players who died during their careers."
37. *The Cincinnati Post,* "Jake Daubert Dies After Heroic Fight," October 9, 1924, p. 1.
38. Ibid.
39. Ibid., "This Is Station Swope Broadcasting," October 10, 1924, p. 22.
40. *Buffalo Courier,* Buffalo, New York, "Silent Tribute to Daubert," October 10, 1924, p. 10.
41. *The Call,* Schuylkill Haven, Pa., "Great Ball Player and a Gentleman," October 17, 1924, p. 5.
42. Ibid.
43. *The Cincinnati Post,* "Bury Daubert on Monday," October 10, 1924, p. 22.
44. *Reading Times,* Reading, Pa., "Thousands Pass Jake Daubert's Bier," October 13, 1924, p. 1.
45. *Pottsville Republican,* Pottsville, Pa., "Jake Daubert Laid at Rest," October 13, 1924, p. 5.

ENDNOTES

46. *The Call*, Schuylkill Haven, Pa., "Fine Tribute to Jake Daubert," October 17, 1924, p. 1.
47. *The Cincinnati Post*, "This Is Station Swope Broadcasting," October 10, 1924, p. 22.
48. *The Call*, Schuylkill Haven, Pa., "Great Ball Player and a Gentleman," October 17, 1924, p. 5.
49. Ibid., "In Tears They Laid Him Away," October 17, 1924, p. 4.
50. *Dayton Daily News*, Dayton, Ohio, "Daubert's Widow Makes Claim," July 2, 1925, p. 19.
51. *Pottsville Republican*, Pottsville, Pa., "Autopsy on Jake Daubert," September 16, 1925, p. 1.
52. *Pittsburgh Gazette Times*, "Jake Daubert's Skull Not Fracture, Autopsy Reveals," September 30, 1925, p. 13.
53. Gertrude V. Daubert, plaintiff, vs. The Cincinnati Base Ball Club Company, a corporation under the law of Ohio, defendant, Court of Common Pleas, Hamilton County, Ohio, by J.W. Heintzman, attorney for plaintiff, August 10, 1929.
54. Ibid., Entry of Dismissal, October 21, 1931.
55. *Pottsville Republican*, Pottsville, Pa., "Daubert Cup Shoot April 18," April 15, 1926, p. 11.
56. Ibid., "Senior Daubert Passes On," November 6, 1928, p. 9.
57. *The Morning Call*, Allentown, Pa., "Jake Daubert Inducted Into Cincy Hall of Fame," July 29, 1966, p. 40.
58. *The West Schuylkill Press*, Tremont, Pa., "'He Deserves It,' Says His Widow," October 13, 1966, p. 1.

Chapter 12

1. Minor League Baseball, milb.com, "Looking Back: Is Jake Daubert a Hall of Famer?" by Bill Traughber, quoting 1989 *New York Post* article, May 4, 2017.
2. *The Pittsburgh Press*, "Jake Says He Is French," April 9, 1919, p. 26.
3. From letter by Joan Daubert Becker to Robert Edward Auction, 2011.
4. Robert Edward Auction.
5. *The Cincinnati Post*, "Daubert Discards Small Glove for a Larger One," March 20, 1924, p. 14.
6. *The Patriot*, Harrisburg, Pa., "Many Ball Players Have Their Pet Superstitions," December 26, 1911, p. 6.
7. *The Brooklyn Daily Eagle*, "Daubert Patented His Bat," April 6, 1919, p. 47.
8. *The Scranton Republican*, Scranton, Pa., "Consider Jake Daubert Lucky Ball Player," May 20, 1918, p. 16.
9. *The Cincinnati Post*, "Jake Has Smallest Head in Majors," April 3, 1924, p. 15.
10. *The Buffalo American*, "Sterling First Baseman of Cincinnati Reds Takes Up Tobacco in Place of Gum," September 30, 1920, p. 4.
11. *The Brooklyn Daily Times*, March 1, 1916, p. 10.

Chapter 13

1. *The Pittsburgh Post*, "Connie Mack Squarest Man in Game, Says Charley Dooin," July 2, 1914, p. 12.
2. *Pottsville Republican*, Pottsville, Pa., "Jake Daubert as a Player," October 12, 1914, p. 5.
3. *The Pittsburgh Press*, "The Ty of the N.L.," December 4, 1914, p. 35.
4. *The Brooklyn Daily Eagle, Junior Eagle Section*, Brooklyn, "A Fine Quality," May 20, 1917, p. 4.
5. *Baseball Magazine*, "The Greatest of All First Basemen," by F.C. Lane, October 1912.
6. *The Morning Call*, Allentown, Pa., "Fans and Players Laud Jake Daubert," October 11, 1924, p. 15.
7. *The Cincinnati Post*, "Bohne and Daubert 'Most Particular," April 26, 1923, p. 14.
8. *Baseball Magazine*, "Jake Daubert—A Self-Made Success" by F.C. Lane, February 1914.

Chapter 14

1. *West Schuylkill Press*, Tremont, Pa., June 10, 1911, p. 3.
2. *Baseball Magazine*, "Jake Daubert, the Hal Chase of the National League" by F.C. Lane, July 1912, p. 46.
3. Ibid., p. 47.
4. Ibid., p. 48.
5. Ibid., p.49.
6. *Baseball Magazine*, "Jake Daubert—a Self-Made Success" by F.C. Lane, February 1914, pp. 35-36.
7. Ibid., p. 38.
8. Ibid., p. 39.
9. Ibid., p.4090.

10. Ibid., p. 44.
11. Ibid., p. 45.
12. *The Tribune-Republican,* Scranton, Pa., "Who Is the Greatest Pitcher in the Big Leagues Today?" August 30, 1912, p.12.
13. *The Pittsburgh Gazette Times,* "The Six Best Pitchers I've Ever Faced," February 19, 1916, p. 10.
14. *The Brooklyn Times,* "Just Fanning," May 1, 1914, p. 10.
15. *The New Castle Herald,* "Jake Tells His System," October 12, 1916, p. 10.
16. *The Brooklyn Daily Eagle,* "The Greatest Play I Ever Made," July 30, 1916, p. 53.
17. *The Brooklyn Citizen,* "Jake Daubert, at Thirty-seven, Is Going Better Than Ever" by Billy Evans, February 23, 1923, p. 4.

Chapter 15

1. baseball-reference.com, Doug Pappas, and the Society for American Baseball Research.

Afterword

1. *The 1919 World Series: What Really Happened?* by William A. Cook, McFarland & Company, Inc., Publishers, 2001, Reprinted with permission of the author.
2. *The Cracker Jack Collection . . . Baseball's Prized Players,* By Tom Zappala and Ellen Zappala, Peter E. Randall Publisher, 201.
3. Minor League Baseball, milb.com, "Looking Back: Is Jake Daubert a Hall of Famer?" by Bill Traughber, quoting 1989 *New York Post* article, May 4, 2017.

Acknowledgments and Credits

Special thanks to:

Dr. Ann Yezerski for her genealogy research and direction in tracking down information about Jake's family and his early life.

Jack Daubert and Jill Malone, two of Jake's great-grandchildren, for sharing their family photos and documents and for overall assistance, support and encouragement.

Cody Swords, Vintage Baseball Memorabilia, for sharing numerous photos

Chris Whitehouse, They Played in Color Galleries, for providing the colorized photo of Jake for the cover.

Richard Goldstein, the author of *Superstars and Screwballs,* allowed me to share comments by Jake Daubert's son, George.

William A. Cook, Tom Zappala, and John McMurray for sharing their perspectives on Jake's Hall of Fame consideration.

Jason Alexander, Central Services Division Manager, Hamilton County Clerk of Courts, Cincinnati, Ohio

Lawrence Knorr, who committed to publishing this book before I had written a word for it.

Photo Credits

Photos of Jake Daubert are in the public domain. Most of the photos in this book were acquired from collections of the following and used with permission and appreciation:

Jack Daubert	Jill Daubert Malone
Mancave Pictures	Vintage Baseball Memorabilia
Library of Congress archives	National Baseball Hall of Fame
Detroit Public Library	Steve Steinberg
Various newspaper and magazine archives	

Bibliography

Superstars and Screwballs: 100 Years of Brooklyn baseball by Richard Goldstein, Penguin Books USA Inc., 1991. Excerpts used with permission of the author.
Deadball Stars of the National League, written by the Deadball Era Committee of the Society for American Baseball Research, edited by Tom Simon, Brassey's, Inc. 2004
Society for American Baseball Research
Society for American Baseball Research Biography Project
Baseball Magazine
National Baseball Hall of Fame, Jake Daubert file
Numerous newspapers on file through newspapers.com

Statistics credit

Information was obtained free of charge from and is copyrighted by Retrosheet. Interested parties may contact Retrosheet at "www.retrosheet.org."

Additional statistics compiled from
Baseball-reference.com, Sports Reference LLC
Baseball-almanac.com

About the Author

Harry J. Deitz Jr. worked in the newspaper business for 45 years as a photographer, sportswriter, sports editor, design editor, and editor. He retired in 2018 after ten years as editor-in-chief of the *Reading Eagle*, Reading, Pa.

In his weekly "Editor's Notebook" column, he wrote extensively about his family—parents, grandparents, three children and especially six grandchildren—and shared his personal story of his six years as the primary caregiver for his late wife during her battle with Parkinson's disease and cancer.

He has served as president and board member of the Pennsylvania Newsmedia Association and the Pennsylvania Associated Press Managing Editors and has won numerous awards for his columns, sportswriting, and newspaper design work.

In his spare time, he has hiked the entire Pennsylvania section of the Appalachian Trail and has read every book by novelist Ken Follett.

Harry is a native of Shamokin, Pa., where he followed his father into newspaper work. He is the author of *Our Father's Journey: A Path Out of Poverty*, *Journal of a Caregiver: A Story of Love and Devotion*, and *Covey: A Stone's Throw from a Coal Mine to the Hall of Fame*.

www.ingramcontent.com/pod-product-compliance
Lightning Source LLC
Chambersburg PA
CBHW021145160426
43194CB00007B/697